Treasures of the World's Religions
Series

About the Editor and This Book

"Patrick Laude has provided a rich resource that is at once spiritual and scholarly. Extraordinary foundational texts on the unceasing invocation of the Divine Name are complemented by illuminating analytical essays on the remembrance of God. *Pray Without Ceasing* is a wonderful introduction to the experience of prayer; it also comprises an initiation into the world of prayer itself. Whether the reader is seeking silent inspiration or pursuing academic aspirations, this book is a powerful reminder that 'praying is like breathing' (Gregory Nazianzus) and that 'the Spirit blows where it wills' (John 3:8)."

> — **John Chryssavgis,** author of *In the Heart of the Desert,*
> *The Spirituality of the Desert Fathers and Mothers*

"*Pray Without Ceasing*, edited by Patrick Laude, is for anyone seeking inner union with the Divine. A Name of God, divinely revealed, legitimately bestowed by a proper spiritual authority, and frequently invoked, reconsecrates the altar of the temple, or the heart of the believer, and functions in a direct way to reanimate the Holy Spirit or latent Divine breath within. When the finite and temporal human heart is rhythmically impressed with a Divine Name, which by its very nature participates in the infinite and the eternal, the heart cannot resist and invariably recalls its theomorphic essence."

> — **Virginia Gray Henry**, author of *Beads of Faith: Pathways*
> *to Meditation and Spirituality using Rosaries, Prayer Beads, and*
> *Sacred Words*

"Patrick Laude has given us here a superb anthology where prayer is the human condition's focal point. Through a wide array of texts across traditions, prayer shines as a most desired and most innate act. Its transformative light restores dignity to human beings who glow in its dwellings. All religions seem to agree that to pray is to reside in the Divine Name that is none other than the Divine Presence itself."

> — **Amira El-Zein,** Director of the Arabic Program, Tufts
> University

"The common ground of the spirit is more than a concept. It is realized through the experience of deep prayer and spiritual practice that radiates through every page of Patrick Laude's immensely interesting and valuable book on a universal tradition of important potential for creating unity in our divided world.

"Simplicity and depth. These qualities of the spiritual journey fill the pages of Patrick Laude's rich and inspiring pilgrimage through the centuries and cultures of the human search for God. He shows us how our own practice connects us with this great living tradition."

— **Laurence Freeman OSB**, Georgetown University

"How does one travel from the abstract to the concrete in religion, assimilate spiritually that which is conceived mentally, render intimate and transformative that which appears to be remote and inaccessible? *Pray Without Ceasing* gives us a resounding answer, a veritable symphony of voices from a dazzling variety of religious traditions, proclaiming in harmonious unity: the perpetual invocation of the Name of the Absolute."

— **Reza Shah-Kazemi**, Institute of Ismaili Studies, and author of *Paths to Transcendence: According to Shankara, Ibn Arabi, and Meister Eckhart*

World Wisdom
The Library of Perennial Philosophy

The Library of Perennial Philosophy is dedicated to the exposition of the timeless Truth underlying the diverse religions. This Truth, often referred to as the *Sophia Perennis*—or Perennial Wisdom—finds its expression in the revealed Scriptures as well as the writings of the great sages and the artistic creations of the traditional worlds.

The Perennial Philosophy provides the intellectual principles capable of explaining both the formal contradictions and the transcendent unity of the great religions.

Ranging from the writings of the great sages of the past, to the perennialist authors of our time, each series of our Library has a different focus. As a whole, they express the inner unanimity, transforming radiance, and irreplaceable values of the great spiritual traditions.

Pray Without Ceasing: The Way of the Invocation in World Religions appears as one of our selections in the Treasures of the World's Religions series.

Treasures of the World's Religions Series

This series of anthologies presents scriptures and the writings of the great spiritual authorities of the past on fundamental themes. Some titles are devoted to a single spiritual tradition, while others have a unifying topic that touches upon traditions from both the East and West, such as prayer and virtue. Some titles have a companion volume within the Perennial Philosophy series.

PRAY WITHOUT CEASING

The Way of the Invocation
in World Religions

Edited by
PATRICK LAUDE

World Wisdom

Pray Without Ceasing: The Way of the Invocation in World Religions
© 2006 World Wisdom, Inc.

Library of Congress Cataloging-in-Publication Data

Pray without ceasing : the way of the invocation in world religions / edited by Patrick Laude.
    p. cm. -- (Treasures of the world's religions)
  Includes bibliographical references and index.
  ISBN-13: 978-1-933316-14-7 (pbk. : alk. paper)
  ISBN-10: 1-933316-14-4 (pbk. : alk. paper) 1. Prayer. 2. Invocation. I. Laude, Patrick,
1958- II. Series.
  BL560.P665 2006
  204'.3--dc22

                                                                      2006001393

Printed on acid-free paper in Canada.

For information address World Wisdom, Inc.
P.O. Box 2682, Bloomington, Indiana 47402-2682
www.worldwisdom.com

CONTENTS

III. CONTEMPORARY TESTIMONIES

INTRODUCTION

It is widely recognized in all religious worlds that nothing is more important than prayer, since prayer involves a direct relationship between the Divine and the human. Nothing can be deemed more spiritually necessary than prayer since among all possible actions none engages as direct a communication with the Great Mystery. A work of charity, for example, could be considered *prima facie* as important as prayer, or it could be viewed as an extension and a consequence of prayer inasmuch as it is centered on a consciousness of the Divine; but it is nevertheless contingent upon circumstances and particular needs, whereas prayer as such is totally unconditioned since it expresses the very essence of the human station before the One.

Prayer defines the essence of the human condition because man was "created to know, love, and serve God," and how could this be achieved better than through prayer, which is both a gift of oneself to God, and knowledge of his Reality through and in this gift? That prayer be considered as a mode of knowledge may come as a surprise to those who have been conditioned to limit knowledge to matters of the mind, thereby ignoring the fact that the deepest and truest knowledge dwells in the heart, the very center of the human being. In this sense, knowledge involves a sense of totality that points to its relationship with love, understood as a longing for reality, truth, goodness, and beauty. Prayer is the very language of this love, whether it takes the form of a dialogue between the loving soul and the beloved Divine, or that of a nostalgic aspiration toward union with God. And prayer is ultimately service—a point that is often overlooked by a world engrossed with outer actions—because the best way to serve God is to give oneself to him through prayer, and to discover, as a result of this gift, the specific modes in which we may best become his loving servant, as well as be of service to our neighbors.

It should therefore be evident that there is no spiritual tradition that does not place a strong emphasis on prayer as a central connection between the human and the Divine. This holds true whether the mode of this relationship be understood in terms of a verbal communication, or as an instance of silent communion. Even though some of the highest modes of meditation, such as the techniques of Yoga or Japanese *zazen*, do not immediately seem to fit into the category of prayer in its common acceptation, they are no less dependent upon a devotional attitude than others. In the context of Zen, for example,

Huang-po's response to his disciple's perplexity at his paying devotional homage to the Buddha—"I do not seek it through the Buddha, nor through the Dharma, nor through the Sangha; I just go on doing this act of piety to the Buddha"[1]—illustrates the function of prayer, in the most general sense, in any attempt at transcending the limits of the egoic consciousness. For an authentic spiritual life by definition presupposes some measure of relinquishing the hold of psychic subjectivity. In Huang-po's example, a concrete sense of the need to let go of any ego-centered seeking, albeit spiritually disguised, goes hand in hand with an acceptance of one's limitations as expressed in a reverent bowing before the crystalline form of That which passes human understanding and seeking. This point is corroborated by the fact that Indian Yoga itself, as centered as it may be on the purely technical means of awakening the spiritual nexus of latent energies, places devotion among the five prescriptions (*niyama*) that are, together with the five proscriptions (*yama*), strict preliminary requirements for any spiritual realization along the yogic path. This devotion is defined as an effort to act while keeping one's eyes constantly gazing on the Lord.[2]

Prayer is both an act of the individual and a universal demand of the human condition. It is expressed, on the most elementary level, in the urgency of a vocal or silent call to God, or in a dialogue with Him. It is also epitomized, in an eminent and normative manner, in a number of revealed and inspired orisons by which believers of a given faith find consecrated words with which to speak to God. These are often prayers first uttered by the founders of religions, like the Lord's Prayer taught by Jesus or David's Psalms, and they have functioned as the prototypes of all individual prayer. These prayers are also frequently integrated within daily rituals, and synthetically contain all that human beings need to give expression to their relationship with the Divine.

Notwithstanding this recognition of the universal demand for prayer in a general sense, one of the misleading aspects of the common concept of prayer lies in the assumption that it is necessarily associated with an attitude of request, or even begging. It is true that these attitudes can, and in some way must, enter into the economy of devotion. Before the Absolute man cannot but be a "beggar." However the deepest mystery of prayer lies beyond any particular request. It dwells in love, or in the irrepressible desire

---

[1] Daisetz Teitaro Suzuki, *An Introduction to Zen Buddhism*, New York, Grove Press, 1964, p. 52.

[2] See *Upanishads du Yoga*, edited by Jean Varenne, Paris, 1971, pp. 49-51.

to be one with the Beloved, and—even beyond—it pertains to a need for Reality and Self-Knowledge. The true finality of prayer is not the fulfilling of a request—which has led some mystical writers like Simone Weil to reject, no doubt hyperbolically, the latter as incompatible with "pure Love"—but the modification of oneself by contact with the transformative power of the Divine. It is in this context that the way of the invocation appears as the essence and perfection of all prayers, and as the most powerfully transformative of all actions.

The way of the invocation, sometimes referred to as jaculatory prayer or the way of the Name—*nāma-japa* or *japa-yoga* in India—can be defined as the methodical, trusting, and virtually—or actually—permanent invocation of a Divine Name or a sacred formula. The modalities of the practice vary greatly, from singing aloud to silent concentration upon the heart. This path is practiced and lived within the context of a religious tradition—with its various ritual, moral, and legal demands, of which it constitutes the perfection, at least in terms of its ultimate end, i.e., as perfect conformity and union with the Divine. Within the framework of this tradition, the methodical practice of the invocation normally requires an authorization in the form of an induction or initiation into a spiritual rule or a contemplative order under the guidance of a spiritual instructor. As in the case of monastic engagement, it may also take the form of a vow. In other words, this practice cannot be initiated and pursued in a spirit of individualistic improvisation without incurring grave danger; and it cannot be artificially severed from the religious universe in which it unfolds. It may, however, in some instances be substituted—as a continuous and integrated mode of orison—for virtually all the other practices that define a given religion. It bears stressing that if it occasionally does so it is only on the basis of a deep immersion in the invocatory practice and certainly not as a starting point.

Modern individuals, when they still recognize the need for salvation or deliverance, are often willing to pursue it only on condition that it be defined in their own terms. We have been taught from the cradle that we are masters of our own destiny, and that no external constraint should weigh on the way we may "find ourselves" or "be with God." The wide success of improvised, tailor-made, and trivialized liturgies bears witness to this tendency in the modern world. When considered from the highest standpoint this contemporary leaning toward self-made methods may at best echo a diffuse sense of inner freedom and an obscure intuition of the fact that "there are as many paths to God as there are souls." But the matter is neither so simple nor so one-sided, for our free will does not modify in the least the predicament of our human relativity and we cannot reach That which transcends us through means that originate from within the individual domain alone. To seek for salvation or deliverance on one's own terms is a contradiction in terms: salvation or deliverance can take place only on the Other's terms. Only the Other can save us from ourselves, all the more so when it is a matter of going beyond our individuality.

Spiritual liberation, on one level or another, presupposes and coincides with—on the level of the intention—an actual realization, a "change of heart," or an inner modification through which the center of consciousness shifts from the individual to the Divine, namely, Grace, God, or the Supreme Self—He who alone can say "I am That I am." This is why the first step on the spiritual path always entails elements of obedience and submission, of passing through a "narrow gate." As for its peak or summit, it can only emerge triumphantly from the rubbles of an inward death. Human beings cannot save themselves by their own means: the Name or the sacred formula is the synthesis of the transcendent means that they have received from the Divine Other so that they may realize, God willing, that there is ultimately no Other. The invocation is the synthesis of Religion as such, the integral and integrating sacred whole without which man in his ordinary disintegrated state can do nothing. It is because the Name can be envisaged as a synthesis of the whole that Kabbalists can claim that the entire Torah is included in the Tetragrammaton—the four Hebrew consonants of the ineffable Supreme Name of God—or that Sufis can consider that the Koran, source of the whole sacred Law, proceeds from the Name *Allāh*.

*   *   *

Even though jaculatory prayer is a universal phenomenon, it cannot be denied that not all traditions place as central an emphasis on it; indeed, the place of invocatory practices within the spiritual economy of religions may vary somewhat from one tradition to the other. In this respect Hinduism, Eastern Christianity, and Sufism can no doubt be considered as the richest veins, together with Jōdo or Pure Land Buddhism, the Japanese way of the invocation of Amida Buddha. Pure Land Buddhism may appear in some respects as a pure, and almost extreme and exclusive, manifestation of the invocatory path, the foundational manifestations of which may at first sight seem quite distant from the general tenor of Buddhism. In Judaism, given the clear bifurcation between the exoteric and the esoteric, and by reason of the strong "linguistic" and hermeneutic bent of the tradition, the way of the invocation has most often been associated, in Kabbalistic circles, with complex meditational practices on Divine Names, letters, and numbers, while almost always being situated under the sacred jurisdiction of the arcana.

More akin to a full manifestation of the Hidden, Hinduism places the supreme divine utterance, the *Omkara*, at the beginning and at the end of all sacred undertakings, and this privilege of the sacred sound OM accounts, among other factors, for a sense of the divine Presence and spiritual power in formulae such as *Om Namah Shivāya* or *Om Srī Rām Jai Rām Jai Jai Rām*.

The case of Islam is analogous, but in a way that emphasizes the pervasiveness of the "material" substance of the Koranic scripture in daily life. The Divine Name, which is woven into the Book, thereby penetrates the whole course of existence through formulae such as *bismillāh* (in the Name of God) or *al-hamdu-li-llāh* (praise be to God). Sufism extracts the quintessence of this manifold presence in focusing on the Great Name *Allāh*, or the ninety-nine names of God taught by the tradition, fourteen of them being directly Koranic. More rarely the supreme third person "He," *Huwa*, is invoked, and sometimes even just its initial aspiration, *Hu*, which also concludes the name *Allāhu* in the nominative case.

As for Eastern Christianity, particularly in the Orthodox Church, it presents us with a sacramental understanding and practice of the methodical invocation of the Name of Jesus. The prayer formula is a vehicle of grace that is considered as a prolongation of the Eucharist, or even as a direct communion with the divine Presence: the Name of Jesus is in any case a mode of the presence of Christ. It is the spiritual "nutrition" of the Christian faithful, which leads the Russian Pilgrim, absorbed in the invocation of the Name of Jesus, to write: ". . . I tenderly experienced the presence of God all about me."[3]

In shamanistic practices the world over, as in Africa or in Central Asia, invocations are numerous, pervading the whole of life: every qualitative action, in craft for instance, is introduced by a specific invocation that effects an "actualization" of the invisible entities, or an "animation" of the "matter" of the activity. This animation by the word is expressed by a sense of the "power" (*nyame*) inherent in invocations. Although such understandings and practices testify to profound analogies with *japa-yoga*, it must be added, in contradistinction, that shamanism and Taoism rarely rely on this method as a central or exclusive practice on the spiritual way. Why? Probably because

---

[3] *The Way of a Pilgrim*, translated and annotated by Gleb Pokrovsky, Vermont, Woodstock, 2001, p. 55.

the shamanistic path primarily involves an increased receptivity to the presence of the Divine in Nature. In that sense pure receptivity is in itself a kind of invocation. A Cheyenne medicine man once explained that attention to the sounds of Nature is the main mode of invocation for the North American Indian. This is also illustrated by the fact that Mongolian "throat singing," which often consists of an imitation of the sounds of Nature, is sometimes understood as a form of primordial invocation. If the invocation in scriptural religions is the Word as Rāma, Jesus, or Allāh, it is rather the Word as Nature in shamanistic traditions, whence the invocation through and with Nature and its sounds. The "invocatory" modes of this participative and anthropocosmic unity will not be our focus in this anthology, for they escape the realm of words and scriptures, i.e., that of the written word, while pertaining to a different spiritual economy.

In Western Christianity, the practice of presence that has been described by spiritual writers such as Brother Lawrence of the Resurrection, or the "orison of simple attention" proposed by Madame Guyon, are also in a sense manifestations of the way of the invocation. A silent attention to presence is like an inarticulate invocation. However, since we as human beings are forms moving among forms, it befits us better to make use of forms in aspiring toward That which transcends forms: hence the particular benefit of a single form that synthesizes them all, a short and simple form which, as a key, can open the door that leads to the divine Presence.

It is difficult, especially in a world as saturated with agitated and meaningless forms as ours, to "oppose" the Divine Formless to worldly forms, or to "resist" the flow of terrestrial forms in and by the Formless. But a synthetic form can be substituted for the stream of forms, and transmute this stream into the Formless. The invocation does just this, either by "negating" forms inasmuch as they are themselves "negations" of the Formless, or by affirming the Formless which expresses itself through forms. In other words, the invocation of the Name is a form because we cannot do without forms in the formal world; but it is a "minimal" form that can be alchemically "blended" with other forms, without thereby entering into conflict with them on the level of analytical complexity, thoughts, events, etc. This form is the Divine Name: Form of the Formless, Prayer of Silence, Door of the Thousand Things. It is therefore especially suitable for reducing the complexities of modern life to a measure of spiritual simplicity. The Name transforms our hurried time into a contemplative space: the "sacred space" of the Name reabsorbs "our time" in and through the invocation.

The invocation could be compared to the Taoist *yin-yang* symbol, its white half symbolizing its formal aspect—its graphic, phonetic, and "conceptual" form—and the dark half symbolizing its informal dimension—the silence and plenitude of pure being and pure consciousness. The black dot in the white surface will then refer to the informal and essential end or limit of form, while the white dot will represent the "initial" and "minimal" crystallization of the supra-formal. In this sense the two halves of the *yin-yang* represent the same "intermediary" reality perceived from two standpoints: the uttered Name as "expiration" into pure consciousness, and silence as "entrance" into form. The invocation can be either an affirmation of the Divine in form, or a disappearance of form in the Divine, or else both consecutively, as expiration and inspiration. It is, above all, a coincidence of opposites, hence also its aspect of *kōan* (who is it that invokes?) in some traditions.

* * *

The conventional objections to the way of the invocation are not few: among these are its reputation of being mechanical; its danger of superficiality; its excessive facility; its making the words of the scriptures and sacred laws unnecessary, if not dispensable; its depriving religious life of a need for action. To the first kinds of objections, spiritual masters of the invocatory way have answered by stressing the importance of intention in the path, an intention that is inseparable from faith. An invocation that is legitimate in its intention cannot but produce spiritual fruits, whether we are aware of it or not. Whatever might be the source of this intention—whether it stems from a desire to be saved, from a love of the spiritual and the Divine, or from an intellectual recognition of the primacy of the divine Reality—in all cases faith is a prerequisite for the invocation. How could one effectively and consistently perform that in which one has no faith? Here faith can be defined as a sincere trust in the Divine nature and virtue of the Name or sacred formula that is invoked. It is through faith, and through the persevering practice that is buttressed by legitimate intentions, that the invocation may deepen, and—far from being a merely mechanical or superficial utterance—become the center of one's life, the sole contentment of one's heart.

That the way of the invocation is "easy" cannot be denied, since it is formally simple and accessible under all circumstances. It is plain that it is this "easiness" that makes it particularly appropriate for our time of "sounds and fury." It is also more accessible, as a method, to contemporary men and women who are, for the most part, unable, or at least ill-fitted—given their poor psycho-spiritual constitution—to follow more complex and ascetic approaches to the Divine. This "easiness" does not preclude "difficulty" however, as is plain from the fact that the incessant solicitations of the world and the soul cannot but represent a challenge to a consistent practice. Moreover, the idea that an effective spiritual practice should be "difficult" is predicated upon an emphasis on effort, therefore on the individual and human side of the "spiritual equation." By contrast, the *tariki* accentuation of the way of the invocation—its reliance upon the Divine Other—takes stock of the intuition that "with God all things are possible." Unburdening oneself of "what is" might in fact be "easier" than pretending one "is" when one "is not"; it is also much wiser. The categories of "facility" and "difficulty" are too relative and too subjective to be of real import, especially when the matter is a recognition of Reality more than a tension of the will.

The way of the invocation is understood as being so powerful, and its practice places so much emphasis on the divine Presence and Grace, that it is not uncommon to extend its prerogatives and effects to their ultimate consequences. There is a sense that nothing else matters, spiritually speaking, than the Name itself; the exclusive unicity of the means becomes virtually one with the goal. It could even be said that the distinction between means and end becomes moot since "God and His Name are one," as Ramakrishna has said. Even though this overemphasis might be ill-sounding to many who like to think of religion in psychological or moral terms, it must be acknowledged that it is fundamentally no less than a full methodical recognition of the doctrine of essential unity of Reality, such as is expressed in the Hindu Advaita Vedānta or in the Sufi "unicity of existence," or simply—in more implicit and less metaphysical parlance—of the absolute primacy of the Divine. On this level, the invocation is not only a prayer of the human to the Divine, it is also a prayer of the Divine to itself through a human intermediary.

Along with its reputation for "easiness," *japa-yoga* is sometimes considered as a path well suited for individuals who are less intellectually gifted. This was, among others, the opinion of Shankarāchārya, who favored the path of intellective discernment (*viveka*).[4] This reputation is directly connected

---

[4] This did not prevent Shankara from engaging in Hindu devotions, nor from his full recognition of the spiritual validity of *japa*, as he eloquently testifies in the following hymn in honor of Govinda: "Remember, nothing can save thee at the last moment except the shelter of the Lord, so sing thou His sweet Name Govinda! Govinda! . . . Indulge not in formal ceremonies. Dwell in the Atman. Cross the Ocean of transmigration singing the sweet name— Govinda! Govinda! Govinda!" (Bankey Behari, *Sufis, Mystics, and Yogis*, Bombay, Bharatiyah Vidya Bhavan, 1971, pp. 198-200).

to the needs of our time, a time when metaphysical acumen, and the very time to think and meditate, have grown more and more sparse. However, it would be unfair to reduce the way of the invocation to a mere devotional practice involving no intellectual component. In principle, and often in fact, the way of the invocation can be associated with metaphysical meditation. It would also be inaccurate to limit it to the status of a methodical means toward an end—although it is undoubtedly that in some respects—since it also constitutes, and above all, a most direct metaphysical "situation" in the axis of divine Reality, through the Name that makes it present. As such, it may be defined as virtual knowledge. In a sense, the invocation leads to a future salvation, as most commonly understood by Jōdo practitioners who seek to be reborn in the Pure Land; but in a deeper sense the invocation is a participation in Reality, here and now.

The way of the invocation is at the junction of the two paths of "faith" and "works," illustrated theologically by the "*ex opere operato*" of the Catholic Church and the "justification by faith" of the Protestant Church. The principle of "*ex opere operato*" maintains the objective validity of the sacrament, for instance the Eucharist, irrespective of the subjective conditions, such as the moral imperfection of the officiating subject or of the faithful who participate in it. By contrast, and by reaction, the doctrine of justification through faith places an exclusive emphasis, with respect to spiritual and salvific effectiveness, on the subjective reality of the mystery of faith as inner acceptance of truth *ex toto corde*. When analogically applied to the domain of jaculatory prayer these two "extreme" principles correspond, *mutatis mutandis*, to the recognition of the divine inherence in the Name, on the one hand, and to the principle of complete trust in its saving power, on the other hand. The way of the invocation normatively involves a kind of reciprocity between these two terms, in the sense that faith "actualizes" the objective and efficient power of the Name, while the Name "kindles" and nourishes faith within the heart of the practitioner. This reciprocity always pertains to a dimension of mystery because relative consciousness, the starting point of the path, cannot even begin to fathom the depth of absolute consciousness which is ultimately, and *a priori*, the source of spiritual work, and actually its sole agent and subject. In asking the enigmatic question "who invokes?", mentioned above, some Buddhist and Hindu masters have pointed to this mystery as something that will always remain out of reach of the mind.[5]

---

[5] This is what Taitetsu Unno beautifully suggests when he refers to the distinction between "growing rice," "watching rice grow," and "listening to rice growing." These three ways correspond to three types of practice: "practice as a means to an end (growing rice), practice

The relationship between the way of the invocation and the systems of religious prescriptions, proscriptions, and complex practices within which it unfolds and grows nearly always entails tensions, or even oppositions, between its practitioners and their collective context. How could it be otherwise when the religious system that is embodied by an institution and a collective body finds itself confronted with a way that appears to relativize its forms or even transcend them? The fact is that, for *japa-yoga*, the invocation is a synthesis of all laws and prescriptions, while being also the essence of all scriptures. The invocation realizes the *raison d'être* of all religious practices since the latter ultimately aim at recognizing, remembering, and assimilating the supreme Reality. It is true that the multiplicity of rules and practices is intended to address the variegated aspects of the human person and the collectivity on all levels of reality; however, it is no less true that *japa-yoga*, inasmuch as it infuses the whole of life, realizes, or contributes to realizing, all of the objectives of the religious laws and practices: it does so by orienting human activities toward our higher ends and by permeating the former with a greater measure of awareness and beauty, thereby fulfilling the spirit of religion as such. The synthetic character of the invocation can also be brought home by the simple and obvious fact that any state of urgency, and the moment of death is one *par excellence*, evokes a single call to God, not a plunging into complex practices or prayers.[6] Before death, the Name of God is all that can be given and all that is needed; it summarizes our life and our being.

* * *

This anthology is comprised of three parts. The first part, "Foundational Texts," includes excerpts from major classics of spirituality, which introduce

as focusing on the process rather than on the end (watching), and practice in which the end expresses itself (listening)" (*Living in Amida's Universal Vow: Essays in Shin Buddhism*, edited by Albert Bloom, Bloomington, IN, World Wisdom, 2004, p. ix).

[6] The last words of a stewardess who was to be among the victims of the September 11 hijackings are most expressive in this respect: "She said, calmly, 'I see water and buildings.' There was a pause, then, in an entirely different tone of voice, 'Oh, my God!' Again a pause, and again 'Oh, my God!'. . . It is probably safe to say that she was neither a Sufi nor an Hesychast, and that her last words began as an involuntary exclamation wrung from her shocked heart, not a consciously intended prayer. But instinctively and, I believe, unerringly in the final moments of her life, her soul found its true center, and at the last possible instant, she invoked God. Her last words were, I am convinced, truly an invocation . . ." (Vincent Rossi, "Presence, Participation, Performance: The Remembrance of God in the Early Hesychast Fathers," in *Paths to the Heart: Sufism and the Christian East*, edited by James S. Cutsinger, Bloomington, IN, World Wisdom/Louisville, KY, Fons Vitae, 2002, p. 111).

the foundations of the way of the invocation in various traditions. With these texts the reader can sample some of the most celebrated sacred references to jaculatory prayer, references that have nourished the spiritual life of generations of faithful. A second part, "Contemporary Doctrinal Essays," consists of articles by contemporary scholars who have been expositors of the principles of the way of the invocation. It is hoped that this series of texts will help elucidate, in a contemporary conceptual idiom, all that may have remained obscure, elliptical, or implicit in the foundational classics. The final section of this volume, "Contemporary Testimonies," is focused on the contemporary witness of spiritual and literary figures from various traditions, who have either taught, advocated, or simply illustrated the path of jaculatory prayer. In giving the final word to the voices of these sages, saints, and literary figures, we wish to provide the reader with an opportunity to taste of the spiritual flavor and inspiration of the invocatory path. It is also a way to suggest the relevance, actuality, and accessibility of this way in the modern world.

Finally, mention must be made of the contemporary practice of "centering prayer" that has been introduced to wider audiences by Fr. Thomas Keating, and which holds much in common with the universal way of *japa*. While the latter is founded upon the mystery of the divine presence within the uttered name or formula (God is *directly* and *objectively* present in His Name as Christ in the Holy Host, which may ultimately be understood, as often in India, as God and His Name being one), the contemporary forms of "centering prayer," by contrast, conceive the *mantra* as a mere "symbol of the intention" of the contemplative, such an idea being both a more *indirect* or abstract, and a more *subjective* way of envisaging the matter. This relatively subjective aspect might also be related to the modalities of the choice of a *mantra*: it appears that advocates of "centering prayer" envisage this choice exclusively as a matter of affinity and inspiration, whereas the traditional way of the invocation, as we have seen, is normally predicated upon objective criteria and traditional "guarantees," such as a line of authentic transmission, a rite of initiation, and the supervision of a spiritual guide. Finally, it is important to note that "centering prayer" does not seem to be conceived by its practitioners as the highest or most essential mode of prayer since it is not intended to substitute other forms of prayers but, rather, is envisaged as an inner preparation for other formal practices. *Japa*, by contrast, without necessarily replacing all other ritual and contemplative practices, tends to be understood, at its summit, as the very end and essence of the spiritual path, all other practices converging into its synthetic, unifying, and interiorizing power.

—Patrick Laude
Georgetown University

I.

FOUNDATIONAL TEXTS

*Every religious practice, every rite, all liturgy
is a form of the recitation of the name of the Lord.*
SIMONE WEIL

HE WHO THINKS OF ME CONSTANTLY

Bhagavad Gītā

The **Bhagavad Gītā** *(The Song of the Blessed One) is part of the Hindu epic the* Mahābhārata. *The* Bhagavad Gītā *relates the discourse given by Krishna to Arjuna just before the great battle at Kurukshetra. Arjuna, the great warrior of the clan of the Pandavas, hesitates suddenly as he is about to lead his family against the Kuru princes. Krishna, who appears to him as a charioteer, reminds him of the deepest meaning of his* kshatriya *(warrior) caste: to perform his duty without attachment to the fruits of his action. The following excerpts are taken from Song VIII in which Krishna defines* Brahman *as the "supreme imperishable" while describing the disciplines of Union (Yoga) that lead to the supreme goal, among which is the invocation of the Divine mantra.*

And at the hour of death, he who dies
Remembering Me,
Having relinquished the body,
Goes to My state of being.
In this matter there is no doubt. . . .

Therefore, at all times
Meditate on Me (or: Remember Me [*mam anusmara*])
With your mind and intellect
Fixed on Me.
In this way, you shall surely come
To Me. . . .

Uttering the single-syllable "Om"
Brahman
Meditating on Me,
He who goes forth, renouncing the body,
Goes to the supreme goal.

He who thinks of Me constantly,
Whose mind does not ever go elsewhere,
For him, the *yogin* who is constantly
Devoted,
I am easy to reach, Arjuna.

I SHALL REPEAT THY NAME

Chaitanya

Chaitanya Mahāprabhu *was born in West Bengal, India, in 1486. Although he was also known as a scholar, he is chiefly remembered for having revitalized the* bhakti *movement (path of love) in India by gathering thousands of devotees together to play musical instruments and chant the names of Krishna (*sankīrtana*). This chanting of God's names was, in his teachings, the primary source of grace for all. He is also said to have defeated Buddhist scholars by the strength of his arguments. Chaitanya died at the age of forty-eight. He left eight verses, known as the* Shikshashtaka, *which summarize his teachings, and from which the following passages are excerpted.*

1. Praise be to the name of Lord Krishna, which purifies the mind of all sensual images and unholy worldly desires; which allays the heat and fire of all those pains which man is heir to, that which offers eternal joy, which is the essence of all wisdom, and the veritable sea of happiness and fruit of all *sadhanas*, and which satisfies all our holy yearnings towards the Lord.

2. The names of the Lord are many, they are filled with power like Himself and He has laid down no laws regarding their repetition. (They can be repeated anywhere and at all times by anybody of any caste, age, or denomination.) Alas! such is His Grace, and yet we on our part have not yet developed full love and enthusiasm for the name of the Lord .

3. Perform at all times the *kirtan* of Hari with due humility like that of the grass which you tread underfoot, giving honor to the meek, and bearing up with all humiliation like unto a tree.

4. O Lord! I crave not for wealth, or high relationships, nor is it my wish to be a poet O Sri Krishna; I cherish but one desire, to Love you with single-hearted devotion through countless lives.

5. O Darling of Nanda! I, Thy slave, am steeped in the ocean of worldliness. I pray Thee keep me in Thy Lotus Feet as a particle of dust (that I may thereby attain the joy of my life).

6. O Lord Krishna! when will that moment arrive when with my eyes brimful with tears, my heart overflowing with love for Thee, and with words soft with Thy remembrance, and my whole body tense with Thy love—I shall repeat Thy name?

7. O Lord! without Thee, a moment of separation hangs upon me like countless ages and my eyes shed tears incessantly while the whole world appears to be a veritable desert, O Govinda!.

8. O Lord! what matters it if Thou embraceth me: and what if Thou crusheth me underfoot? I can never leave Thee, O Lord of my heart, I am all surrender and sacrifice to Thee, for ever and ever.

RECITE THE NAME OF THE LORD

Kabīr

Kabīr *was born around 1440. He was—and still is—widely recognized as a saint among Hindus, Sikhs, and Muslims alike. According to hagiographic accounts his mother became pregnant after visiting a Hindu shrine. Upon delivery the child was given up for adoption and Kabīr was raised among a Muslim community of weavers. It is said that the only word that he ever learned to write was "Rāma." The spiritual perspective of Kabīr belongs to* bhakti, *the devotional longing for union with God. His poetry is written in a fresh, vernacular style and it is this quality which has made his philosophy accessible to generations of Indians for whom he has remained, beyond confessional boundaries, one of the main sources of religious inspiration.*

1. The true Name is like none other name!
The distinction of the Conditioned from the Unconditioned is but a word:
The Unconditioned is the seed, the Conditioned is the flower and the fruit.
Knowledge is the branch, and the Name is the root.
Look, and see where the root is: Happiness shall be yours when you come to
    the root.
The root will lead you to the branch, the leaf, the flower, and the fruit.
It is the encounter with the Lord, it is the attainment of bliss, it is the
    reconciliation of the Conditioned and the Unconditioned.

2. Of what use is your study and reflection; of what use your reading and
    listening?
If one has not the experience of the Absolute, if you do not call on the Name
    of Hari, O stupid one, of what use is all your reflecting and thinking?

3. Today you say, "tomorrow I shall repeat His Name" and when dawns the
    morrow you say "the following day I shall repeat it."
Thus todays and tomorrows pass away and you lose the golden opportunity.

4. Utter thou the Name of the Creator.
When you lay in the womb you promised to the Lord you would remember
    Him
And day and night you would recite His Name if He would take you out of
    the misery of the womb.
You promised to fix all attention on His feet and attach yourself to His
    Name

And not for an instant to forsake Him whether the body remained happy or suffered.

Dwell upon the feet of the True Teacher,

Hold on to the Name of the Lord fearlessly.

Recite the Name of the Lord, O mind, or else thou shalt have to repent.

Damned be the joy which expels the Name out of the heart.

All praises to pain: that moment by moment compels us to repeat the Name.

The True Name is the only thing to repeat. It is the best gift to make.

You are counting the beads with the hand and with the lips you are repeating the Name; whilst your mind is wandering on all sides. This is not remembrance of God.

I AM FASCINATED BY THY NAME

Mīrābāī

Mīrābāī was born in Rajasthan in 1498 to a Rajput noble family. She was married in 1516. Her husband died before becoming king, and he left no heir. Tradition says that Mīrābāī left the court in her thirties and became a wandering mendicant. Her poems show her devotion to Rāma and Krishna. She may have written them in Gujarati, but they were almost immediately translated into Hindi and other languages. Their spiritual influence quickly spread throughout India. Mīrābāī is the most famous of the women bhakta *poets of north India. Different traditions relate that Mīrābāī met Chaitanya and Tulsīdās. It is thought that Mīrābāī passed away in 1546. In the following excerpts she typically sings the Name of the Lord as the "quintessence of scripture."*

1. My Lord: I am fascinated by Thy Name,
Who can count the merits of Thy Name, which could float stones on which
    it was inscribed?
Though she had no good deed to her credit and on the other hand she
    indulged in many evils, yet because she made her parrot repeat Thy
    Name the courtesan Ganikā ascended to heaven.
Why does not one recite Thy exploits with zest, seeing that Thou answered
    the elephant Gajendra, with alacrity and force?
Thou emancipated him from the bondage of animal life when he called Thee
    by Thy Name.
Even the sinner Ajamil frightened the messengers of Death and escaped their
    clutches by repeating his son's name Nārāyan which bore a resemblance
    to Your Name. The guru taught her the secret behind the Name, and by
    its help she attained to the Lotus Feet of Lord Girdhar.

2. I gained the priceless gift of the Lord's Name—and a veritable treasure it
    is.
The Lord conferred on me a valuable gift; the Teacher owned me as His
    own.
I lost my material wealth sacrificing all that the world holds respectable.
But this treasure is a thing that grows day by day even by spending
    (repeating).
It is the life-saving boat steered by the guru as helmsman, easily taking us
    over the ocean of worldliness.
Mīrā sings full of joy of the grace and goodness of Lord Girdhar.

3. I repeat the Name of the Lord Rāma, day in and day out.

You also remember Him, likewise, and this remembrance of the Name will wash away all your sins.

Aye, even the sins of past lives are all washed away and your past record erased by repeating the Name.

Aye, the Name is like a nectar filling a cup of gold which none can resist the temptation to quaff. O Lord Eternal! all my body and mind is steeped in Thy Name.

4. My heart moves at Thy Name, so sweet does it sound.

The pain of separation consumes my heart, yet the Name of the Dear One is ever on my lips.

I cannot forget the Name of the Lord—which like the Lord's form *līlā* (exploits), *dhāma* (abode), *guna*s (attributes), is like unto Him in efficacy and power. It is *alaukika* (divine) *sat-cit-ānanda svarūpa* (being-consciousness-bliss). It is eternal and leads its followers to the Divine realm of Eternity.

The Name, which I have been repeating for a long time, has now been engrafted in my heart by *satguru*, who is established in Divinity.

My mind is fixed on the Lord, no obstacle in the pursuit of the path can obstruct me.

I have met my guru and he has conferred the boon of realization on me.

The Name has struck roots in my heart and I am ever pining for Thee.

I discovered the great secret in uttering the Name and adhering to this quintessence of *sāstras* (scriptures), I reached my Girdhar through prayers and tears.

COMFORT IN THIS WORLD AND THE NEXT

Tulsīdās

Goswami Tulsīdās *was a medieval Hindi poet and philosopher. He was born in Rajapur, in Uttar Pradesh, in 1532 during the reign of Humayn. He is said to have written the Hindi version of the* Rāmāyana, *the famous epic devoted to Lord Rāma, under the direction of Hanumān. Tulsīdās is regarded as an incarnation of Vālmīki, the author of the classic Sanskrit* Rāmāyana. *He died in 1623 in Varanasi. The following excerpts from the* Rāmāyana *emphasize the protective and purifying powers of the Name of Rāma.*

The Lord's name Rāma fulfills all the devotee's aspirations and desires in this *Kali* (Iron) Age. It comforts them in this world and in the next. It is like a father and mother to a devotee.

In this *Kali* Age salvation is not gained by knowledge, *karma*, and worship. But only by taking shelter in the Name.

It destroys the direst demon and turns poison to nectar. Sri Hanuman performed marvelous feats by using the Name. The Name is like the Lord Narsingh, like Hiranyakasipu is this *Kali* Age, the devotee is like unto Prahlad who by remembering the Name was saved from the demon's tortures. . . .

Who abandons one who has surrendered to him,
Is a disgraceful sinner indeed.
I say to you that even if a man has killed a hundred sacred Brahmans and
then surrenders to Me (Rāma),
I will hold him fast and never forsake him.
Truly the moment anyone appears before Me he is purified of the sins of
millions of lives.
Those whose hearts are pure and know no tricks, they attain Me. I hate a
deceitful nature and egoism in man.
Whoever, driven by fear, surrenders to Me, I hold him dearer and closer to
Me than My heart itself.

GLORIFY THE NAME OF THE LORD AMITĀBHA

Sukhāvatīvyūha

*The **Larger Sukhāvatīvyūha Sūtra** is one of the foundational texts of Pure Land Buddhism. It is a sermon delivered by the Buddha at the Vulture's Peak near Rājagriha before an assembled gathering of 12,000 disciples. In this Sūtra, the Buddha relates how all mankind will be saved through Amitābha Buddha. The Bodhisattva Dharmākara, in order to deliver all beings from the sufferings of this world of illusion, made forty eight sacred vows and worked for many kalpas, according to the scripture, to bring these vows into realization. With the completion of these vows he attained Buddhahood and took the name of Amitābha, meaning "Infinite Light." The Land of Sukhāvatī is the Pure Land of the Western Paradise.*

And all the beings who have been born, who are born, who will be born in this Buddha-field, they all are fixed on the right method of salvation, until they have won Nirvāna. And why? Because there is here no place for and no conception of the two other groups, i.e. of those who are not fixed at all, and those who are fixed on wrong ways. For this reason also that world-system is called the "Happy Land". . . .

And further again, Ānanda, in the ten directions, in each single direction, in Buddha-fields countless like the sands of the river Ganges, Buddhas and Lords countless like the sands of the river Ganges, glorify the name of the Lord Amitābha, the Tathāgata, praise him, proclaim his fame, extol his virtue. And why? Because all beings are irreversible from the supreme enlightenment if they hear the name of the Lord Amitābha, and, on hearing it, with one single thought only raise their hearts to him with a resolve connected with serene faith.

And if any beings, Ānanda, again and again reverently attend to this Tathāgata, if they will plant a large and immeasurable root of good, having raised their hearts to enlightenment, and if they vow to be reborn in that world system, then, when the hour of their death approaches, that Tathāgata Amitābha, the Arhat, the fully Enlightened One, will stand before them, surrounded by hosts of monks. Then, having seen that Lord, and having died with hearts serene, they will be reborn in just that world-system Sukhāvatī. And if there are sons or daughters of good family, who may desire to see that Tathāgata Amitābha in this very life, they should raise their hearts to the supreme enlightenment, they should direct their thought with extreme resoluteness and perseverance unto this Buddha-field and they should dedicate their store of merit to being reborn therein.

THE BUDDHA OF BOUNDLESS LIGHT

Hōnen

Hōnen (1133-1212) is the patriarch of Japanese Amidism, or the School of the Pure Land (Jōdo-Shū). In his forties, he was exposed to the Pure Land teachings of the great Chinese Master Shan-tao, of which he became the propagator and chief representative in Japan. The appeal of his teaching of complete trust in the saving power of Amida's Name was widespread, especially among popular classes. His focus on the practice of nembutsu, or invocation of the Name of Amida, gave rise to the most popular form of Buddhism in Japan through the work of his disciple Shinran and the School of the True Pure Land (Jōdo-Shin-Shū). In the following text Hōnen replies to the questions of one of his devotees—Lady Kanezane Tsukinowa—on the subject of the practice of nembutsu.

I have the honor of addressing you regarding your inquiry about the Nembutsu. I am delighted to know that you are invoking the sacred name. Indeed the practice of the Nembutsu is the best of all for bringing us to *ojo*,[1] because it is the discipline prescribed in Amida's Original Vow. The discipline required in the Shingon, and the meditation of the Tendai, are indeed excellent, but they are not in the Vow. This Nembutsu is the very thing that Shakya himself entrusted[2] to his disciple, Ananda. As to all other forms of religious practice belonging to either the meditative or non-meditative classes, however excellent they may be in themselves, the great Master did not specially entrust them to Ananda to be handed down to posterity. Moreover, the Nembutsu has the endorsement of all the Buddhas of the six quarters; and, while the disciples of the exoteric and esoteric schools, whether in relation to the phenomenal or noumenal worlds, are indeed most excellent, the Buddhas do not give them their final approval. And so, although there are many kinds of religious exercise, the Nembutsu far excels them all in its way of attaining *ojo*. Now there are some people who are unacquainted with the way of birth into the Pure Land, who say, that because the Nembutsu is so easy, it is all right for those who are incapable of keeping up the practices required in the Shingon, and the meditation of the Tendai sects, but such a

---

[1] Rebirth in the Pure Land.

[2] This refers to the passage in the Meditation Sutra which says: "Buddha said to Ananda, 'Preserve well these words. I mean to preserve well the name of the Buddha of Endless Life.'"

cavil is absurd. What I mean is: that I throw aside those practices not included in Amida's Vow, nor prescribed by Shakyamuni, nor having the endorsement of the Buddhas of all quarters of the universe, and now only throw myself upon the Original Vow of Amida, according to the authoritative teaching of Shakyamuni, and in harmony with what the many Buddhas of the six quarters have definitely approved. I give up my own foolish plans of salvation, and devote myself exclusively to the practice of that mightily effective discipline of the Nembutsu, with earnest prayer for birth into the Pure Land. This is the reason why the abbot of the Eshin-in Temple in his work "Essentials of Salvation" (*Ojoyoshu*) makes the Nembutsu the most fundamental of all. And so you should now cease from all other religious practices, apply yourself to the Nembutsu alone, and in this it is all-important to do it with undivided attention. Zendo,[3] who himself attained to that perfect insight (*samadhi*) which apprehends the truth, clearly expounds the full meaning of this in his "Commentary on the Meditation Sutra," and in the two-volumed Sutra, the Buddha (Shakya) says, "Give yourself with undivided mind to the repetition of the name of the Buddha who is in Himself endless life." And by "undivided mind" he means to present a contrast to a mind which is broken up into two or three sections, each pursuing its own separate object, and to exhort to the laying aside of everything but this one thing only. In the prayers which you offer for your loved ones, you will find that the Nembutsu is the one most conducive to happiness. In the "Essentials of Salvation," it says that the Nembutsu is superior to all other works. Also Dengyo Daishi, when telling how to put an end to the misfortunes which result from the seven evils, exhorts to the practice of the Nembutsu. Is there indeed anything anywhere that is superior to it for bringing happiness in the present or the future life? You ought by all means to give yourself up to it alone.

---

[3] Chinese Patriarch of the Pure Land Sect.

TAKING REFUGE IN THE RIGHT PRACTICE

Hōnen

Shan-tao says in the fourth book of his *Kuan wu-liang-shou ching shu* (Commentary on the Meditation Sūtra):

> As to establishing faith with respect to practice, we should first note that practice is of two kinds: the first is right practice, and the second is miscellaneous practice. Right practice consists in performing only the kinds of discipline derived from the sūtras on birth in the Pure Land; hence the name "right practice." What disciplines are they? They are (1) single-mindedly and wholeheartedly reading and reciting the *Kuan wu-liang-shou ching* (Meditation Sūtra), the *A-mi-t'o ching* (Amida Sūtra), and the *Wu-liang-shou ching* (Sūtra of Immeasurable Life); (2) single-mindedly and wholeheartedly thinking of, contemplating, and meditating on the splendid view of the two (principal and dependent) rewards in that land; (3) when doing prostrations is in order, single-mindedly and wholeheartedly prostrating oneself before that buddha (A-mi-t'o Fo); (4) when reciting (holy names) is in order, single-mindedly and wholeheartedly reciting the name of that buddha; and (5) when giving praises and offerings is in order, single-mindedly and wholeheartedly giving them (to that buddha). These are called the "right (practices)."
>
> Further, within these right practices there are two types. The first is to recite single-mindedly and wholeheartedly the name of A-mi-t'o Fo, whether walking or standing still, whether seated or lying down, without considering whether the time involved is long or short and without ceasing even for an instant. This is called the rightly established act. It is so called because such a practice accords with (the intent of) A-mi-t'o Fo's vow. The other acts, such as doing prostrations to the Buddha and reading and reciting (the sūtras), are called the auxiliary acts. Besides these two (kinds of right practice), the rightly established and the auxiliary practices, all the other good practices are collectively called miscellaneous practices. If we perform the rightly established and the auxiliary practices (acts), our heart always remains intimately with and near (to A-mi-t'o Fo), and we never cease to bear him in mind. Hence these are called uninterrupted. When we perform the other miscellaneous practices, however, our concentration is always liable to be broken. Even though we can be born by dedicating the merit (of such practices to that end), they are called estranged miscellaneous practices.

14

The following is my own opinion: This passage has two purposes. The first is to make clear the types of practice proper for birth. The second is to determine the advantages and disadvantages of the two kinds of practice. As to the first, elucidation of the practice proper for birth, according to Master Shan-tao, the practices leading to birth are many but can be grouped under two major divisions: right practice and miscellaneous practice. Speaking first of right practice, there are two (ways of elucidating their) import: analysis and summation. In the first, they are divided into five kinds; later they are merged into two. First, regarding the division into five kinds, these are (1) the right practice of reading and reciting (sūtras), (2) the right practice of contemplation, (3) the right practice of doing prostrations, (4) the right practice of reciting the name, and (5) the right practice of giving praises and offerings.

The first, the right practice of reading and reciting (sūtras), is to read and recite wholeheartedly the *Kuan wu-liang-shou ching* and the other (Pure Land) sūtras; or, in the words of the above-quoted passage, "single-mindedly and wholeheartedly reading and reciting the *Kuan wu-liang-shou ching*, the *A-mi-t'o ching*, and the *Wu-liang-shou ching*." The second, the right practice of contemplation, is to contemplate wholeheartedly the two principal and dependent rewards of that land; or, as it is said in the text above, "single-mindedly and wholeheartedly thinking of, contemplating, and meditating on the splendid view of the two rewards." The third, the right practice of doing prostrations, is wholeheartedly to prostrate oneself before Amida; or, as in the text above, "when doing prostrations is in order, single-mindedly and wholeheartedly prostrating oneself before that buddha." The fourth, the right practice of reciting the name, is to recite the name Amida wholeheartedly; or, as in the words of the text above, "when reciting (holy names) is in order, single-mindedly and wholeheartedly reciting the name of that buddha." The fifth, the right practice of giving praises and offerings, is to give praises and offerings wholeheartedly to Amida; or, as in the text above, "when giving praises and offerings is in order, single-mindedly and wholeheartedly giving them (to A-mi-t'o Fo). These are called the right (practices)." If we treat "praising" and "making offerings" as two separate practices, then we must speak of "the six kinds of right practice." Here, these two are joined together, and so we speak of "the five kinds (of right practice)."

Next, regarding the two merged types of (right) practice: These are the right act and the auxiliary acts. First, the right act is reciting the name, which is the fourth of the above-listed five kinds of right practice, which is called the rightly established act. As the above-cited text says: ". . . to recite single-mindedly and wholeheartedly the name of A-mi-t'o Fo, whether walking or standing still, whether seated or lying down, without considering whether the time involved is long or short and without ceasing even for an instant. This is called the rightly established act. It is so called because such a practice accords with (the intent of) A-mi-t'o Fo's vow."

Next, the auxiliary acts are the four other kinds of acts, such as reading and reciting sūtras, with the exception of the fourth, reciting (the name). As the above text says: "Other practices, such as doing prostrations to the Buddha and reading and reciting sūtras, are called the auxiliary acts."

Question: Why, among the five kinds of practice, is only reciting the name of the Buddha called the rightly established act?

Answer: It is because this is in accord with the intent of that Buddha's vow. That is to say, reciting the name (of Amida) is the practice specified in the original vow of the Buddha. Therefore, one who dedicates oneself to this practice is carried forward by the power of the Buddha's vow and will certainly attain birth in the Pure Land. The meaning of the (Buddha's) original vow will be made clear below. Next, we will discuss the miscellaneous practices. Above, we read the following words: "Besides these two (kinds of right practice), the rightly established and the auxiliary practices (acts), all the other good practices are collectively called miscellaneous practices."

That is to say, there being endless numbers of such miscellaneous practices, we do not have the time here to discuss them in detail. We will now merely explain the five kinds of miscellaneous practice in contrast to the five kinds of right practice: (1) the miscellaneous practice of reading and reciting sūtras, (2) the miscellaneous practice of contemplation, (3) the miscellaneous practice of doing prostrations, (4) the miscellaneous practice of reciting (holy names), and (5) the miscellaneous practice of giving praises and offerings.

Regarding the first, the miscellaneous practice of reading and reciting (sūtras), with the exception of the above-mentioned *Kuan wu-liang-shou ching* and others pertaining to birth in the Pure Land, embracing and chanting the sūtras, whether Mahāyāna or Hīnayāna, whether exoteric or esoteric, is called the miscellaneous practice of reading and reciting sūtras.

Regarding the second, the miscellaneous practice of contemplation, with the exception of the above-mentioned contemplation of the principal and the dependent rewards in the Land of Sukhāvati, all practices of contemplation, whether of phenomena or of principle, set forth in the Mahāyāna or Hīnayāna, exoteric or esoteric teachings, are called the miscellaneous practice of contemplation.

Regarding the third, the miscellaneous practice of doing prostrations, with the exception of the above-mentioned prostrations to Amida, all forms of doing prostrations and showing reverence to buddhas and bodhisattvas, as well as to the various divinities, are called the miscellaneous practice of doing prostrations.

Regarding the fourth, the miscellaneous practice of reciting (holy names), with the exception of the above-mentioned practice of reciting the name of Amida, all forms of the practice of reciting the names of buddhas and bodhisattvas, as well as the names of various divinities, are called the miscellaneous practice of reciting (holy names).

Regarding the fifth, the miscellaneous practice of giving praises and offerings, with the exception of the above-mentioned practice of giving praises and offerings to Amida Buddha, all forms of giving praises and offerings to buddhas and bodhisattvas as well as to various divinities are called the miscellaneous practice of giving praises and offerings.

In addition to these five, there are also countless numbers of other practices, such as *dāna* and observance of the precepts. All of these should be included under the name of miscellaneous practice.

Next, I will determine the advantages and disadvantages of the two kinds of practice. It is said in the text above:

> If we perform the rightly (established) and the auxiliary practices (acts), our heart always remains intimate with and near (to A-mi-t'o Fo), and we never cease to remember him. Hence these are called uninterrupted. When we perform the other miscellaneous practices, however, our concentration is always liable to be broken. Even though we can indeed be born by dedicating the merit (of such practices to that end), they are called estranged miscellaneous practices.

Considering the meaning of these words, we find that with regard to these two, the right and the miscellaneous practices, there are five pairs of contrasts: (1) intimate versus estranged, (2) near versus far, (3) intermittent versus uninterrupted, (4) necessary to dedicate merit versus unnecessary to dedicate merit, and (5) pure versus miscellaneous.

As regards the first pair, the intimate versus the estranged, "intimate" means that those who perform both the rightly (established) and the auxiliary practices (acts) are brought into exceedingly close intimacy with Amida Buddha. Thus, it is said in the preceding part (that is, the third book) of the commentary (*Kuan wu-liang-shou ching shu*):

When sentient beings arouse themselves to practice and always recite with their lips the name of the Buddha, the Buddha will hear them. When they constantly and reverently bow down to the Buddha with their bodies, the Buddha will see them. When they constantly think of the Buddha in their hearts, the Buddha will know them. When sentient beings remember the Buddha, the Buddha, also, remembers them. In these three acts, the Buddha and sentient beings are not separate from each other. Hence, they are called the intimate karmic relations.

Next, "estranged" refers to miscellaneous practices. When sentient beings do not call the Buddha, the Buddha does not hear them. When they do not offer prostrations before the Buddha, the Buddha does not see them. When they do not think of the Buddha in their hearts, the Buddha does not know them. When they do not remember the Buddha, the Buddha does not remember them. In these three acts, the Buddha and sentient beings are separate from each other. Hence they are called "estranged practice."

As regards the second pair, the near versus the far, "near" means that those who perform the two, the rightly (established) and the auxiliary practices (acts), are very close to Amida Buddha. Thus, in the preceding part of the commentary, it is said: "If sentient beings desire to see the Buddha, he, responding to their desire, will appear before their eyes. Hence, this is called the close karmic relations."

Next, "far" refers to those who perform the miscellaneous practices. If sentient beings do not desire to see the Buddha, he will respond to their lack of desire and not appear before their eyes. Hence, this is called "far."

The meanings of "intimate" and "near" seem to be identical, but Shan-tao distinguishes between them. This appears in his commentary. Therefore, I have quoted these passages here and explained them.

Regarding the third pair, the uninterrupted versus the intermittent, "uninterrupted" means that those who perform the two, the rightly (established) and the auxiliary practices (acts), never cease to remember Amida Buddha. Hence, this is called "uninterrupted." Next, "intermittent" means that those who perform miscellaneous practices will constantly find their concentration on Amida Buddha broken. That is why the text says, "Our concentration is always liable to be broken."

As regards the fourth pair, "unnecessary to dedicate merit" versus "necessary to dedicate merit," for those who perform the two, the rightly (established) and the auxiliary practices (acts), even though they do not deliberately intend to dedicate the merit (of these practices toward attaining birth), their practice by its very nature forms the karma for birth. Thus, it is said in the preceding part of the commentary:

> Now the "ten recitations of the Buddha's name" in this *Kuan wu-liang-shou ching* contain and accomplish ten vows and ten practices. How do they accomplish them? "Nan-wu" indicates "devoting one's life (to the Buddha)." It also means "to launch a vow (to attain birth) and to dedicate one's merits (to that end)." (To recite) "A-mi-t'o Fo" indicates "practice." For this reason, one can attain birth (by reciting it).

Next, as for "necessary to dedicate merit," those who perform the miscellaneous practices can make them serve as sufficient cause for birth only when they intend their merits to be dedicated (to this end). When they do not intend dedicating merit, then their practice does not become sufficient cause for birth. That is why the text says, "Even though we can indeed be born by dedicating the merit (of such practices to that end). . . ."

As regards the fifth pair, the pure versus the miscellaneous, "pure" means that the two practices (acts), the rightly established and the auxiliary, are purely directed toward birth in the Land of Sukhāvatī. Next, "miscellaneous" refers to those practices that are not purely directed toward the Land of Sukhāvatī. They are practices leading to the realms of human and heavenly beings, to the three vehicles, or to (birth in other) pure lands of the ten directions. Therefore, they are called "miscellaneous." Hence, practitioners longing for the Western Land should necessarily cast aside the miscellaneous and perform the right practice.

Question: Can evidence for this understanding of the pure and the miscellaneous practices be found in the sūtras and *shāstras*?

Answer: There is more than one instance in the sūtras, *vinayas*, and *shāstras* of both Mahāyāna and Hīnayāna in which the two gateways of "pure" and "miscellaneous" practices are distinguished. The Mahāyāna establishes the "miscellaneous storehouse" among the "eight storehouses." It should be understood that seven of these eight are "pure" and one "miscellaneous." The Hīnayāna sets up the "miscellaneous" *āgama* as one of the four *āgama*s. It should be understood that three of them are "pure" and one is "miscellaneous." In the (*Ssu fen*) *lü* (*hsin-shih-ch'ao tzu-ch'ih-chi*) (Commentary on the Four-Part *Vinaya*), twenty sections are established to explain practice in accord with the precepts. Among these, the first nineteen are "pure," and the last one is "miscellaneous." In the (*abhidharma*) *shāstras*, eight sections are distinguished to explain the nature and aspects of various dharmas. The first seven are "pure," and the last is "miscellaneous." In the biographies of holy monks compiled in the T'ang and Sung dynasties, which are contained in the *Hsien-sheng-chi* (Collection of Wise and Holy Men's Biographies), it is said that the virtuous conduct of noble monks is explained under ten headings of (virtuous conduct regarding) the Dharma. Of these, the first nine are "pure," and the last is "miscellaneous." Furthermore, in the *Ta-ch'eng-ichang* (A Collection of Passages on the Meaning of Mahāyāna), there are five groups of teachings, of which the first four are "pure," and the last is "miscellaneous." Moreover, not only in the exoteric teachings, but also in the esoteric teachings, there are pure and miscellaneous divisions. It is stated in the *Sange buppō kechimyakufu* (Records of the Lines of the Dharma Transmission), by Saichō: "The first is the record of the Matrix Realm Mandala Line of Transmission. The second is the record of the Diamond Realm Mandala Line of Transmission. The third is the record of the Miscellaneous Mandala Line of Transmission." The first two are "pure," and the last is "miscellaneous." The cases in which the pure versus miscellaneous mode of classification is employed are many. Here I have briefly presented only a few of them. It should be noticed that, in their various contexts, the delineations of "pure" and "miscellaneous" are not fixed. In the light of this, the intention of Master Shan-tao in the above passage was to discuss the "pure" and "miscellaneous" with regard to Pure Land practice. The notion of the "pure" versus "miscellaneous" is not limited to canonical Buddhist writings. Many examples are also found in non-Buddhist sources. To avoid unnecessary complexity, I will not treat these here.

Shan-tao is not the only master who divides practice for birth in the Pure Land into two kinds. According to the view of the Dhyāna master Tao-ch'o, practices for birth (in the Pure Land) are many but are grouped into two categories: (1) birth through the *nembutsu* and (2) birth through the myriad practices. Next, according to the view of the Dhyāna master Huai-kan, practices for birth in the Pure Land are also many, but they are grouped into two categories: (1) birth through the *nembutsu* and (2) birth through the various practices. (Eshin makes the same division.) These three masters indeed made a very appropriate interpretation when each set up two kinds of practice to group practices for birth. Other masters did not make such an interpretation. Practitioners should certainly take notice of this fact.

The *Wang-sheng li-tsan* says:

> If people practice the *nien-fo* constantly in the above-mentioned manner until the end of their lives, then ten out of ten and a hundred out of a hundred will attain birth. Why is this so? It is because this practice keeps away other miscellaneous karmic conditions and enables one to achieve Right Mindfulness. It is because it agrees with the intent of the Buddha's original vow. It is also because it does not contradict the teaching. Further, it is because it accords with (Shākyamuni) Buddha's words.

As for those who select to cast aside the wholehearted practice and perform miscellaneous practices, it is rare for even one or two out of a hundred, or even four or five out of a thousand, to attain birth. Why? It is because their practice is disturbed by miscellaneous karmic conditions, and so they lose Right Mindfulness. It is because their practices do not agree with the Buddha's original vow. It is because they differ from the teaching. It is because they do not accord with (Shākyamuni) Buddha's words. It is because these people do not keep their minds continually fixed (on Amida Buddha). It is because their concentration is broken. It is because their desire to dedicate their merits (toward birth) is not sincere and true. It is because the passions of greed, anger, and wrong views arise and obstruct them. It is because they lack repentance and contrite hearts. Moreover, it is because they do not continually remember their indebtedness to that buddha (Amida). It is because pride arises in their hearts and, though they engage in practice, they always have desire for fame and self-benefit. It is because their hearts are filled with self-attachment, and so they do not enjoy close intimacy with their fellow practitioners and religious teachers. It is because they seek miscellaneous karmic conditions, and so they create hindrances to themselves and others in the performance of the right practice for birth.

Why do I make these assertions? It is because I have myself recently seen and heard that everywhere practitioners, whether monks or laity, differ from one another in understanding and practice and, in particular, with regard to the right and the miscellaneous practices. Only people who concentrate their minds on the right practice will attain birth, ten people out of ten. As for people who perform miscellaneous practices and so fail to attain sincerity of heart, not even one out of a thousand will be born. The advantages and disadvantages of these two practices have already been stated above.

It is my desire that all those aspiring to the Pure Land should ponder this well. Those who already in this lifetime desire birth in the land should unfailingly exert themselves in the performance of this practice, whether moving or standing still, whether sitting or lying down; they should conquer their own egos and should never cease practicing, day and night, until the end of their lives. To practice thus all through life may appear to be somewhat painful, but when life comes to an end, at that very moment they will be born into that land, where they will continue to enjoy the bliss of the unconditioned (Dharma) throughout the length of eternal *kalpas*. Until they attain buddhahood, they will never again have to pass through the cycle of birth-and-death. Is this not a joyful thing? One should take careful note of it.

The following also is my own opinion; I believe that anyone who reads these words ought to cast aside the miscellaneous and take up the exclusive practice. Why should anyone cast aside the exclusive and right practice, by which a hundred out of a hundred attain birth, and stubbornly cling to the miscellaneous practices, by which not even one out of a thousand attain birth? Practitioners ought seriously to ponder this.

PASSAGES ON THE PURE LAND WAY

Shinran

Shinran *(1173-1262) was the chief disciple of Hōnen and the founder of the School of the True Pure Land (Jōdo-Shin-Shū) form of Buddhism in Japan. Shinran was born at the close of the Heian period, a time of dramatic transition between imperial supremacy and the rise to power of the warrior clans. As befits a time of profound upheaval and uncertainty, this period saw Japanese Buddhism undergo a profound and lasting renewal, with the advent of new paths to enlightenment spreading throughout the entire Japanese society. The Pure Land School encourages its practitioners to rely on the vow of the Buddha Amida to save all beings from suffering. Shinran's innovation in Pure Land Buddhism was to take this teaching to its most extreme consequences. For him, the blessing of* nembutsu *can and should be experienced here and now and not only in a posthumous state of bliss in Amida's Pure Land.*

PREFACE

The radiant light, unhindered and inconceivable, eradicates suffering and brings realization of joy; the excellent Name, perfectly embodying all practices, eliminates obstacles and dispels doubt. This is the teaching and practice for our latter age; devote yourself solely to it. It is eye and limb in this defiled world; do not fail to endeavor in it. Accepting and living the supreme, universal Vow, then, abandon the defiled and aspire for the pure. Reverently embracing the Tathagata's teaching, respond in gratitude to his benevolence and be thankful for his compassion.

Here I, Gutoku (Shinran), of outlying islands, relying on the treatises from India and the western regions and looking to the explanations of the teachers of China and Japan, reverently entrust myself to the teaching, practice, and realization that are the true essence of the Pure Land way. And knowing keenly that the Buddha's benevolence is difficult to fathom, I seek to clarify it through this collection of passages on the Pure Land way.

TEACHING

To begin, the teaching of the Pure Land way is found in the *Larger Sutra of the Buddha of Immeasurable Life*. The central purport of this sutra is that Amida, by establishing the incomparable Vows, has opened wide the dharma-storehouse, and full of compassion for small, foolish beings, selects and bestows the treasure of virtues. It reveals that Shakyamuni appeared in this world and expounded the teachings of the way to enlightenment, seeking to save the multitudes of living beings by blessing them with the benefit that is true and real. Assuredly this sutra is the true teaching for which the Tathagata appeared in the world. It is the wondrous scripture, rare and most excellent. It is the conclusive and ultimate exposition of the One Vehicle. It is the right teaching, praised by all the Buddhas throughout the ten quarters. To teach Tathagata's Primal Vow is the true intent of this sutra; the Name of the Buddha is its essence.

PRACTICE

The practice of the Pure Land way is the great practice that embodies Amida's perfect benefiting of others. It is revealed in the Vow that all the Buddhas praise the Name, also known as "the Vow that all the Buddhas say the Name." It may further be called "the Vow of the right act, which is Amida's directing of virtue for our going forth." Amida's directing of virtue to beings through the power of the Primal Vow has two aspects: the aspect for our going forth to the Pure Land and the aspect for our return to this world. Regarding the aspect for going forth, there is great practice, there is pure *shinjin*.

The great practice is to say the Name of the Tathagata of unhindered light. This practice, comprehensively encompassing all practices, is perfect and most rapid in bringing them to fullness. For this reason, it is called "great practice." Saying the Name, then, breaks through all the ignorance of sentient beings and readily brings all their aspirations to fulfillment. Saying the Name is in itself mindfulness; mindfulness is *nembutsu*; *nembutsu* is *Namu-amida-butsu*.

The passage declaring the fulfillment of the Vows in the *Larger Sutra* states:

> The Buddha-tathagatas throughout the ten quarters, countless as the sands of the Ganges, are one in praising the majestic power and the virtues, inconceivably profound, of the Buddha of immeasurable life. All sentient beings, as they hear the Name, realize even one thought-moment of *shinjin* and joy, which is directed to them from Amida's sincere mind, and aspiring to be born in that land, they then attain birth and dwell in the stage of nonretrogression.

Further the sutra states:

> The Buddha said to Maitreya, "If there are persons who, having heard the Name of that Buddha, leap and dance with joy and say it even once,

know that they receive the great benefit; that they acquire the unexcelled virtues."

Bodhisattva Nagarjuna states in the *Commentary on the Ten Bodhisattva Stages*:

> If a person desires quickly to attain
> The stage of nonretrogression,
> He or she should, with a reverent heart,
> Say the Name, holding steadfast to it.
>
> When persons doubt as they plant roots of good,
> The lotus (in which they gain birth) will not open;
> But for those whose *shinjin* is pure,
> The flower opens, and immediately they see the Buddha.

Bodhisattva Vasubandhu states in the *Treatise on the Pure Land*:

> O World-honored one, with the mind that is single
> I take refuge in the Tathagata of unhindered light
> Filling the ten quarters
> And aspire to be born in the land of happiness.
>
> Relying on the sutras
> In which the manifestation of true and real virtues is taught,
> I compose a *gatha* of aspiration, a condensation,
> That accords with the Buddha's teaching.
>
> Contemplating the power of the Buddha's Primal Vow,
> I see that no one who encounters it passes by in vain;
> It quickly brings to fullness and perfection
> The great treasure ocean of virtues.

With these passages from the sacred words of the Buddha and from the treatises, we know in particular that the great practice is not a foolish being's practice of directing his or her own merit toward attainment of birth. It is the fulfilled practice that Amida directs to beings out of great compassion, and therefore is called "not-directing virtue (on the part of beings)." This practice indeed embodies the Primal Vow, in which the *nembutsu* is selected and adopted. It is the supreme, all-surpassing universal Vow. It is the true and wondrous right *dharma* that is the One Vehicle. It is the unexcelled practice that perfectly embodies all good acts.

24

The word *naishi* (even) in the passages from the *Larger Sutra* is used to indicate an upper or lower limit while omitting what is between. (In the second passage,) *ichinen* (saying of the Name once) indicates single-heartedly practicing the *nembutsu*. Single-heartedly practicing the *nembutsu* is a single voicing. A single voicing is saying the Name. Saying the Name is constant mindfulness. Constant mindfulness is right-mindedness. Right-mindedness is the true act (that brings about birth in the Pure Land).

Further, *naishi ichinen* in no way refers to one thought in contemplation on the Buddha's virtue or to one utterance in repeated recitation of the Name. (As the first passage shows), *naishi ichinen* (even one thought-moment) refers to the ultimate brevity and expansion of the length of time in which one attains the mind and practice (i.e., *shinjin* and *nembutsu*) that result in birth in the Pure Land. Let this be known.

THE HOLY ONE SPEAKS HIS NAME

Zohar

The **Zohar** *(Book of Splendor) is the seminal work of the Kabbalah, written by Rabbi Shimon bar Yochai (in the second century A.D.) and his students. It is one of the basic texts of the oral Torah and Kabbalah. Under the form of a commentary on the Pentateuch, written partly in Aramaic and partly in Hebrew, it presents an integral Kabbalistic doctrine, treating of metaphysics, cosmogony and cosmology, spiritual psychology, good and evil, sin and redemption. It first appeared in Spain in the thirteenth century, being made known through the Kabbalist Moses de Leon. The* Zohar *contains and elaborates upon much of the material found in the* Sefer Yetzirah *(Book of Creation) and* Sefer Bahir *(Book of Illumination). The following passage hallows the divine Tetragrammaton as God's supreme utterance, the source of both mercy and awe.*

The secret Garden
In worlds of light hidden
—Two hundred and fifty
Encompassing worlds—
Where Shekhinah's splendor
From splendor proceeding
Its splendor sends forth
To the ends of creation,
In the fullness of glory
Is revealed in its beauty
To the eyes made seeing—
The garden of Eden.

The Ancient, the Father,
The Holy One speaks
His Name again pronouncing
"Yod He Vau He" again
Gloriously crying.
Then speak the lightful Hosts
Making brave music:
His thirteen paths of mercy
They gladly proclaim.

Who sees the mighty ones
High in the Heavens
Mighty in beauty?
Who sees the Chariots
Holy and glorious?
Who sees the Hosts in
The bright courts of glory
Exalting and praising
In awe and in fear
In joy and in wonder
The Holy One's Name?

THE LIGHT OF THE INTELLECT

Abraham Abulafia

Abraham ben Samuel Abulafia *was a Sicilian Kabbalist born in Saragossa, Spain, in 1240. He is considered as one of the most important, but also most complex, figures in Jewish mysticism. During his early youth he traveled to Palestine and Italy, studying philosophy under Hillel ben Samuel ben Eliezer of Verona. Upon his return to Spain, his thirst for knowledge led him, in his thirties, to the world of speculative and operative Kabbalah. He immersed himself in the* Sefer Yetzirah *(Book of Creation) and began to teach a kind of Kabbalistic "Yoga" based upon the ontological value of Hebrew letters, numbers, and vowel points, as well as a rigorous moral and spiritual ascesis. He taught that a complex science of combinations, permutations, and invocations of these symbols gives access to the highest spiritual realities and may even confer a "prophetic" status. After his attempt to convert the Pope—who died from apoplexy one day before Abulafia's arrival—in 1280, he appeared as a prophet and Messiah in Sicily. He was condemned by Rabbi Solomon ben Adret and had to leave Sicily. His end is unknown. With him the Kabbalah took a definitely visionary and prophetic turn, with a special emphasis on the mysteries of the Tetragrammaton.*

It is well known that the letters (of the Hebrew alphabet) have no vibration of their own, and therefore the Blessed God set into nature, in accordance with the Intellect, powers into the whole mouth in order to bring the letters into pronunciation, according to the form of their existence as found in books. And vowel-points were set into the letters to demonstrate the vibration of pronunciation in their translation from the book to the mouth. Thus the vibrations are essentially the letters of the mouth, and accidentally, the letters in the book. And joined to this by necessity with the places of the various vibrations, for nothing will vibrate without place and time. The elements of space are the dimensions, and the elements of time that are the cycles through which it is measured in divisions such as years, months, days and the like. And because of the dimensions, a person must know (how) to lengthen the pronunciation of each of the letters.

And this is the secret of the pronunciation when you wish to mention this glorious (divine) Name: Make yourself right and isolate yourself in a special place, so that no one will hear your voice except you, then purify your heart and your soul from all thoughts of this world. Then imagine in that moment that your soul is separated from your body, removed from this world, and living in the world-to-come, which is the source of the life that exists distributed in all that lives. This is (identical with the Active) Intellect, which is the source of all wisdom, understanding, and knowledge of the Supreme King of kings, the Holy, Blessed One, whom all revere with a great awe—and this awe of one who has attained (such spiritual heights) is a double awe: (comprising) the awe (that comes of) love (of God) and the awe (that comes from) ascent. When your mind (*da'at*) comes to cleave to (the divine) Mind (*da'at*), it puts knowledge (*da'at*) into you. Your mind must turn aside from itself all extraneous knowledge, apart from the knowledge (*da'at*) of (God), which joins you and (God) by virtue of (God's) honored and awesome Name. And therefore, you must know the form of its pronunciation, and this is its configuration: These are the twenty-five "forward" (permutations). There are another twenty-five "backward" (permutations), and here they are: In this same way, (permute) with (the letter) *hay*, and similarly with *vav*, and similarly with the last *hay*. (Note by Moses Cordovero: We have abbreviated this, and even corrected it accordingly, because the author of *Sefer HaNikkud* confused the issue by means of a poem to obscure it, but he reveals it at the end of his work, so we will explain it as is fitting and proper. Now we return to his words:)

This is the configuration: When we begin to pronounce the *'alef*, in whatever configuration you pronounce it (i.e. with whatever vowel), because it alludes to the secret of (divine) unity, you should not lengthen it beyond one breathe. And do not interrupt it in any way at all until you have completed its pronunciation. Lengthen this particular breath, according to your breathing ability, for as long as you are able to hold it. And chant the *'alef*, or whatever letter, while in the form of the vowel-point (as explained below): Thus the *cholem* (with the sound of "o") is above (the letter). When you begin to pronounce it, turn your face to the east, (looking) neither up nor down, and sit wrapped in clean, pure white robes over all your garments, or with your *tallit* over your head, wearing *tefillin* (and) facing east because that is the direction from which light enters the world. With (each of) the twenty-five (pairs of letters) you must move your head (correctly).

In the case of *cholem*, begin facing due east, purify your thoughts, and raise your head little by little as you breathe (out), until you are finished with your head facing upwards. After you have finished, prostrate yourself on the ground once. Do not make a distinction between the breath of the *'alef* and that of the letter attached to it (in the pair), apart from one breath, either short or long. Alternatively, between each letter of the name, whether "forward" or the reverse, you may breathe twice without pronouncing (anything), but no more; however, you have the option of fewer. When you have completed each row, you have the option of breathing five times only, but no more; however, you have the option of fewer. If you change or deviate from this order while (proceeding through) the row, return to the beginning of that row, until you have said it correctly.

By analogy with the shape of the *cholem* which draws (one) upwards, (you must) sing the *chirek* (with the sound of "ee," which) draws (one) downwards. Thus you may draw down supernal power to adhere to you. In the case of *shuruk* (with the sound of "oo"), neither raise nor lower your head, but push it forwards at a middle level. In the case of *tsere* (with a sound of "ay") push your head from left to right, and in the case of *kamatz* (with the sound of "ah") from right to left.

In any case, if after completing this, you see a form before you, prostrate yourself before it immediately. And if you hear a voice, either loud or soft, and want to understand what it is saying, answer it immediately. Say: "Speak my lord, for your servant is listening" (I Samuel 3:9). (But then) do not speak at all, but listen carefully to what it may tell you. If you experience great terror, which you cannot bear, even in the middle of the pronunciation, prostrate yourself immediately. And if you do not hear or see (anything), abandon this for the rest of that week. It is good to use this pronunciation (technique) once a week, in a form that "runs and returns" (Ezekiel 1:14), for with regard to this matter a covenant has been made.

So, what can I add further, to make this known to you? For it is well known that if you are wise, you can understand this entire order from hints. If you feel that your intellect is weak in wisdom, or in (knowledge of) *kabbalah*, or that your thought is strongly bound to the vanities of time, do not pronounce the name, lest you sin more.

THE QUESTION OF PROPHECY

Abraham Abulafia

You, my son, if wise and loving the Name with all your heart, must put your mind to the root you were drawn from, and learn that you were taken from the honored throne, influxed by the enlightened mind, created from the image of God and His likeness, found wrapped in the abundance of the truth of His existence, did not in short come from nothing; and so come back to me for He will save you, Holy Israel by Name, the saint who adores you. Now listen to these words, my son, and wear them at your throat and write them on the tablet of your heart. Trust in the Name and not in a man, for the man who secures himself by way of man is crushed, and this is what you must study day and night in the Torah of God, the Torah of Moses, man of God in the wisdom of God. You must read the books of the prophets with good sense, and sing the written word and its knowledge, and immerse yourself in the sayings of the wise men (may their memory be blessed) in clean and mindful study, and look into the company of the kabbalists with Godly wisdom and you will find the desired things through them, find that all are shouting about wisdom's lack and the want of true actions and the diminution of sense; for there is no wisdom, knowledge, speech, or act in all the Torah, the prophets, the scriptures, and sayings of the wise men (blessed be their memory) that is not within the kabbalists. And as you plunge on, let your heart afterward pay attention to the knowledge of the honored and faithful Name, which shall be blessed, and carve it deep into your heart so that it cannot be erased; for with it our rabbis (may their memory be blessed) have said: The Holy Names will not be erased for they all point to the image of God, and how may the artist erase the ineradicable image? Neither mouth the Names without purpose but respect and bless them, believing they are angels of the blessed Name, sent to raise you, higher and higher, above all the nations of the world; so that all will see the sign of God upon you and will fear you. This is the strong foundation I give into your hands, to know and carve into your heart the Holy Names and the whole Torah and all the scriptures and prophetics filled with Names and fearful things, connecting one with the other, imaging them, trying them, testing them, purifying them and believing they are the writings of the king delivered to you for your own good all the length of your days, as you carry on with them, dealing clearly and lucidly, cleansing yourself of all sins, crimes, guilts, and mean acts—in preparation for the time when you are raised to the level of love and are beloved above and below, and commence to combine the first Name YOD HAY VAV HAY (YHVH), and observe its infinite connections and combinations uplifting and whirling like a cycling wheel, this way and that, like a scroll; so that you may not rest until you behold that He strengthens through much motion and much confusion in your imagination amid the whirling of your ideas; and even when you stop you will return to Him asking for the wisdom that you cannot forsake because of the beginnings and ends of the alphabet and the *gematria* and *notarikon* and the combinations of the letters and their changes and rhythms and the recognitions of their different shapes and the knowledge of their names and the understanding of their meaning and the fashioning out of the letter ALEPH many words and from the many words, One: they are the truths of the Kabbalah of the prophets which, through their knowledge, raised your cry to God, who will answer; for you will be attached to His company.

And now, my son, the secret of God to the ones who fear Him and his covenant: He who fears God and His total covenant will be told His covenant, and it will be kept from the others, for honor is not befitting fools.

GAZING AT THE LETTERS

Rabbi Isaac of Akko

Isaac of Akko (1250-1350) was, like Abulafia, a Kabbalist of the School of Segovia. In his youth he studied in Akko (Acre) at the School of Rabbi Shlomo. He arrived in Spain, via Italy, in 1305 where he met with Rabbi Moses de Leon and learned from him the secrets of the composition of the Zohar. His writings include a Commentary on the Secrets of Rabbi Moses ben Nachman *(Nachmanides) and a* Commentary on the Sefer Yetzirah *(Book of Creation). The following two brief excerpts express the mystery of the Divine Name as the intermediary form between the finite and the Infinite, and its consequent power as a means of spiritual union.*

Remember God and God's love constantly. Let your thought not be separated from God. I declare, both to individuals and to the masses: If you want to know the secret of binding your soul above and joining your thought to God—so that by means of such continuous contemplation you attain incessantly the world that is coming, and so that God be with you always, in this life and the next—then place in front of the eyes of your mind the letters of God's name, as if they were written in a book in Hebrew script. Visualize every letter extending to infinity. What I mean is: when you visualize the letters, focus on them with your mind's eye as you contemplate infinity. Both together: gazing and meditating.

CLIMBING THE LADDER

Rabbi Isaac of Akko

I, Rabbi Isaac of Akko, was contemplating, according to the method I received from the great one of his generation—great in humility, the wisdom of Kabbalah, philosophy, and the science of permutation of letters. He insisted that I set the ten *Sefirot* in front of me, as it is written: "I set YHVH before me always." I saw them today above my head like a pillar, with their feet on my head and their heads high above, beyond all the four worlds: emanation, creation, formation, and actualization. As long as I was contemplating this ladder—the name of the Blessed Holy One—I saw my soul cleaving to *Ein Sof.*

PHILOKALIA

The **Philokalia** (literally "Love of the Beautiful") is a collection of texts written between the fourth and fifteenth centuries by Hesychast spiritual masters of the Eastern Orthodox Christian tradition. Although these texts were widely known prior to their publication as the Philokalia, their influence grew considerably after they appeared as a compilation in Greek in Venice in 1782. They were then translated into Church Slavonic by Paissy Velichovsky, and later into Russian by St. Theophan the Recluse. The Philokalia has exercised an influence far greater than any book, other than the Bible, in the recent history of the Orthodox Church. The following excerpts are from St. Philotheos of Sinai (ninth century), Ilias the Presbyter (early twelfth century), St. Symeon the New Theologian (949-1022), and St. Gregory of Sinai (thirteenth century.)

St. Philotheos of Sinai

The blessed remembrance of God—which is the very presence of Jesus—with a heart full of wrath and a saving animosity against the demons, dissolves all trickeries of thought, plots, argumentation, fantasies, obscure conjectures and, in short, everything with which the destroyer arms himself and which he insolently deploys in his attempt to swallow our souls. When Jesus is invoked, He promptly burns up everything. For our salvation lies in Christ Jesus alone. The Savior Himself made this clear when He said: "Without Me you can do nothing" (John 15:5).

Ilias the Presbyter

96. Not all have the same purpose in prayer: one man has one purpose, another has another. One prays that, if possible, his heart may always be absorbed in prayer; another, that he may even transcend prayer; and a third, that he may not be hindered by thoughts during prayer. But all pray either to be preserved in what is good, or not to be carried away by evil.

97. If everyone is humbled by prayer—for he who prays with humility is brought to compunction—it follows that anyone outwardly boastful is not praying in a state of humility.

98. Bearing in mind the widow who persuaded the cruel judge to avenge her (cf. Luke 18: 2-5), the man who prays will never lose heart because the blessings to be gained through prayer are slow in arriving.

99. Prayer deserts you if you give attention to thoughts within and to conversations without. But if you largely ignore both in order to concentrate on it, it will return to you.

100. Unless the words of prayer penetrate to the soul's depths no tears will moisten your cheeks.

101. Corn will spring up for the farmer who has hidden seed in the earth; tears will flow for the monk who diligently attends to the words of prayer.

102. The key to the kingdom of heaven is prayer. He who uses this key as he should sees what blessings the kingdom holds in store for those who love it. He who has no communion with the kingdom gives his attention merely to worldly matters.

103. The intellect cannot say boldly to God at the time of prayer: "Thou hast burst my bonds asunder; I will offer to Thee the sacrifice of praise" (Psalm 116:16-17. LXX), unless out of a desire for higher things it frees itself from cowardice, indolence, excessive sleep, and gluttony, all of which lead it to sin.

104. He who is distracted during prayer stands outside the first veil. He who undistractedly offers the single-phrased Jesus Prayer is within the veil. But he alone has glimpsed the holy of holies who, with his natural thoughts at rest, contemplates that which transcends every intellect, and who has in this way been granted to some extent a vision of the divine light.

St. Symeon the New Theologian

True and unerring attentiveness and prayer mean that the intellect keeps watch over the heart while it prays; it should always be on patrol within the heart, and from within—from the depths of the heart—it should offer up its prayers to God. Once it has tasted within the heart that the Lord is bountiful (cf. Psalm 34:8. LXX), then the intellect will have no desire to leave the heart, and it will repeat the words of the Apostle Peter, "It is good for us to be here" (Matthew 17:4). It will keep watch always within the heart, repulsing and expelling all thoughts sown there by the enemy. To those who have no knowledge of this practice it appears extremely harsh and arduous; and indeed it is oppressive and laborious, not only to the uninitiated, but also to those who, although genuinely experienced, have not yet felt the delight to be found in the depths of the heart. But those who have savored this delight proclaim with St. Paul, "Who will separate us from the love of Christ?" (Romans 8:35).

Our holy fathers hearkened to the Lord's words, "Out of the heart proceed evil thoughts, murders, adulteries, unchastity, thefts, perjuries, blasphemies; these are the things that defile a man" (Matthew 15:19-20); and they also hearkened to Him when He enjoins us to cleanse the inside of the cup so that the outside may also be clean (cf. Matthew 23:26). Hence they abandoned all other forms of spiritual labor and concentrated wholly on this one task of guarding the heart, convinced that through this practice they would also possess every other virtue, whereas without it no virtue could be firmly established. Some of the fathers have called this practice stillness of the heart, others attentiveness, others the guarding of the heart, others watchfulness and rebuttal, and others again the investigation of thoughts and the guarding of the intellect. But all of them alike worked the earth of their own heart, and in this way they were fed on the divine manna (cf. Exodus 16:15).

Ecclesiastes is referring to this when he says, "Rejoice, O young man, in your youth; and walk in the ways of your heart" (Ecclesiastes 11:9), blameless, expelling anger from your heart; and "if the spirit of the ruler rises up against you, do not desert your place" (Ecclesiastes 10:4), by "place" meaning the heart. Similarly our Lord also says, "Out of the heart proceed evil thoughts" (Matthew 15:19), and "Do not be distracted" (Luke 12:29). And again, "Strait is the gate and narrow is the way that leads to life" (Matthew 7:14). Elsewhere He also says, "Blessed are the poor in spirit" (Matthew 5:3); that is to say, blessed are those who are destitute of every worldly thought. St. Peter says likewise, "Be watchful, be vigilant, because your adversary, the devil, walks about like a roaring lion, seeking whom he may devour" (I Peter 5:8). And St. Paul writes very plainly to the Ephesians about the guarding of the heart, "We do not wrestle against flesh and blood" (Eph. 6:12), and so on. And our holy fathers have also spoken in their writings about guarding the heart, as those who wish can see for themselves by reading what St. Mark the Ascetic, St. John Klimakos, St. Hesychios the Priest, St. Philotheos of Sinai, St. Isaiah the Solitary, and St. Varsanuphios, and the entire book known as *The Paradise of the Fathers*,[1] have to say about the subject.

In short, if you do not guard your intellect you cannot attain purity of heart, so as to be counted worthy to see God (cf. Matthew 5:18). Without such watchfulness you cannot become poor in spirit, or grieve, or hunger and thirst after righteousness, or be truly merciful, or pure in heart, or a peacemaker, or be persecuted for the sake of justice (cf. Matthew 5:3-10). To speak generally, it is impossible to acquire all the other virtues except through watchfulness. For this reason you must pursue it more diligently

---

[1] The title *Paradise* is applied in particular to the *Lausiac History* of Palladius, but also more broadly to any work on Egyptian monasticism, such as the *Historia Monachorum in Aegypto* or the *Apophthegmata*. Cf. the Syriac collection compiled by Anan-Isho, *The Paradise or Garden of the Holy Fathers*, English translation by E. A. Wallis Budge (2 vols., London, 1907).

than anything else, so as to learn from experience these things, unknown to others, that I am speaking to you about. Now if you would like to learn also about the method of prayer, with God's help I will tell you about this too, in so far as I can.

Above all else you should strive to acquire three things, and so begin to attain what you seek. The first is freedom from anxiety with respect to everything, whether reasonable or senseless—in other words, you should be dead to everything. Secondly, you should strive to preserve a pure conscience, so that it has nothing to reproach you with. Thirdly, you should he completely detached, so that your thoughts incline towards nothing worldly, not even your own body.

Then sit down in a quiet cell, in a corner by yourself, and do what I tell you. Close the door, and withdraw your intellect from everything worthless and transient. Rest your beard on your chest, and focus your physical gaze, together with the whole of your intellect, upon the center of your belly or your navel. Restrain the drawing-in of breath through your nostrils, so as not to breathe easily, and search inside yourself with your intellect so as to find the place of the heart, where all the powers of the soul reside. To start with you will find there darkness and an impenetrable density. Later, when you persist and practice this task day and night, you will find, as though miraculously, an unceasing joy. For as soon as the intellect attains the place of the heart, at once it sees things of which it previously knew nothing. It sees the open space within the heart and it beholds itself entirely luminous and full of discrimination. From then on, from whatever side a distractive thought may appear, before it has come to completion and assumed a form, the intellect immediately drives it away and destroys it with the invocation of Jesus Christ. From this point onwards the intellect begins to be full of rancor against the demons and, rousing its natural anger against its noetic enemies, it pursues them and strikes them down. The rest you will learn for yourself, with God's help, by keeping guard over your intellect and by retaining Jesus in your heart. As the saying goes, "Sit in your cell and it will teach you everything."[2]

---

[2] *Apophthegmata*, alphabetical collection, Moses 6; English translation by Sister Benedicta Ward, *The Sayings of the Desert Fathers: The Alphabetical Collection* (2nd ed., London/Oxford, 1981), p. 139.

St. Gregory of Sinai

"In the morning sow your seed," says Solomon—and by "seed" is to be understood the seed of prayer—"and in the evening do not withhold your hand," so that there may be no break in the continuity of your prayer, no moment when through lack of attention you cease to pray; "for you do not know which will flourish, this or that" (Ecclesiastes 11:6). Sitting from dawn on a seat about nine inches high, compel your intellect to descend from your head into your heart, and retain it there. Keeping your head forcibly bent downwards, and suffering acute pain in your chest, shoulders, and neck, persevere in repeating noetically or in your soul "Lord Jesus Christ, have mercy." Then, since that may become constrictive and wearisome, and even galling because of the constant repetition—though this is not because you are constantly eating the one food of the threefold name, for "those who eat Me," says Scripture, "will still he hungry" (Ecclesiastes 24:21)—let your intellect concentrate on the second half of the prayer and repeat the words "Son of God, have mercy." You must say this half over and over again and not out of laziness constantly change the words. For plants which are frequently transplanted do not put down roots. Restrain your breathing, so as not to breathe unimpededly; for when you exhale, the air, rising from the heart, beclouds the intellect and ruffles your thinking, keeping the intellect away from the heart. Then the intellect is either enslaved by forgetfulness or induced to give its attention to all manner of things, insensibly becoming preoccupied with what it should ignore. If you see impure evil thoughts rising up and assuming various forms in your intellect, do not be startled. Even if images of good things appear to you, pay no attention to them. But restraining your breathing as much as possible and enclosing your intellect in your heart, invoke the Lord Jesus continuously and diligently and you will swiftly consume and subdue them, flaying them invisibly with the divine name. For St. John Klimakos says, "With the name of Jesus lash your enemies, for there is no more powerful weapon in heaven or on earth."[3] . . . Some of the fathers advise us to say the whole prayer, "Lord Jesus Christ, Son of God, have mercy," while others specify that we say it in two parts—"Lord Jesus Christ, have mercy," and then "Son of God, help me"—because this is easier, given the immaturity and feebleness of our intellect. For no one on his own account and without the help of the Spirit can mystically invoke the Lord Jesus, for this can be done with purity and in its fullness only with the help of

---

[3] *The Ladder of Divine Ascent*, Step 21 (*P.G.* lxxxviii, 945C), English translation, p. 200.

the Holy Spirit (cf. I Corinthians 12:3). Like children who can still speak only falteringly, we are unable by ourselves to articulate the prayer properly. Yet we must not out of laziness frequently change the words of the invocation, but only do this rarely, so as to ensure continuity. Again, some fathers teach that the prayer should be said aloud; others, that it should be said silently with the intellect. On the basis of my personal experience I recommend both ways. For at times the intellect grows listless and cannot repeat the prayer, while at other times the same thing happens to the voice. Thus we should pray both vocally and in the intellect. But when we pray vocally we should speak quietly and calmly and not loudly, so that the voice does not disturb and hinder the intellect's consciousness and concentration. This is always a danger until the intellect grows accustomed to its work, makes progress, and receives power from the Spirit to pray firmly and with complete attention. Then there will be no need to pray aloud—indeed, it will be impossible, for we shall be content to carry out the whole work with the intellect alone.

UNCEASING INTERIOR PRAYER

The Way of a Pilgrim

The Way of a Pilgrim *is the best-known classic of Russian Orthodox spirituality. It is an anonymous text from the mid-nineteenth century. It was first published in Russia in 1881 under the title* Intimate Conversations of a Pilgrim with his Spiritual Father. *It is a fresh and inspiring account of a wandering pilgrim's search for the perfection of prayer, following St. Paul's admonition, "Pray without ceasing" (I Thess. 5:17), which he heard during a religious service. The text has become a classic of Hesychasm, the way of "quietness" (Greek:* hesychia*) in Eastern Orthodox Christianity, which practices the jaculatory Jesus Prayer, or Prayer of the Heart.*

"Be so kind, Reverend Father, as to show me what prayer without ceasing means and how it is learnt. I see you know all about these things."

He took my request kindly and asked me into his cell. "Come in," said he; "I will give you a volume of the holy Fathers from which with God's help you can learn about prayer clearly and in detail."

We went into his cell and he began to speak as follows. "The continuous interior Prayer of Jesus is a constant uninterrupted calling upon the divine Name of Jesus with the lips, in the spirit, in the heart; while forming a mental picture of His constant presence, and imploring His grace, during every occupation, at all times, in all places, even during sleep. The appeal is couched in these terms, 'Lord Jesus Christ, have mercy on me.' One who accustoms himself to this appeal experiences as a result so deep a consolation and so great a need to offer the prayer always, that he can no longer live without it, and it will continue to voice itself within him of its own accord. Now do you understand what prayer without ceasing is?"

"Yes indeed, Father, and in God's name teach me how to gain the habit of it," I cried, filled with joy.

"Read this book," he said. "It is called the *Philokalia*, and it contains the full and detailed science of constant interior prayer, set forth by twenty-five holy Fathers. The book is marked by a lofty wisdom and is so profitable to use that it is considered the foremost and best manual of the contemplative spiritual life. As the revered Nicephorus said, 'It leads one to salvation without labor and sweat.'"

"Is it then more sublime and holy than the Bible?" I asked.

"No, it is not that. But it contains clear explanations of what the Bible holds in secret and which cannot be easily grasped by our short-sighted understanding. I will give you an illustration. The sun is the greatest, the most resplendent, and the most wonderful of heavenly luminaries, but you cannot contemplate and examine it simply with unprotected eyes. You have to use a piece of artificial glass which is many millions of times smaller and darker than the sun. But through this little piece of glass you can examine the magnificent monarch of stars, delight in it, and endure its fiery rays. Holy Scripture also is a dazzling sun, and this book, the *Philokalia*, is the piece of glass which we use to enable us to contemplate the sun in its imperial splendor. Listen now, I am going to read you the sort of instruction it gives on unceasing interior prayer."

He opened the book, found the instruction by St. Simeon the New Theologian, and read: "Sit down alone and in silence. Lower your head, shut your eyes, breathe out gently and imagine yourself looking into your own heart. Carry your mind, i.e., your thoughts, from your head to your heart. As you breathe out, say 'Lord Jesus Christ, have mercy on me.' Say it moving your lips gently, or simply say it in your mind. Try to put all other thoughts aside. Be calm, be patient, and repeat the process very frequently."

The old man explained all this to me and illustrated its meaning. We went on reading from the *Philokalia* passages of St. Gregory of Sinai, St. Callistus, and St. Ignatius, and what we read from the book the *starets* explained in his own words. I listened closely and with great delight, fixed it in my memory, and tried as far as possible to remember every detail. In this way we spent the whole night together and went to Matins without having slept at all.

The *starets* sent me away with his blessing and told me that while learning the Prayer I must always come back to him and tell him everything, making a very frank confession and report; for the inward process could not go on properly and successfully without the guidance of a teacher.

In church I felt a glowing eagerness to take all the pains I could to learn unceasing interior prayer, and I prayed to God to come to my help. Then I began to wonder how I should manage to see my *starets* again for counsel or confession, since leave was not given to remain for more than three days in the monastery guest-house, and there were no houses near.

However, I learned that there was a village between two and three miles from the monastery. I went there to look for a place to live, and to my great happiness God showed me the thing I needed. A peasant hired me for the whole summer to look after his kitchen garden, and what is more gave me the use of a little thatched hut in it where I could live alone. God be praised!

I had found a quiet place. And in this manner I took up my abode and began to learn interior prayer in the way I had been shown, and to go to see my *starets* from time to time.

For a week, alone in my garden, I steadily set myself to learn to pray without ceasing exactly as the *starets* had explained. At first things seemed to go very well. But then it tired me very much. I felt lazy and bored and overwhelmingly sleepy, and a cloud of all sorts of other thoughts closed round me. I went in distress to my *starets* and told him the state I was in.

He greeted me in a friendly way and said, "My dear brother, it is the attack of the world of darkness upon you. To that world, nothing is worse than heartfelt prayer on our part. And it is trying by every means to hinder you and to turn you aside from learning the Prayer. But all the same the enemy only does what God sees fit to allow, and no more than is necessary for us. It would appear that you need a further testing of your humility, and that it is too soon, therefore, for your unmeasured zeal to approach the loftiest entrance to the heart. You might fall into spiritual covetousness. I will read you a little instruction from the *Philokalia* upon such cases."

He turned to the teaching of Nicephorus and read, "'If after a few attempts you do not succeed in reaching the realm of your heart in the way you have been taught, do what I am about to say, and by God's help you will find what you seek. The faculty of pronouncing words lies in the throat. Reject all other thoughts (you can do this if you will) and allow that faculty to repeat only the following words constantly, "Lord Jesus Christ, have mercy on me." Compel yourself to do it always. If you succeed for a time, then without a doubt your heart also will open to prayer. We know it from experience.'

"There you have the teaching of the holy Fathers on such cases," said my *starets*, "and therefore you ought from today onwards to carry out my directions with confidence, and repeat the Prayer of Jesus as often as possible. Here is a rosary. Take it, and to start with say the Prayer three thousand times a day. Whether you are standing or sitting, walking or lying down, continually repeat, 'Lord Jesus Christ, have mercy on me.' Say it quietly and without hurry, but without fail exactly three thousand times a day without deliberately increasing or diminishing the number. God will help you and by this means you will reach also the unceasing activity of the heart."

I gladly accepted this guidance and went home and began to carry out faithfully and exactly what my *starets* had bidden. For two days I found it rather difficult, but after that it became so easy and likeable, that as soon as I stopped, I felt a sort of need to go on saying the Prayer of Jesus, and I did it freely and willingly, not forcing myself to it as before.

I reported to my *starets*, and he bade me say the Prayer six thousand times a day, saying, "Be calm, just try as faithfully as possible to carry out the set number of prayers. God will vouchsafe you His grace."

In my lonely hut I said the Prayer of Jesus six thousand times a day for a whole week. I felt no anxiety. Taking no notice of any other thoughts however much they assailed me, I had but one object, i.e., to carry out my *starets'* bidding exactly. And what happened? I grew so used to my Prayer that when I stopped for a single moment, I felt, so to speak, as though something were missing, as though I had lost something. The very moment I started the Prayer again, it went on easily and joyously. If I met anyone, I had no wish to talk to him. All I wanted was to be alone and to say my Prayer, so used to it had I become in a week.

My *starets* had not seen me for ten days. On the eleventh day he came to see me himself, and I told him how things were going. He listened and said, "Now you have got used to the Prayer. See that you preserve the habit and strengthen it. Waste no time, therefore, but make up your mind by God's help from today to say the Prayer of Jesus twelve thousand times a day. Remain in your solitude, get up early, go to bed late, and come and ask advice of me every fortnight."

I did as he bade me. The first day I scarcely succeeded in finishing my task of saying twelve thousand prayers by late evening. The second day I did it easily and contentedly. To begin with, this ceaseless saying of the Prayer brought a certain amount of weariness, my tongue felt numbed, I had a stiff sort of feeling in my jaws, I had a feeling at first pleasant but afterwards slightly painful in the roof of my mouth. The thumb of my left hand, with which I counted my beads, hurt a little. I felt a slight inflammation in the whole of that wrist, and even up to the elbow, which was not unpleasant. Moreover, all this aroused me, as it were, and urged me on to frequent saying of the Prayer. For five days I did my set number of twelve thousand prayers, and as I formed the habit I found at the same time pleasure and satisfaction in it.

Early one morning the Prayer woke me up as it were. I started to say my usual morning prayers, but my tongue refused to say them easily or exactly. My whole desire was fixed upon one thing only—to say the Prayer of Jesus, and as soon as I went on with it I was filled with joy and relief. It was as though my lips and my tongue pronounced the words entirely of themselves without any urging from me. I spent the whole day in a state of the greatest contentment, I felt as though I was cut off from everything else. I lived as though in another world, and I easily finished my twelve thousand prayers by the early evening. I felt very much like still going on with them, but I did not dare to go beyond the number my *starets* had set me. Every day following I went on in the same way with my calling on the Name of Jesus Christ, and that with great readiness and liking. Then I went to see my *starets* and told him everything frankly and in detail.

He heard me out and then said, "Be thankful to God that this desire for the Prayer and this facility in it have been manifested in you. It is a natural consequence which follows constant effort and spiritual achievement. So a machine to the principal wheel of which one gives a drive, works for a long while afterwards by itself; but if it is to go on working still longer, one must oil it and give it another drive. Now you see with what admirable gifts God in His love for mankind has endowed even the bodily nature of man. You see what feelings can be produced even outside a state of grace in a soul which is sinful and with passions unsubdued, as you yourself have experienced. But how wonderful, how delightful, and how consoling a thing it is when God is pleased to grant the gift of self-acting spiritual prayer, and to cleanse the soul from all sensuality! It is a condition which is impossible to describe, and the discovery of this mystery of prayer is a foretaste on earth of the bliss of Heaven. Such happiness is reserved for those who seek after God in the simplicity of a loving heart. Now I give you my permission to say your Prayer as often as you wish and as often as you can. Try to devote every moment you are awake to the Prayer, call on the Name of Jesus Christ without counting the number of times, and submit yourself humbly to the will of God, looking to Him for help. I am sure He will not forsake you, and that He will lead you into the right path."

Under this guidance I spent the whole summer in ceaseless oral prayer to Jesus Christ, and I felt absolute peace in my soul. During sleep I often dreamed that I was saying the Prayer. And during the day if I happened to meet anyone, all men without exception were as dear to me as if they had been my nearest relations. But I did not concern myself with them much. All my ideas were quite calmed of their own accord. I thought of nothing whatever but my Prayer, my mind tended to listen to it, and my heart began of itself to feel at times a certain warmth and pleasure. If I happened to go to church the lengthy service of the monastery seemed short to me, and no longer wearied me as it had in time past. My lonely hut seemed like a splendid palace, and I knew not how to thank God for having sent to me, a lost sinner, so wholesome a guide and master.

But I was not long to enjoy the teaching of my dear *starets*, who was so full of divine wisdom. He died at the end of the summer. Weeping freely I bade him farewell, and thanked him for the fatherly teaching he had given my wretched self, and as a blessing and a keepsake I begged for the rosary with which he said his prayers.

And so I was left alone. Summer came to an end and the kitchen garden was cleared. I had no longer anywhere to live. My peasant sent me away, giving me by way of wages two roubles, and filling up my bag with dried bread for my journey. Again I started off on my wanderings. But now I did not walk along as before, filled with care. The calling upon the Name of Jesus Christ gladdened my way. Everybody was kind to me, it was as though everyone loved me.

Then it occurred to me to wonder what I was to do with the money I had earned by my care of the kitchen garden. What good was it to me? Yet stay! I no longer had a *starets*, there was no one to go on teaching me. Why not buy the *Philokalia* and continue to learn from it more about interior prayer?

I crossed myself and set off with my Prayer. I came to a large town, where I asked for the book in all the shops. In the end I found it, but they asked me three roubles for it, and I had only two. I bargained for a long time, but the shopkeeper would not budge an inch. Finally he said, "Go to this church nearby, and speak to the church warden. He has a book like that, but it's a very old copy. Perhaps he will let you have it for two roubles." I went, and sure enough I found and bought for my two roubles a worn and old copy of the *Philokalia*. I was delighted with it. I mended my book as much as I could; I made a cover for it with a piece of cloth, and put it into my breast pocket with my Bible.

And that is how I go about now, and ceaselessly repeat the Prayer of Jesus, which is more precious and sweet to me than anything in the world. At times I do as much as forty-three or four miles a day, and do not feel that I am walking at all. I am aware only of the fact that I am saying my Prayer. When the bitter cold pierces me, I begin to say my Prayer more earnestly and I quickly get warm all over. When hunger begins to overcome me, I call more often on the Name of Jesus, and I forget my wish for food. When I fall ill and get rheumatism in my back and legs, I fix my thoughts on the Prayer and do not notice the pain. If anyone harms me I have only to think, "How sweet is the Prayer of Jesus!" and the injury and the anger alike pass away and I forget it all. I have become a sort of half-conscious person. I have no cares and no interests. The fussy business of the world I would not give a glance to. The one thing I wish for is to be alone, and all by myself to pray, to pray without ceasing; and doing this, I am filled with joy. God knows what is happening to me! Of course, all this is sensuous, or as my departed *starets* said, an artificial state which follows naturally upon routine. But because of my unworthiness and stupidity I dare not venture yet to go on further, and learn and make my own, spiritual prayer within the depths of my heart. I await God's time. And in the meanwhile I rest my hope on the prayers of my departed *starets*. Thus, although I have not yet reached that ceaseless spiritual prayer which is self-acting in the heart, yet I thank God I do now understand the meaning of those words I heard in the Epistle—*"Pray without ceasing."*

STRIKE DOWN EVERY KIND OF THOUGHT

The Cloud of Unknowing

The Cloud of Unknowing, *written around 1375, first appeared in Middle English. It is an anonymous manual on contemplation that owes as much to the deep spiritual experience of its author as to the influence of the medieval mystical tradition. It was most likely written by a monk, of whom we know nothing. The treatise is addressed to a contemplative aspirant. The author of* The Cloud of Unknowing *also wrote or translated several works, including a translation of a work by Pseudo-Dionysius. The* Cloud of Unknowing *advocates an apophatic spirituality, that is, a way of placing images and concepts beneath a "cloud of forgetting," and then striving to love God who is hidden from our soul by a "cloud of unknowing." The excerpt is from Chapter VII which treats of "how to deal with all thoughts."*

How to deal with all thoughts during this exercise, particularly those which result from one's own investigation, knowledge, and natural acumen.
If any thought should rise and continue to press in, above you and between you and that darkness, and should ask you and say: "What do you seek and what would you have?" you must say that it is God whom you would have. "Him I covet, him I seek, and nothing but him." And if the thought should ask you who that God is, you must answer that it is the God who made you and ransomed you, and with his grace has called you to his love.[1] And say: "You have no part to play." So say to the thought: "Go down again."[2] Tread it down quickly with an impulse of love, even though it seems to you to be very holy; even though it seems that it could help you to seek him.[3] Perhaps the thought will bring to your mind a variety of excellent and wonderful instances of his kindness; it will say that he is most sweet and most loving,

---

[1] Gallus, in quoting the verse I Peter 4:1, "Christ having suffered in the flesh, you must arm yourselves with a mind like his," makes the point that "the mysteries of the divine humanity are like a ladder which bring(s) us up to the contemplation of the divinity" (Explanation on the *Ecclesiastical Hierarchy*, chap. III).

[2] The Middle English reads: "In him sei thou kanst no skile." The "thou" is ambiguous: Does it refer to the thought or the thinker? The Latin version could definitely be rendered: "I am unable to express what he is; and so, thought, go down again!"

[3] Gregory the Great, speaking of the grades of contemplation, says that in the third, the mind is to rise above itself and turn to the contemplation of the invisible creature; but that it cannot begin to do this unless it learns to reject and tread under foot (*calcare*) whatever comes into its mind by way of the senses and imagination. Cf. *Homilies on Ezekiel* II, V, 9 (PL 76, 993-4).

gracious and merciful. The thought will want nothing better than that you should listen to it; for in the end it will increase its chattering more and more until it brings you lower down to the recollection of his passion.[4] There it will let you see the wonderful kindness of God; it looks for nothing better than that you should listen to it. For soon after that he will let you see your former wretched state of life;[5] and perhaps as you see and think upon it, the thought will bring to your mind some place in which you used to live.[6] And so at the end, before you are even aware of it, your concentration is gone, scattered about you know not where. The cause of this dissipation is that in the beginning you deliberately listened to the thought, answered it, took it to yourself and let it continue unheeded.[7]

Yet what it said was nonetheless both good and holy. Yes indeed, so holy that if any man or woman should think to come to contemplation without many sweet meditations of this sort, on their own wretched state, on the passion, the kindness and the great goodness and the worthiness of God, they will certainly be deceived and fail in their purpose.[8] At the same time, those men and women who are long practiced in these meditations must leave them aside,[9] put them down and hold them far under the cloud of forgetting, if they are ever to pierce the cloud of unknowing between them and their God.

---

[4] The author continues his teaching that in this exercise, the purgative and illuminative ways, and the exercises proper to them, must be rejected. So de Balma on the purgative life makes the point that reflections on the Lord's passion are especially necessary for beginners.

[5] Prior to such meditations on the passion, the novice must first bring to mind his sinfulness—and particularly the grave sins he has committed in the past (de Balma).

[6] In the *Spiritual Exercises* of Ignatius Loyola, the author first deals with the purgative life; and in offering a meditation on the "tale of one's personal sins," directs the "worker" to think of the places where he used to live (Exx 36).

[7] "Those who are called to this exercise of dark contemplation cannot afford to relax in the ascent to God; they must never turn away their concentration deliberately, but only when necessity demands" (Gallus, on the *Divine Names*, chap. 1).

[8] "That most excellent of speculative contemplations (viz. of the trinitarian processions) must be relinquished, not because it is not good and noble, but because there is an apprehension by which alone the supreme Spirit can be grasped: and this alone is the best part of Mary" (Gallus, Explanation on the *Mystical Theology*).

[9] The teaching of John of the Cross is exactly the same: e.g., in the *Ascent of Mount Carmel* II, 12:6: "Great, therefore, is the error of spiritual persons who have practiced approaching God by means of images and forms and meditations, as befits beginners. God would now lead them on to further spiritual blessings, interior and invisible, by taking from them the pleasure and sweetness of discursive meditation."

Therefore, when you set yourself to this exercise, and experience by grace that you are called by God to it, then lift up your heart to God by a humble impulse of love, and mean the God who made you and ransomed you, and has in his grace called you to this exercise. Have no other thought of God; and not even any of these thoughts unless it should please you. For a simple reaching out directly towards God is sufficient, without any other cause except himself.[10] If you like, you can have this reaching out, wrapped up and enfolded in a single word. So as to have a better grasp of it, take first a little word, of one syllable rather than of two; for the shorter it is the better it is in agreement with this exercise of the spirit.[11] Such a one is the word "God" or the word "love." Choose which one you prefer, or any other according to your liking—the word of one syllable that you like best. Fasten this word to your heart, so that whatever happens it will never go away. This word is to be your shield and your spear,[12] whether you are riding in peace or in war. With this word you are to beat upon this cloud and this darkness above you. With this word you are to strike down every kind of thought under the cloud of forgetting; so that if any thought should press upon you and ask you what you would have, answer it with no other word but with this one. If the thought should offer you, out of its great learning, to analyze that word for you and to tell you its meanings, say to the thought that you want to keep it whole, and not taken apart or unfastened. If you will hold fast to this purpose, you may be sure that the thought will not stay for very long. And why? Because you will not allow it to feed itself on the sort of sweet meditations that we mentioned before.

---

[10] "He is attained and perceived by the grasp of the affection which reaches out for him above mind and thought" (*The Ascent to Contemplative Wisdom*, p. 247).

[11] This is the author's practical application of Denis' teaching in the *Mystical Theology*, chap. III: "We ascend from the lowest to the highest . . . and when the ascent is complete, there will be no words at all."

[12] Cassian (or Abbot Isaac) *Collationes* X, 10: "Take a short verse of a psalm and it shall be your shield and buckler." "This short verse," says Cassian, in his conferences of the Abbot Moses—he is speaking of the invocation "O God, come to my aid: O Lord, make haste to help me"—"shall be your impenetrable breastplate and stoutest shield" (*Collationes* X, 10, PL 49, 833). De Balma chooses to offer a spiritual exegesis of Exodus 17:11-12: "Moses merited to be Israel's victor by lifting up his hands in burning prayer to heaven—a shield and a spear of love and courage reaching out to God."

THE SERMON FOR PALM SUNDAY

St. Bernardino of Siena

St. Bernardino of Siena *was born of noble parents at Massa, Italy, in 1350. He entered the Franciscan order in 1402 and became its vicar-general in 1437. He was the most famous preacher of his time and spoke in all parts of Italy with exceptional charisma. Three times he refused to become a bishop. He died in 1444. He was canonized by Pope Nicholas V six years later. It was found that blood drawn from his dead body continued to remain in a liquid state. His writings were first printed in Lyons (1501) and Paris (1636). Bernardino's writings are, for the most part, formal treatises upon morality, asceticism, and mysticism. He is known as one of the foremost advocates of the grace of the Name of Jesus in the Western Church.*

That those who extol and proclaim the singular Name of Jesus who is the Savior, come to fruition in the Word of God.

The repetition of the Name of Jesus is the most wonderful thing that can be advocated, because, by this, as St. Bernard says, His Word is heard and proclaimed in all its luminous splendor. In what other way can you find the light of God so greatly, so unexpectedly, and so fervently manifested, unless it be in the repetition of the Name of Jesus. With all the brilliance and sweetness of this Name, God has called us to enter into His wonderful glory—that we might be illuminated and in this light be able to apprehend His glory. As the Apostle says in his letter to the Ephesians 5: "for you were once in darkness, but now you are light in the Lord: walk then as children of light." So also, in like manner, this Name should be extolled and proclaimed, that it might shine forth. It should not be hidden, nor exposed in speech that reflects an evil heart, or a polluted tongue, but rather brought forth from a person who is like a vessel of election. Hence God says in Acts 9: "this man is a chosen vessel to me to carry My Name among the nations and kings and children of Israel." "A chosen vessel," He says—and is this not a container where the sweetest liquor is kept, a liquor that can be poured forth and imbibed while at the same time it continues to shimmer and glow in the vessel? "To carry" He says, "My Name"—this is like the fire lit in the autumn to burn the dry and useless stubble left after harvesting; it is like the risen sun dispelling the darkness of light that covers the acts of thieves that wander about and rifle houses. Thus it was that Paul spoke to the people, like thunder pealing forth; like an overpowering fire; like the burning sun—consuming all perfidy, dispersing error, and clarifying the truth, much as a strong fire burns up wax. Truly, the Name of Jesus was spread broad by voice, by letter, by miracles, and by examples, for Paul raised this Name of Jesus continuously. He extolled it in all things, and above all, he extolled it before kings, before the nations, and to the sons of Israel. The Apostle carried this Name as if it were a torch with which he illuminated his fatherland. He proclaimed it, saying in Romans 13: "the night is far advanced, and the day is at hand. Let us therefore put aside the works of darkness and put on the armor of light. Let us walk becomingly as in the day." He showed to all this shining lamp, like the light over the candelabrum—announcing in every place Jesus and His crucifixion. And how greatly did that light shine forth in Paul, blinding the eyes of those who listened as if with wonder and astonishment. Peter describes this in Acts 3: "like lightning flashing, curing, and making strong the crippled limbs of their bodies and illuminating the spiritual blindness of many." Did he not dispense fire when he said: "In the Name of Jesus Christ arise and walk"? St. Bernard tells us, both in the source quoted above, and also in his treatise on the Apostle Mark, that "the perfect have extolled it always"—that is to say, the Name of Jesus, "and, God cooperating, the Word having been as it were confirmed, signs follow"—which signs were truly shown in the Name of Jesus. And how are these signs shown? They are shown by miracles, by the persecution that tyrants imposed upon the faithful, and by those shining lights, who by explaining the scriptures have destroyed the false teachings of heretics—and what is more, it is daily demonstrated in our own sweet meditations and in the frequent illuminations of the elect. Thus it is that the Church, the Bride of Christ, in support of this testimony, rejoices in singing from Psalm 95: "Lord Thou hast taught me from my youth, and even now I shall pronounce Thy miraculous Name"—that is to say, invoking it continuously. And the prophet further exhorts us to this, saying: "sing to the Lord and bless His Name: announce His Salvation from day to day"—which is to say, constantly invoke the Name of Jesus, our Savior.

How by the power of this Name, merit is gained in good works.
With respect to our actions, the Name of Jesus is a labor of merit, for by the virtue of this Name, grace and merit are accumulated as is testified to by the Apostle in his first letter to the Corinthians 12: "no one can say 'Jesus is Lord' except in the Holy Spirit." Now, Alex of Ales understands in this passage a triple definition: namely, no one can say Jesus is God in his heart, with his mouth, or in his actions unless he does it through the strength of the Holy Spirit. He says "no one" because if anyone is able to bear this most Holy Name

worthily, it will inevitably be efficacious in producing in him a worthy life and eternal glory. This is so because all acts that are elicited of the Holy Spirit are worthy of eternal glory. Great indeed the is the richness and treasure with which this most Holy Name of Jesus overflows. Indeed, when the Name of Jesus is continuously praised and glorified, with humble devotion and with sweetness, this hidden treasure is shared and spread abroad in the manner that is recommended in Ecclesiastes 51: "*I will praise Thy Name continuously and will extol it in all things.*" St. Chrysostom in commenting on this passage says that it refers to a person who deeply loves and invokes the Name of God repeatedly, and who is, by this invoking, exulted in the Most High Lord—that is to say, by the accumulation of merit and the acquisition of graces.

THE NAME ADMIRABLE ABOVE ALL NAMES

St. Jean Eudes

St. Jean Eudes (1601-1680) was a disciple of Cardinal Bérulle and belonged to the "French School," a movement for the renewal of religious life in the seventeenth century. Ordained in 1625, he founded the women's congregation of Our Lady of Charity of the Refuge in 1641. His major contribution to the Church as a whole was his foundation of public devotion to the Sacred Heart. Eudes composed the mass and office of the Sacred Heart in 1668-1669, and a feast of the Sacred Heart was first celebrated by Eudist communities in 1672. His devotion to the invocation of the name of Mary and Jesus is evidenced in several of his writings.

If I were to follow my own convictions, I should never speak or write any word but one, *Jesus*, for it seems to me that the tongue which has once pronounced, and the pen that has once written this adorable name and this divine word, *Jesus*, should never again be used to speak or write anything else. Besides, to say *Jesus* is to say everything, and after having said *Jesus*, there is nothing more to add, inasmuch as *Jesus* is an abridged word which in itself contains everything great that can be said or thought. *Jesus* is the name admirable above all names which, through its immense grandeur, fills heaven and earth, time and eternity, the minds and hearts of all the angels and saints; it even fills and possesses, from all eternity, the infinite capacity of the Heart of God, of the Father, Son, and Holy Ghost. Even if I could write nothing, therefore, save the one word *Jesus*, and could go everywhere in the world crying out unceasingly and pronouncing no other name except this one *Jesus, Jesus, Jesus*, I believe that I should be saying and writing enough to fill to capacity the minds and hearts of all the inhabitants of the earth.

THE SACRAMENT OF THE PRESENT MOMENT

Jean-Pierre de Caussade

Jean-Pierre de Caussade *was born in 1675 in Toulouse, France. He joined the Jesuit novitiate at eighteen and was ordained priest in 1708. After teaching at the Jesuit College in Toulouse, he was appointed spiritual director in charge of the Jesuit retreat house in Nancy. There he was spiritual director of the Nuns of the Visitation between 1731 and 1740. In 1740 he was back in Toulouse, and for the next three years was appointed rector at various Jesuit colleges. His letters at the time describe his dislike of administrative duties, having to deal with important officials, and so on, and of his attempts to resign himself to them through surrender to the will of God. In 1746 he returned to the house of the Professed at Toulouse, where he died in 1751 at the age of 76. Notes made of talks given by Caussade and excerpts from his correspondence were preserved by the nuns whom he directed and were first published in 1860 under the title* Self-Abandonment to Divine Providence.

If everything that happens to souls who have surrendered themselves to God is all that matters, it must be true that having everything there is nothing to complain of, and if they do complain, they are lacking in faith and living by their reason and their senses, which do not perceive the sufficiency of grace and can never be satisfied. According to the scriptures, to glorify the name of God is to recognize that he is holy, to adore and love him for everything he utters. Everything God does each moment tells us something significant, manifesting his purpose in so many words and sentences. His purpose is but one in itself, incomprehensible, unutterable; but its effects are countless and known by as many names. To glorify the name of God is to know, worship, and love that adorable, incomprehensible word which is his very essence. It is also to recognize and adore and worship his ineffable will every moment in all its manifestations, seeing everything as mere glimmers and shadows of that eternally divine purpose, divine in all its works, all its utterance, all its manifestations, and by what ever name. This is how Job called down the blessing on the name of God. The total desolation by which his will was made known was blessed by this holy man in the name of God—not cursed—and, in blessing it, Job affirmed that the most terrible manifestation of God's divine purpose was nevertheless sacred whatever form it might take, just as David blessed it always in whatever circumstances. And so it is by this continual discovery, this manifestation, this revelation of the divine purpose of God in all things, that his kingdom is in us, that his will is done on earth as it is in heaven, that he gives us our daily bread. His purpose includes and contains the substance of that incomparable prayer, dictated by Jesus, which, as ordained by God and the holy Church, we recite aloud several times a day, but which we also repeat every moment from the bottom of our heart as we rejoice in all we do and suffer in obedience to his word. What the lips take many syllables, sentences, and time to pronounce, the heart is really saying all the time. This is how faithful souls must glorify God in the depths of their being, though they groan at being powerless to do so in any other way, so like adversity are the means God employs to bestow his grace and favors on them. Herein lies the secret of divine wisdom, to impoverish the senses while enriching the heart. The emptiness of one makes the fullness of the other, and this is so universally true that the more holy the heart, the less the outward eye can detect it.

THE KEY TO SALVATION

Ibn 'Atā' Allāh Al-Iskandarī

Ibn 'Atā' Allāh Al-Iskandarī (1259-1309) was born in Alexandria. He met Abū'l-Abbās Al-Mursī at age seventeen and converted to tasawwuf *(Sufism), the mystical dimension of Islam. In 1287 he succeeded his master as head of the Shādhilī order. He devoted his life to teaching, spiritual direction, and writing. The following lines are excerpted from his treatise* The Key to Salvation and the Lamp of the Soul *(Miftāh Al-Falāh wa Misbāh Al-Arwāh), which was written as a spiritual manual for his disciples.*

BENEFITS OF THE INVOCATION IN GENERAL

Let whosoever desires the benefits of invoking follow the established texts, inasmuch as its benefits are not insignificant nor can they be exhausted. The invocation of the traditional authorities has numerous advantages, so let us mention what comes to mind. We say: invoking repels, subdues, and tames Satan, but pleases the Compassionate (*ar-Rahmān*). It angers Satan, removes worry and grief from the heart, attracts joy and happiness, and eliminates sadness and evils.

Invoking strengthens the heart and the body, puts inner and outer affairs in order, gladdens the heart and face, making the latter radiant. Moreover, it procures sustenance and facilitates obtaining it. It clothes the invoker in dignity; it inspires correct behavior in every affair. Its permanence is one of the means of obtaining the love of God; it is one of the greatest of the gateways leading to that love.

Invoking causes the vigilance that leads to the station of spiritual virtue (*ihsān*), wherein the servant adores God as if he saw Him with his very own eyes. It causes one to turn to God often; for whoever turns to God by remembering Him frequently will eventually turn to Him in all his affairs. Invoking brings closeness to the Lord and opens the door of gnosis within the heart. It bestows on the servant the veneration and reverential fear (*haybah*) of his Lord, while for the forgetful man the veil of reverential fear over his heart is very thin.

Invoking causes God's remembrance of the servant, which is the greatest honor and loftiest distinction. Through the invocation, the heart of man lives just as the seed lives through the downpour of rain. The invocation is the nourishment of the soul just as food is the nourishment of the body. Invoking polishes the heart of its rust, which is forgetfulness (*ghaflah*) and the pursuit

57

of its passions. It is to meditation like a lamp that guides one in the dark towards an open road. It thwarts sinful actions: ". . . Verily, good deeds annul bad deeds . . ." (Qur'ān 11:114). Invoking puts an end to the estrangement that occurs between the Lord and the forgetful servant.

Whatever the formula used by the servant to remember God with, such as: "Glory be to God!" (*subhāna'llāh*) or "God is Most Great" (*Allāhu Akbar*) or "There is no divinity but God" (*Lā ilāha illa'llāh*) or any formula or praise, it calls the attention of God on the Glorious Throne to the servant. All acts of worship withdraw from the servant on the Day of Resurrection except the remembrance of God, the belief in His Oneness (*tawhīd*), and praise of Him. Whoever gets to know God in times of prosperity through his invoking, gets to know Him in times of adversity through his piety.

A tradition states,

> Indeed, when misfortune befalls the obedient servant who frequently remembers God Most High, or when he asks of God a need, the angels say, "My Lord, there is a familiar voice from a familiar servant." When the forgetful person who shuns God calls upon Him or asks something of Him, the angels say, "My Lord, there is an unknown voice from an unknown servant."

Of all deeds there is none more redemptive from the chastisement of God, Who possesses Majesty, than the invocation. For the servant it is the cause for the descent of peace (*sakīnah*) upon him, for the encircling of angels around him, for their alighting by him, and for his being enveloped by Mercifulness. How sublime is such a grace! The invocation is for a tongue undistracted by slander, lying, and every falsehood!

The companion who sits with the invoker is not troubled by him; the invoker's close friend is happy with him. On the Day of Judgment, the invoker's encounters with others will not be a source of sorrow for him or of harm or remorse.

Invoking with tears and lamentation is a cause for obtaining the shelter of the umbral Throne on the great Day of Requital, when mankind stands for a period awaiting judgment. Whoever is diverted by the remembrance of God from making a request will be given the best of what is given to the one who does ask; and things will be made easy for the servant most of the time and in most situations.

The movement of invoking with the tongue is the easiest movement for a person. The plants of the gardens of Paradise are the invocation. Paradise is a good earth and sweet water; it is composed, indeed, of plains, and the plants therein are "Glory be to God" (*subhāna'llāh*), "Praise be to God" (*al-hamdu li'llāh*), "There is no divinity but God" (*Lā ilāha illa'llāh*), and "God is Most Great" (*Allāhu Akbar*), as are found in the sound *hadīth*s. These formulas are a means of liberating oneself from the fires of Hell and are a protection from forgetfulness in this world, the world of ignomy. The textual proof of this, as found in the Qur'ān, is: "Therefore remember Me, I will remember you" (Qur'ān 2:152). Forgetfulness of God is what makes servants forget their souls and that is the extreme of corruption.

Invoking is a light for the servant in this world, his grave, his resurrection, and his assembling with others on the Day of Judgment. It is the fundamental principle and the door to spiritual union; it is the sign of authority whereby it assails the ego and passional desires. When the invocation is firmly rooted in the heart and drops down in it and the tongue becomes subordinate to it, the invoker is in need of nothing; so he progresses and ascends. As for the forgetful man, even if he be wealthy, he is in reality poor, and if he be powerful, he is actually base.

For the one who remembers God, invoking unites his dispersed heart and pervades his will and his broken resolve. It scatters his sadness, his sin, and the forces of Satan and his followers. Invoking brings the heart closer to the Hereafter and keeps the world away from the heart, even though the world is around it. Invoking warns the heedless heart to abandon its pleasures and deceptions. It redresses what has passed and prepares itself for what is to come.

The invocation is a tree whose fruit is gnosis; it is the treasure of every gnostic: God is with the invoker through His nearness, authority, love, bestowal of success and protection. The invocation puts in proper perspective the emancipation of slaves, the holy war and its hardships, fighting in the way of God, injury, and the expenditure of money and gold. The invocation is the summit, source, and basis of gratitude of God. He whose tongue does not cease being moist with the remembrance of God and who fears God in His prohibitions and commands is granted entrance into the Paradise of the beloved ones and nearness to the Lord of Lords. ". . . Lo! the noblest of you, in the sight of God, is the best in conduct . . ." (Qur'ān 49:13).

The invoker enters Paradise laughing and smiling and is at home therein, living in ease. Invoking removes hardness from the heart and engenders tenderness and mildness. Forgetfulness of the heart is a disease and an ailment, while remembrance is a cure for the invoker from every malady and symptom, as was said by a poet:

When we became ill, by Your remembrance we were cured,
And when at times we abandon it, a relapse do we suffer.

Remembrance is the source and foundation of God's friendship; forgetfulness is the origin and summit of His enmity. When forgetfulness takes possession of the servant, it drives him back to God's enmity in the ugliest way. Invoking removes misfortunes, pushing them to one side, and draws unto itself blessings and every beneficial thing. It is a cause for the blessings of God and the noble angels upon him, so that he emerges out of the darkness into the light and enters the abode of peace. The gatherings to invoke are gardens of Paradise, and indulging therein pleases the Compassionate. God Most High boasts of those who remember Him to the angels of heaven, for its place among the acts of worship is the highest and most sublime.

The most excellent of those who perform good deeds are those who most often remember God in all situations. Remembrance takes the place of all deeds, it being alike whether they are connected with wealth or with something else. Invoking strengthens the limbs and facilitates pious work. It eases difficult matters, opens locked doors, mitigates hardships, and lessens toil. It is a security for the fearful and deliverance from desert wastelands. Among the participants in the race track for the winning trophy, the invoker is triumphant. Soon you will see, when the dust settles: was it a horse you rode—or a donkey?

Invoking is a cause for God's approval of His servant, because the invocation has made him aware of His Majesty and Beauty and praise. Through the invocation the dwellings of Paradise are built; but for the forgetful, no dwelling in Paradise is built. Invocations are a barrier between the servant and hellfire. If the remembrance is continuous and permanent, then the barrier is good and solid; if not, it is fragile and torn.

Remembrance is a fire that neither stays nor spreads. When it enters a house, it leaves no substance or trace therein. It eliminates the portions of food remaining which exceed one's bodily need or are forbidden to consume. Invoking removes darkness and brings forth radiant lights. Angels ask forgiveness for the servant when he perseveres in the remembrance and praise of God. Lands and mountains are proud of the one who, amongst men, remembers God while on them.

Remembrance is the sign of the thankful believer, whereas the hypocrite is rarely found to be invoking. He whose wealth or children distract him from remembering God is lost; but the one who remembers God experiences delights sweeter than the pleasure of food and drink. In this world the invoker's face and heart are covered with beauty and happiness; in the Hereafter his face is whiter and more luminous than the moon. The earth witnesses on his behalf just as it does for every person who obeys or disobeys God. Invoking elevates the participant to the most exalted of ranks and conveys him to the highest of stations.

The invoker is alive even if he be dead; while the forgetful man, even though he is alive, is actually to be counted among the dead. The invoker has his thirst quenched at death and is safe from the apprehensions of the perils associated with death. Among the forgetful, the one who remembers God is like a lamp in a dark house, while the forgetful are themselves like a dark night with no morning to follow.

If something occupies the invoker and distracts him from the remembrance of God, then he risks chastisement. If he is unmindful of this point, then it is like someone sitting with a king without the proper conduct: that will expose him to being punished. Concentrating on the remembrance of God for a while is being careful not to mix sins with pious deeds. "Being careful," if only for a short while, has tremendous benefit.

ON CHOOSING THE TYPE OF REMEMBRANCE

Note that there are those who choose *Lā ilāha illa'llāh, Muhammadun rasūlu'llāh* (There is no divinity but God, Muhammad is the Messenger of God) at the beginning and at the end, and there are others who choose *Lā ilāha illa'llāh* in the beginning, and in the end confine themselves to *Allāh*. These latter are the majority. Then there are those who choose *Allāh, Allāh* and others who choose *Huwa* (He). He who affirms the first view advances as his proof that faith is not sound nor acceptable unless the Testimony of Messengerhood is connected with the Testimony of the Unity of God. They maintain:

> If you say, "That is so only at the beginning of faith, but that if one's faith is established and becomes stable, then the two formulas can be separated," the answer is that if separation is not permitted in the beginning, then it is all the more fitting that it not be permitted in the end.

Do you not see that the call to prayer, which is one of the rituals of Islam, is not valid except on condition that the two Testimonies be always together? Just as the call to prayer never varies from the condition prescribing that the two Testimonies be joined together, so similarly the believer cannot change the condition that makes his faith acceptable through his uttering the two

Testimonies. Hence, there is no way one can separate the two Testimonies. God Most High has said, ". . . He misleadeth many thereby, and He guideth many thereby," (Qur'ān 2:26) up to His word (exalted be He!), ". . . and they sever that which God ordered to be joined . . ." (Qur'ān 2:27).

One of the commentators has said, "God has commanded that the mention of the Prophet be connected with the mention of Himself; so whosoever separates them separates what God has decreed should be joined; and whosoever separates what God has commanded should be joined is called 'lost.'"

God Most High has said, "We have exalted thy fame (*dhikrak*)" (Qur'ān 94:4). Another of the commentators has said, "The verse means: 'I am not to be mentioned unless you are mentioned with Me.'" It is maintained that if a claimant alleges that he is in the station of extinction (*maqām al fanā'*) and says "I see naught but God, and I contemplate naught but Him; therefore, I do not remember anyone but Him," the response is that, when Abū Bakr as-Siddīq (may God be pleased with him!), brought all his wealth to the Prophet the latter said to Abū Bakr, "What have you left for your family?" He replied, "I left God and His Messenger for them." He did not confine himself to saying *Allāh*, but rather he combined the two remembrances. Similarly, in the circumambulation of the Ka'bah, sand is prescribed for a reason; but when the reason vanishes, the sand remains.

As for the second invocation, it is *Lā ilāha illa'llāh* (There is no divinity but God), and its textual proof is in the words of God (exalted be He!): "Know that there is no divinity but God . . ." (Qur'ān 47:19); and in the words of the Prophet: "The best thing that I and the Prophets before me have said is 'There is no divinity but God.'"

In this Testimony there is the negation (*nafy*) of any divinity apart from God and the affirmation (*ithbāt*) of the divinity of God Most High. No worship exists without there being implicit in it the meaning of "There is no divinity but God." Thus, ritual purity implies the negation of uncleanness and the affirmation of ritual purity. In almsgiving, there is negation of the love of money and affirmation of the love of God; there is the manifestation of being in no need of the world, of being in need of God Most High, and of being satisfied with Him.

Also, for the heart filled with that which is other-than-God (*ghayru'llāh*), there must be a formula of negation to negate the alterities (*al-aghyār*). When the heart becomes empty, the *mimbar* of the Divine Oneness is placed therein and the sultan of gnosis sits upon it. In general, only the best of things, the most universally beneficial, and the most significant are placed therein, because they are the prototypes against which the heart measures their opposites. Enough power must exist in that locus of the heart to permit it to confront every opposite. For that reason the Prophet said, "The best thing that I and the Prophets before me have said is 'There is no divinity but God.'"

Thus, it is apparent that a certain preponderance must be given to the statement of anyone who maintains that the invocation *Allāh, Allāh* is special. For the knowers of God, it is one of the total number of invocations amongst which "There is no divinity but God" is the best of all.

You must find the most appropriate and generally constant invocation, for that is the most powerful one; it has the most radiant light and loftiest rank. No one has the good fortune of sharing in all that except him who perseveres in it and acts in accordance with it until he masters it. For verily, God has not established mercifulness except as something all-embracing that helps one reach the desired goal. So whosoever negates his nature by "There is no divinity" (*Lā ilāha*) affirms His Being by "but God" (*illaʾllah*).

The third invocation is the one that rejects all comparability (*tanzīh*) between creature and God. It is found in the phrases "Glory be to God" (*subhānaʾllāh*) and "Praise be to God" (*al-hamdu liʾllāh*). When that is manifest to the seeker, it is the fruit of the invocation of negation and of affirmation.

The fourth invocation is *Allāh*. It is called the single invocation, because the invoker contemplates the Majesty and Sublimity of God, while being extinguished from himself. God Most High has said, ". . . Say: *Allāh.* Then leave them to disport themselves with their idle talk" (Qurʾān 6:91).

It is related that ash-Shiblī was asked by a man, "Why do you say *Allāh* and not *Lā ilāha illaʾllāh*?" So ash-Shiblī answered,

> Because Abū Bakr gave all his wealth to the point where not a thing remained with him. Then he took off a garment in front of the Prophet. So the Messenger of God said, "What did you leave for your family?" He answered, "*Allāh.*" Likewise I say *Allāh.*

Then the questioner said, "I want a higher explanation than this." So ash-Shiblī said, "I am embarrassed to mention an expression of negation in His presence, while everything is His light." Then the man said, "I want a higher explanation than this." Ash-Shiblī answered, "I am afraid that I will die during the negation of the phrase before reaching the affirmation." The questioner again said, "I want a higher explanation than this." So ash-Shiblī said, "God Most High said to His Prophet '. . . Say *Allāh*. Then leave them to disport themselves with their idle talk'" (Qur'ān 6:91).

Then the young man got up and let out a shriek. Ash-Shiblī said *Allāh*. He screamed again; and ash-Shiblī said *Allāh*; then he screamed a third time and died, may God Most High have mercy upon him! The relatives of the young man gathered together and grabbed ash-Shiblī, charging him with murder. They took him to the caliph and were given permission to enter, and they accused him of murder. The caliph said to ash-Shiblī, "What is your response?" He answered, "A soul yearned, then wailed and aspired, then screamed, then was summoned, then heard, then learned, then answered. So what is my crime?" The caliph shouted, "Let him go!"

The reason for this teaching on the simple invocation is because God is the goal and the most worthy of being invoked; because the invoker of "There is no divinity but God" (*Lā ilāha illa'llāh*) might die between the negation and the affirmation; because saying *Allāh* only is easier on the tongue and closer to the heart's grasp; because the negation of imperfection in One for Whom imperfection is impossible is an imperfection; because being occupied with this formula conveys to one the grandeur of the Truth through the negation of alterities, since the negation of alterities actually derives from the heart's preoccupation with those very alterities. That is impossible for the person who is absorbed in the Light of Divine Unity.

Whoever says, "There is no divinity but God" (*Lā ilāha illa'llāh*) is indeed occupied with what is other than the Truth; whereas whoever says *Allāh* is indeed occupied with the Truth. Hence, what a difference between the two positions! Likewise, negating the existence of something is needed only when that thing comes to mind; but it does not come to mind save through the imperfection of one's state.

As for those who are perfect, for whom the existence of a partner alongside God would never occur to them, it is impossible that they be put under the obligation of negating the partner. Rather, for these people, only the remembrance of God comes to their minds or enters their imagination. So it suffices them to say *Allāh*. Also, God has said, ". . . Say: *Allāh*. Then leave them to disport themselves with their idle talk" (Qur'ān 6:91). Thus, he has enjoined upon the Prophet the remembrance of God (*dhikru'llāh*) and has forbidden him idle discussion with them in their vanities and diversions. Holding to associationism (*shirk*) is idle talk and constitutes rushing headlong into that state of affairs.

It is more appropriate to be content with saying *Allāh*. The response of the one who upholds negation and affirmation with respect to the meaning of this Name is that the negation is for purification and the affirmation is for illumination. If you wished, you could say that the negation is for emptying oneself and the affirmation is for adorning oneself. If a tablet is not wiped clean of its figures, nothing can be written upon it. A single heart cannot serve as the place for two things, let alone for several things. If the heart is filled with the forms of sensory perceptions, it is rare that it would perceive the meaning of *Allāh*, even if one were to say *Allāh* a thousand times. When the heart is empty of all that is other-than-God, if one uttered *Allāh* only once, one would find such bliss that the tongue could not describe.

The fifth invocation is *Huwa* (He). Know that *Huwa* is a personal pronoun, having an indicative function. Among the exoterists, a sentence is not complete without its predicate, as in the case for "standing" (*qāʾim*) or "sitting" (*qāʿid*); so you say, "He is standing" (*huwa qāʾim*) or "He is sitting" (*huwa qāʿid*). But among the esoterists, *Huwa* indicates the ultimate goal of realization, and they are content with it and need no further explanation. They recite it to extinguish themselves in the realities of nearness to God and in order to have the invocation of the Truth take possession of their innermost being. Therefore, what is other-than-He is nothing at all that one should refer to it.

One of the mentally confused was asked, "What is your name?" He said, "*Huwa.*"

"Where are you from?" He said, "*Huwa.*"

"Where did you come from?" He said, "*Huwa.*" Whatever he was asked, he would only reply "*Huwa.*" So someone said, "Perhaps you desire God." Then he screamed loudly and died.

If you say, "You have mentioned proofs for every invocation to the point where the observer thinks that each invocation is the best, which causes confusion when choosing a remembrance," I respond: Each invocation has its own state and time wherein it is better than another type of remembrance. For every station there is a particular utterance which is more appropriate to it; and for every invocation there is a spiritual state, which is more suitable to it, as will follow. Just as the Qurʾān is better than the invocation, the invocation in some situations is better than it for the invoker, as in bowing during prayer.

II.

CONTEMPORARY
DOCTRINAL ESSAYS

God and His Name are one.

RAMAKRISHNA

MODES OF PRAYER

Frithjof Schuon

Frithjof Schuon is best known as the foremost spokesman of the perennial philosophy or religio perennis. *During the past fifty years, he wrote more than twenty books on metaphysical and spiritual topics. Schuon was born in 1907 in Basle, Switzerland, of German parents. As a youth he went to Paris, where he studied for a few years before undertaking a number of trips to North Africa, the Near East, and India in order to contact spiritual authorities and witness traditional cultures. Following World War II, he accepted an invitation to travel to the American West, where he lived for several months among the Plains Indians, in whom he always had a deep interest. Having received his education in France, Schuon wrote all his major works in French, which began to appear in English translation in 1953. He moved to the United States in 1980 and died there in 1998.*

We have distinguished canonical prayer from individual prayer by saying that it is a particular individual who is the subject in the second, whereas the subject is man as such in the first; now there is a form of orison wherein God Himself is the subject in a certain way, and this is the pronouncing of a revealed divine Name.[1] The foundation of this mystery is, on the one hand, that "God and His Name are identical" (Ramakrishna) and, on the other hand, that God Himself pronounces His Name in Himself, thus in eternity and outside all creation, so that His unique and uncreated Word is the prototype of ejaculatory prayer and even, in a less direct sense, of all orison. The first distinction that the Intellect conceives in the divine nature is that of Beyond-Being and Being; now since Being is as it were the "crystallization" of Beyond-Being, it is like the "Word" of the Absolute, through which the Absolute expresses itself, determines itself, or names itself.[2] Another

---

[1] In his *Cudgel for Illusion*, Shankara sings: "Control thy soul, restrain thy breathing, distinguish the transitory from the True, repeat the holy Name of God, and thus calm the agitated mind. To this universal rule apply thyself with all thy heart and all thy soul." The connection between metaphysical discrimination and the practice of invocation is one of capital importance. We find the same connection in this *Stanza on the Ochre Robe* (of *sannyāsins*), also by Shankara: "Singing *Brahma*, the word of Deliverance, meditating uniquely on 'I am *Brahma*', living on alms and wandering freely, blessed certainly is the wearer of the ochre robe."

[2] In the Torah, God says to Moses: "I am that I am" (*Ehyeh asher Ehyeh*); this refers to God as Being, for it is only as Being that God creates, speaks, and legislates, since the world exists

distinction that is essential here, one which is derived from the preceding by principial succession,[3] is that between God and the world, the Creator and creation: just as Being is the Word or Name of Beyond-Being, so too the world—or Existence—is the Word of Being, of the "personal God"; the effect is always the "name" of the cause.[4]

But whereas God, in naming Himself, first determines Himself as Being and second, starting from Being, manifests Himself as Creation—that is, He manifests Himself "within the framework of nothingness" or "outside Himself", thus "in illusory mode"[5]—man for his part follows the opposite movement when pronouncing the same Name, for this Name is not only Being and Creation, but also Mercy and Redemption; in man it does not create, but on the contrary "unmakes", and it does this in a divine manner inasmuch as it brings man back to the Principle. The divine Name is a metaphysical "isthmus"—in the sense of the Arabic word *barzakh*: "seen by God" it is determination, limitation, "sacrifice"; seen by man, it is liberation, limitlessness, plenitude. We have said that this Name, invoked by man, is nonetheless always pronounced by God; human invocation is only the "outward" effect of an eternal and "inward" invocation by the Divinity. The same holds true for every other Revelation: it is sacrificial for the divine Spirit and liberating for man; Revelation, whatever its form or mode, is "descent"

only in relation to Being. In the Koran, this same utterance is rendered as follows: "I am God" (*Anā 'Llāh*); this means that Being (*Anā*, "I") is derived from Beyond-Being (*Allāh*, this Name designating the Divinity in all its aspects without any restriction); thus the Koranic formula refers to the divine Prototype of the pronunciation of the Name of God. *Anā 'Llāh* signifies implicitly that "God and His Name are identical"—since Being "is" Beyond-Being inasmuch as it is its "Name"— and for the same reason the "Son" is God while not being the "Father". What gives metaphysical force to the Hebraic formula is the return of "being" to itself; and what gives force to the Arabic formula is the juxtaposition, without copula, of "subject" and "object".

[3] By "descent" (*tanazzulah*) as Sufis would say.

[4] This relationship is repeated on the plane of Being itself, where it is necessary to distinguish between the "Father" and the "Son"—or between "Power" and "Wisdom"—the "Holy Spirit" being intrinsically "Beatitude-Love" and extrinsically "Goodness" or "Radiation". This is the "horizontal" or ontological perspective of the Trinity; according to the "vertical" or gnostic perspective—ante-Nicene one might say—it would be said that the Holy Spirit "proceeds" from Beyond-Being as All-Possibility and "dwells" in Being as the totality of creative possibilities, while "radiating" forth into Existence, which is related to the concept of "creation by love".

[5] It is absurd to reproach Creation for not being perfect, that is, for not being divine, hence uncreated. God cannot will that the world should be and at the same time that it should not be the world.

or "incarnation" for the Creator and "ascent" or "ex-carnation" for the creature.[6]

The sufficient reason for the invocation of the Name is the "remembering of God"; in the final analysis this is nothing other than consciousness of the Absolute. The Name actualizes this consciousness and, in the end, perpetuates it in the soul and fixes it in the heart, so that it penetrates the whole being and at the same time transmutes and absorbs it. Consciousness of the Absolute is the prerogative of human intelligence and also its aim.

Or again: we are united to the One by our being, by our pure consciousness, and by the symbol. It is by the symbol—the Word—that man, in central and quintessential prayer, realizes both Being and Consciousness, Consciousness in Being and conversely. The perfection of Being, which is Extinction, is prefigured by deep sleep and also, in other ways, by beauty and virtue; the perfection of Consciousness, which is Identity—or Union, if one prefers—is prefigured by concentration, and also *a priori* by intelligence and contemplation. Beauty does not produce virtue, of course, but it favors in a certain way a pre-existing virtue; likewise intelligence does not produce contemplation, but it broadens or deepens a contemplation that is natural. Being is passive perfection and Consciousness active perfection. "I sleep, but my heart waketh."

[6] In Japanese Amidism, there have been controversies over the question of whether invocations of the Buddha must be innumerable or whether on the contrary one single invocation suffices for salvation, the sole condition in both cases being a perfect faith and—as a function of that faith—abstention from evil or the sincere intention to abstain. In the first case invocation is viewed from the human side, that is, from the standpoint of duration, whereas in the second case it is conceived in its principial, hence divine and therefore timeless, reality; *Jōdo-Shinshū*, like Hindu *japa-yoga*, combines both perspectives.

COMMUNION AND INVOCATION

Frithjof Schuon

Every method of spiritual realization comprises a fundamental means of concentration or actualization; in most, if not all, traditions, this means, or support, is an invocation of a divine Name, an invocation which can take on the most diverse modes, from calling in the strict sense, of which psalmody and litany are secondary modalities, to the respiratory act and even silence—the latter, in its undifferentiated state, synthesizing all words.[1]

Christian communion, too, is one of these modes, through its connection with the symbolism of the Word and the mouth; however, owing to its very particularity, the presence of this exceptional mode of "invocation" cannot exclude the practice of invocation in the strict sense of the term; but in this case this invocation must have a less fundamental importance than is the case in traditions which, like the Sufi tradition—for it is always esoterism that is in question—do not have the Eucharist, or rather, possess its equivalent only in the form of an invocation of the Name, or Names, of the Divinity. Between the Christian and Sufi paths there appears a sort of compensation: it could be said that the initiate of the early Churches, possessing the invocatory rite in Eucharistic mode and being unable, despite this mode, to deprive himself of the eminently important and powerful practice of vocal invocation, no longer had to invoke the supreme Name, the excellence of this invocation being already contained, for this initiate, in the Eucharistic mode; therefore, apart from litanies and psalms, he invoked one Name or several Names attributed to the Word, for: "Whosoever shall call on the name of the Lord shall be saved" (Acts 2:21). On the other hand, it could be said that the Christians, dazzled by the manifestation of the Word and attaching themselves to It alone, no longer had access to the invocation of the integral and supreme Name of God, an invocation which was reserved for the followers of the Paracletic tradition, Islam, not to mention traditions anterior to Christianity. This substitution of the communion for the invocation is directly related to

---

[1] In Sufism silent "invocation" is practiced above all in the *Tarīqah Naqshabandiyyah*, whereas silence as such plays a preponderant role in the Taoist methods, just as it did in the Pythagorean methods. For the Trappist monks, the practice of silence is unfortunately reduced to a purely moral and penitential rigor, the profound meaning of silence—which is of a speculative, thus intellectual, order—having been lost like so many elements of Christian spirituality.

the fact that Christianity has no sacred language—an indispensable element for the rite of invocation.[2]

The verse we have just quoted from the prophet Joel situates this invocation in a set of conditions which are those of the end of the Iron Age (*Kali Yuga*), but which also characterize the entire Iron Age, if one considers the whole cycle of the four ages (*Manvantara*); now the Hindu scriptures also teach that the spiritual practice most suited to the conditions of the Iron Age is the invocation of a divine Name; we know that the invocation practiced by Shrī Ramakrishna was addressed to Kali, the "divine Mother", whereas his illustrious spiritual ancestor, Shrī Chaitanya, had invoked the name of the Word: *Krishna*. Analogously, the Christian invocation is an invocation of the Word: Κύριε ἐλείσον and: Χρίστε ἐλείσον,[3] or again, and perhaps above all: *Marana ta!* ("Our Lord, come!"), an Aramaic formula used in the liturgy of the early Church.

Because of Islam's simple, synthetic, and primordial character as a traditional form, the invocation is addressed to the supreme Principle: *Allāh*. To this invocation is added that of the divine Names (*asmā'u Llāhi*) of which there are ninety-nine, such as: *ar-Rahmān* ("The Clement"), *ar-Rahīm* ("The Merciful"), *al-Malik* ("The King"), *al-Quddūs* ("The Holy"), *as-Salām* ("Peace"), as well as litanies on the Prophet (*salawāt 'alan-Nabī*) or "Universal Man" (*al-Insān al-Kāmil*), glorifying the aspects of the Word; and above all

---

[2] It is the possibility of the Eucharistic mode that appears as the fundamental reason why Christianity has not had a sacred language. It can be noted that the Koran recognizes the rite of Christian communion, which it even indicates as a spiritual means characteristic of Christ. In this connection, let us mention two passages from the *Sūrah* of the Table [5]: verse 75, speaking of Jesus and Mary, says that "they both ate food", which of course does not refer only to ordinary food; the verses 112-115 refer to the very establishment of the rite: "When the Apostles said, 'O Jesus, son of Mary! Is thy Lord able to send down for us a table spread with food from Heaven?' He said, 'Fear Allah, if you are believers.' They said, 'We desire that we should eat of it and our hearts be at rest; and that we may know that thou hast spoken true to us, and that we may be among its witnesses.' Said Jesus, son of Mary, 'O Allah, our Lord, send down upon us a table out of Heaven, that shall be for us a festival, the first and last of us, and a sign from Thee. And provide for us; Thou art the best of providers.' Then Allah said, 'Verily I do send it down on you; whoso of you hereafter disbelieveth, verily I shall chastise him with a chastisement wherewith I chastise no other being.'" etc. The association established between Jesus and Mary in the first quotation will take on its full significance in the light of what we say later about the symbolism of the *Virgo Genetrix*.

[3] There is an analogy worth noting between the name "Jesus of Nazareth" and the Buddhist invocation: "*Om mani padmē hum*"; the literal meaning of the name Nazareth is actually "flower", and *mani padmē* means: "jewel in the lotus".

the recitation of the Koran, to which the chanting of psalms for the Christians and the reading of the *Torah* for the Jews correspond in certain respects.[4]

* * *

Just as there are two Species in the Eucharist, there are two elements in the invocation of the Name *Allāh* corresponding to them: the *alif* and the final *hā*. Just as the bread, image of the sacred body, is broken by Christ, so, too, the *alif* comprises a break, shown graphically by the *hamzat al-qat'* (an orthographic sign indicating a "break") and represented phonetically by the discontinuity between the silence that precedes the word and the sound "a" which suddenly breaks that silence;[5] and just as the wine, image of the sacred blood, is poured, so, too, the sound "h" melts, without perceptible discontinuity and by its apparent and symbolical indefiniteness, into the silence that follows the word and in which it is drowned.

In a quite general way, this pair of elements symbolizes respectively "form" and "spirit", or the "support" and the "reality" of which this support is the vehicle, or again, in a more outward sense, exoterism and esoterism, the latter being represented by the final *hā* of the supreme Name as well as by the Eucharistic wine, or in other words, by the blood as well as by the breath. In this order of ideas, let us note the symbolical correspondence existing between the fact that, in the Roman Church, communion with wine is reserved for the priests alone,[6] and the fact that the breathing of the Sufi

---

[4] The ritual invocation of a divine Name essentially implies a qualification, either corresponding to It or a general one, and for this reason it is never practiced without the supervision or authorization of a spiritual master (the Sufi *shaykh* and the Hindu *guru*) of authorized and orthodox lineage; if this condition is not fulfilled, the foolhardy person who gives himself up to attempts in this order of things exposes himself to extremely serious repercussions, such as mental disequilibrium or death, precisely because of his lack of qualifications.

[5] This discontinuity reflects that which separates manifestation from its Principle, or effect from cause, and in an inverse order, the "Supreme Identity" from the work of realization. Moreover, this *alif* is also pronounced in a purely natural way in the form of the newborn child's first cry, while the final *hā* is pronounced by the dying man in the form of his last sigh.

[6] It is only because the deeper meaning of things has been forgotten that the perfect equivalence of the two Species has come to be admitted; in reality it is impossible that they could be absolutely equivalent, otherwise their difference would have no justification; moreover, the difference—essential in a certain sense—between the physical body and the blood shows clearly that their principial and universal prototypes must comprise a profound difference *a fortiori*. The body and blood of Christ can be compared respectively to the states of "amplitude" and "exaltation" in Muslim esoterism, or again, to the "lesser" and "greater Mysteries", just as

is equivalent to the indefinitely or perpetually repeated pronunciation of the Name *Allāh*, of which the quintessential letter is precisely the final *hā*, that is, the breath; for it is in the breath that the Name *Allāh* is resorbed, and in silence that the breath is resorbed.

We said earlier that the Christian communion—which is originally, and by its nature, an initiatic rite—refers to the symbolism of the mouth, like all invocation in fact; however, between invocation in the strict sense and its Eucharistic mode there is a difference: in the latter the mouth is considered in its capacity as the organ of nutrition, whereas in the former, it is envisaged in its capacity as the organ of speech. Between these two aspects of the mouth there is a close symbolical link, manifested in the physical order precisely by the fact that the two faculties, that of speech and that of nutrition, share the same organ;[7] this symbolic solidarity results moreover from the complexity of the Eucharistic symbol itself: the Word which is "said" by God is "eaten" by man. In the Sufi invocation, the symbol, which always remains fundamentally the same and thus retains its efficacy in all its modes, is applied inversely; it

one can view them in connection respectively with "Universal Man" (whose highest reality corresponds to *al-ulāhiyyah*, "divinity", that is, to the sum of all the realities included in Allah), and with the Supreme Principle (to which corresponds *al-ahadiyyah*, absolutely transcendent "unity"). Every being who is a constituent part of "Universal Man", or in other terms, of Christ's "mystical body", is a manifestation of the Eucharistic "bread" and thus a "brother of Christ"; it is in this sense that Christ said: "Inasmuch as ye have done it unto one of the least of these my brethren, ye have done it unto me" (Matthew 25:40).

[7] Apart from the two natural functions of the mouth, language and nutrition, whose sacred modalities are respectively invocation and communion—the latter being found in other traditions in the form of different "draughts of immortality" (*amrita, soma, haoma*—nectar, ambrosia, the "living water" of Christ)—there is yet another natural function of the mouth, secondary in relation to the first two: the kiss, which refers both to the symbolism of speech and to that of nutrition, and which in itself is related to the spiritual symbolism of love and adoration. Let us note the ritual practice of kissing the crucifix, relics, and icons, a practice which refers to the love of Christ or, in a general way, to divine Love; when the priest presents the crucifix, this invitation to kiss is connected more particularly with the aspect of the mercy of the Cross. Let us recall also, in a quite general way, the practice of hand-kissing and more particularly the kissing of prelates' hands and the spiritual master's hand, which, being the right hand, symbolizes "the hand of Mercy".

The kissing of the black stone enshrined in the Kaaba at Mecca is analogous to the communion, just as the stone itself is analogous to the Eucharist; it was white and radiant when Allah gave it to *Sayyidna* Ibrahīm, and turned black through the sins of those who kissed it to free themselves from these sins; but on the day of the Last Judgment, the stone will have two large eyes, and will turn white again; it will rest in Allah's hand, and will have the power of intercession with Him. The analogy with the whole mystery of the Eucharist and of Christ is remarkable.

is man who "says" the Word by pronouncing the divine Name, and is then absorbed by the divine Mouth; he is himself transformed by his "rebirth" as Eucharistic bread—an image meant to illustrate the process of assimilation and identification of the individual "fact" with the universal Principle.[8] The symbolic relation between the double function of the mouth and the profound equivalence of food and speech is contained in Christ's reply to the tempter: "Man shall not live by bread alone, but by every word that proceedeth out of the mouth of God"; this indicates the initiatic meaning of participation in Christ's body, for which the Eucharistic bread of the communion is the substitute.

From another point of view, there is a most important connection between the invocation of the Name and the birth of Christ;[9] in the first case,

---

[8] There are *pratīka*, or Hindu sacred images, which represent Parvati holding a human body between her teeth; this refers not only to the return—destructive from the point of view of manifestation—to the universal Essence, but also to reintegration through Knowledge; let us add that the image of the crucified Christ, which was of course originally a *pratīka*, like all the important motifs of medieval art, is the exact equivalent of the image of man devoured by a divinity. The reduction of a symbol to a single, more or less exclusive, meaning is a degeneration which does not prevent the symbol from containing everything that is inherent to it by its very form. In a sacrifice in which blood is shed, it is the sacrificer's weapon which serves the role of Kali's tooth; in the holy war, it is the enemy's weapon; this obviously applies not only to the Moslem *jihād*, but to every form of holy war, such as the Crusade, or even traditional war in general, the meaning of which is expounded in the *Bhagavad Gītā*. This war can be a conflict between clans, tribes, or peoples and can degenerate, like blood sacrifice, through the fact that the support comes to be substituted for the end or is even taken for the end itself.

Let us also note that certain forms of voluntary sacrifices, such as death beneath the wheels of the triumphal chariot of *Jagannāth*, or between the teeth of sacred animals, or again the Japanese *seppuku* or *hara-kiri*, are all forms connected by their nature to the same symbolism as the devouring mouth of Kali.

In a quite general way, that is to say in the natural order, the being is "eaten" by the Divinity when it dies; this contains a very clear allusion to the initiatic death of the *dhākir* who is "eaten", as a holocaust, by Allah, in other words who is extinguished in Him and becomes like unto Him. Christ is at once Word and Sacrifice, just as the Universe comprises these two aspects.

[9] The fact that the ox, a docile animal, and the ass, a stubborn animal, figure in images of the Nativity, can be interpreted as follows: the ox, which moreover was sacred to the ancient Semites, is armed with horns and combines gentleness and strength in its nature; in the invocation it represents the "guardian of the sanctuary"; it is the spirit of submission, fidelity, perseverance, effort of concentration; the ass, a "profane" animal whose braying is called "Satan's invocation" (*dhikr ash-Shaytān*), is the Satanic witness in the invocation, that is to say, the spirit of insubordination and dissipation.

In this same figuration, the Virgin, as we shall see later, is identified with him who invokes; Saint Joseph, the adoptive father of Christ, represents the invisible presence of the spiritual master in the invocation; the visitors, summed up, as it were, in the Three Kings, the Word emerges from the mouth of man, in the second case, from the womb of the Virgin, a parallel that reveals the symbolic analogy between speech and birth.[10] It results from this analogy that the mouth of the *dhākir* who invokes *Allāh* is identical to the Virgin's womb, thus to the generative Virgin (*Virgo genetrix*), which very clearly indicates that "virginity" is the indispensable attribute of the *dhākir*'s mouth;[11] these considerations also bring out the connection between the reception of the Spirit of God by the Virgin's body[12]—expressed in Genesis by the "Spirit of God moving upon the face of the waters"—and the reception of the Eucharist by the mouth of man; and man, symbolically identified with the Virgin, must be pure, that is to say, in the sanctifying state of grace brought about, from the sacramental point of view, by confession, or rather by its initiatic prototype, such as it existed for the masters of the early Churches.

The body of Christ—or his individual substance—comes from the Virgin;[13] his Spirit is God; and this is why Christ is called *Rūhu Llāh*, "Spirit of Allāh", in Islam. Just as the body of Christ comes from the generative Virgin, and the Spirit of Christ is God, so, too, the divine Name comes from the mouth of the *dhākir*, while the breath, which comes from the interior of the

---

represent what could be called the "cosmic homage" that flows towards the sanctified man; the Hindu scriptures speak of this by saying that "the Heavens are resplendent with the glory of the *mukta*" ("the delivered one"), which suggests a parallel with the adoration of Adam by the angels in the Koran; finally, the night which enfolds the scene of the Nativity but which is illuminated by the star, the Divine testimony, represents initiatic death or solitude, or again the extinction of the mind, a state whose ritual support is the *khalwah* or "retreat" of the Sufi schools. Then again, the night of the Nativity as well as the *khalwah* correspond to the *Laylat al-Qadr* of the Koran.

[10] The saying of Saint Paul, that woman shall be saved by having children, is obviously not without a deep connection with another saying: "whosoever invokes the Name of the Lord shall be saved".

[11] Let us recall here the importance, stressed by all spiritual masters, notably Saint Paul, of discipline in language and abstention from lying, a discipline to which the practice of secrecy and silence is added.

By symbolic extension, every action is a "Word" or a manifestation "issuing" from man, and capable, in consequence, of defiling him; there is indeed a close connection between the Taoist "non-acting" (*wu-wei*) and the Christian "virginity", attributed eminently to the "beloved disciple".

[12] This reception is undergone symbolically by the mouth of the *dhākir*, in the form of the rhythmic panting of the "sacred dance", the *dhikr as-sadr*.

[13] This is so because the universal body of the Word, namely, the manifested Universe, proceeds from the universal Substance (*Prakriti*) of which the Virgin is the human hypostasis.

body and not from the mouth, yet fills and vivifies the mouth, corresponds to *Rūhu Llāh* or to "the Spirit which bloweth where it listeth"; in a deeper and more real sense, it is the invocation as such that corresponds to the Virgin, because the invocation is the support of the "divine Act" or of the "divine Presence" which, in the *dhākir*, is *Rūhu Llāh*. For just as the Eucharist is the support of the "real Presence", of the *Shekhinah* of the Holy of Holies in the Temple, so, too, the divine Name is the support of this same "Presence", the *sakīnah* which resides in the Holy of Holies or "secret" (*sirr*) of the heart (*qalb*) of the "believer" (*mu'min*).

RITES

Titus Burckhardt

Titus Burckhardt, *a German Swiss, was born in Florence in 1908 and died in Lausanne in 1984. In an age of modern science and technology, Burckhardt was a crystalline exponent of traditional metaphysics, cosmology, psychology, and traditional art. Although he was born in Florence, Burckhardt belonged to a patrician family of Basle. He was the great-nephew of the famous art historian Jacob Burckhardt and the son of the sculptor Carl Burckhardt. Titus Burckhardt was a close associate of Frithjof Schuon—who was destined to become the leading exponent of traditionalist thought in the twentieth century—and the two spent their early school days together in Basle around the time of the First World War. This was the beginning of an intimate friendship and a deeply harmonious intellectual and spiritual relationship that was to last a lifetime.*

All repetitive recitation of sacred formulas or sacred speech whether it be aloud or inward, is designated by the generic term *dhikr*. As has already been noted this term bears at the same time the meanings "mention," "recollection," "evocation," and "memory." Sufism makes of invocation, which is *dhikr* in the strict and narrow sense of the term, the central instrument of its method. In this it is in agreement with most traditions of the present cycle of humanity.[1] To understand the scope of this method we must recall that, according to the revealed expression, the world was created by the Speech (*al-Amr, al-Kalīmah*) of God, and this indicates a real analogy between the Universal Spirit (*ar-Rūh*) and speech. In invocation the ontological character of the ritual act is very directly expressed: here the simple enunciation of the Divine Name, analogous to the primordial and limitless "enunciation" of Being, is the symbol of a state or an undifferentiated knowledge superior to mere rational "knowing."

The Divine Name, revealed by God Himself, implies a Divine Presence which becomes operative to the extent that the Name takes possession of the

---

[1] This cycle begins approximately with what is called the "historical" period. The analogy between the Muslim *dhikr* and the Hindu *japa-yoga* and also with the methods of incantation of Hesychast Christianity and of certain schools of Buddhism is very remarkable. It would, however, be false to attribute a non-Islamic origin to the Muslim *dhikr*, first because this hypothesis is quite unnecessary, secondly because it is contradicted by the facts, and thirdly because fundamental spiritual realities cannot fail to manifest themselves at the core of every traditional civilization.

mind of him who invokes It. Man cannot concentrate directly on the Infinite, but, by concentrating on the symbol of the Infinite, attains to the Infinite Itself. When the individual subject is identified with the Name to the point where every mental projection has been absorbed by the form of the Name, the Divine Essence of the Name manifests spontaneously, for this sacred form leads to nothing outside itself; it has no positive relationship except with its Essence and finally its limits are dissolved in that Essence. Thus union with the Divine Name becomes Union (*al-wasl*) with God Himself.

The meaning "recollection" implied in the word *dhikr* indirectly shows up man's ordinary state of forgetfulness and unconsciousness (*ghaflah*). Man has forgotten his own pretemporal state in God and this fundamental forgetfulness carries in its train other forms of forgetfulness and of unconsciousness. According to a saying of the Prophet, "this world is accursed and all it contains is accursed save only the invocation (or: the memory) of God (*dhikru-'Llāh*)." The Qur'ān says: "Assuredly prayer prevents passionate transgressions and grave sins but the invocation of God (*dhikru-'Llāh*) is greater" (29:45). According to some this means that the mentioning, or the remembering, of God constitutes the quintessence of prayer; according to others it indicates the excellence of invocation as compared with prayer.

Other Scriptural foundations of the invocation of the Name—or the Names—of God are to be found in the following passages of the Qur'ān: "Remember Me and I will remember you . . ." or: "Mention Me and I will mention you . . ." (2:152); "Invoke your Lord with humility and in secret. . . . And invoke Him with fear and desire; Verily the Mercy of God is nigh to those who practice the 'virtues' (*al-muhsinīn*), those who practice *al-ihsān*, the deepening by 'poverty' (*al-faqr*) or by 'sincerity' (*al-ikhlās*) of 'faith' (*al-imān*) and 'submission' to God (*al-islām*)" (7:55, 56). The mention in this passage of "humility" (*tadarru'*), of "secrecy" (*khufyah*), of "fear" (*khawf*) and of "desire" (*tama'*) is of the very greatest technical importance. "To God belong the Fairest Names: invoke Him by them" (7:180); "O ye who believe! when ye meet a (hostile) band be firm and remember God often in order that ye may succeed" (8:45). The esoteric meaning of this "band" is "the soul which incites to evil" (*an-nafs al-ammārah*) and with this goes a transposition of the literal meaning, which concerns the "lesser holy war" (*al-jihād al-asghar*), to the plane of the "greater holy war" (*al jihād al-akbar*). "Those who believe and whose hearts rest in security in the recollection (or: the invocation) of God; Verily is it not through the recollection of God that their hearts find rest in security?" (13:28).

By implication the state of the soul of the profane man is here compared to a disturbance or agitation through its being dispersed in multiplicity, which is at the very antipodes of the Divine Unity. "Say: Call on *Allāh* (the synthesis of all the Divine Names which is also transcendent as compared with their differentiation) or call on *Ar-Rahmān* (the Bliss-with-Mercy or the Beauty-with-Goodness intrinsic in God); in whatever manner ye invoke Him, His are the most beautiful Names" (17:110); "In the Messenger of God ye have a beautiful example of him whose hope is in God and the Last Day and who invokes God much" (33:21); "O ye who believe! invoke God with a frequent invocation *(dhikran kathīrā)*" (33:41); "And call on God with a pure heart (or: with a pure religion) *(mukhlisīna lahu-d-dīn)* . . ." (40:14); "Your Lord has said: Call Me and I will answer you . . ." (40:60); "Is it not time for those who believe to humble their hearts at the remembrance of God? . . ." (57:16); "Call on (or: Remember) the Name of thy Lord and consecrate thyself to Him with (perfect) consecration" (63:8); "Happy is he who purifies himself and invokes the Name of his Lord and prayeth" (87:14, 15).

To these passages from the Qur'ān must be added some of the sayings of the Prophet: "It is in pronouncing Thy Name that I must die and live." Here the connection between the Name, "death," and "life" includes a most important initiatic meaning. "'There is a means for polishing everything which removes rust; what polishes the heart is the invocation of God, and no action puts so far off the chastisement of God as this invocation.'[2] The companions said: 'Is not fighting against infidels like unto it?' He replied: 'No: not even if you fight on till your sword is broken'"; "Never do men gather together to invoke (or: to remember) God without their being surrounded by angels, without the Divine Favor covering them, without Peace *(as-sakīnah)* descending on them and without God remembering them with those who surround Him"; "The Prophet said: 'The solitaries shall be the first.' They asked: 'Who are the solitaries *(al-mufridūn)*?' And he replied: 'Those who invoke much'"; "A Bedouin came to the Prophet and asked: 'Who is the best among men.' The Prophet answered: 'Blessed is that person whose life is long and his actions

---

[2] According to the *Vishnu-Dharma-Uttara* "water suffices to put out fire and the rising of the sun (to drive away) shadows; in the age of Kali repetition of the Name of *Hari* (*Vishnu*) suffices to destroy all errors. The Name of *Hari,* precisely the Name, the Name which is my life; there is not, no, there surely is no other way." In the *Mānava Dharma-Shāstra* it is said: "Beyond doubt a brahmin (priest) will succeed by nothing but *japa* (invocation). Whether he carries out other rites or not he is a perfect brahmin." Likewise also the *Mahābhārata* teaches that "of all functions *(dharmas) japa* (invocation) is for me the highest function" and that "of all sacrifices I am the sacrifice of *japa*."

good.' The Bedouin said: 'O Prophet! What is the best and the best rewarded of actions?' He replied: 'The best of actions is this: to separate yourself from the world and to die while your tongue is moist with repeating the Name of God'";[3] "A man said: 'O Prophet of God, truly the laws of Islam are many. Tell me a thing by which I can obtain the rewards.' The Prophet answered: 'Let your tongue be ever moist with mentioning God.'"

[3] Kabīr said: "Just as a fish loves water and the miser loves silver and a mother loves her child so also Bhagat loves the Name. The eyes stream through looking at the path and the heart has become a pustule from ceaselessly invoking the Name."

THE METHOD

Martin Lings

Martin Lings *was born in Burnage, Lancashire, in 1909. After taking a degree at Oxford in 1932, he was appointed Lecturer in Anglo-Saxon at the University of Kaunas. His interest in Islam and in Arabic took him to Egypt in 1939, and in the following year he was given a lectureship at Cairo University. In 1952 he returned to England and took a degree in Arabic at London University. From 1970-74 he was Keeper of Oriental Manuscripts and Printed Books at the British Museum (in 1973 his Department became part of the British Library), where he was in special charge of the Quranic manuscripts, amongst other treasures, from 1955. Dr. Lings died in 2005. The following excerpts are from his book* What is Sufism?, *which has become an authoritative source for both mystical doctrine and method.*

Of the voluntary rites of Islam as performed by the Sufis, the invocation of the Name *Allāh* has already been mentioned as by far the most important. There might seem to be a certain contradiction between the opening of the Holy Tradition quoted at the outset of this chapter[1] which sets the obligatory above the voluntary and the Quranic affirmation that *dhikr Allāh*, which is voluntary, is *greater* (see Qur'ān 29:45) even than the ritual prayer, which is obligatory. But it must be remembered that although what is obligatory serves to confer a spiritual rhythm on the flow of the hours, the time that it actually takes is relatively short. The voluntary has therefore a potential precedence over it by being capable of embracing and penetrating the whole of life, and this is what those who practice methodically the invocation aim at making it do. The meaning of the Holy Tradition is clearly that what is a legal obligation cannot be replaced, at the whim of an individual, by something which is not. Thus the Sufis are in agreement that the invocation of the Name, in itself the most powerful of all rites, is only acceptable to God on the basis of the invoker's having performed what is obligatory. It could not be a legal obligation itself for power necessarily means danger; and by no means every novice is allowed to proceed at once to the invocation of the Supreme Name.

[1] Editor's Note: "Nothing is more pleasing to Me, as a means for My slave to draw near unto Me, than worship which I have made binding upon him; and My slave ceaseth not to draw near unto Me with added devotions of his free will until I love him; and when I love him I am the Hearing wherewith he heareth and the Sight wherewith he seeth and the Hand whereby he graspeth and the Foot whereon he walketh" (Bukhārī, Riqāq, 37).

The recitation of the Qur'ān is no doubt the voluntary rite which is most widely spread throughout the Islamic community as a whole. The Sufis may be said to differ from the majority in that when they recite it—or when they listen to it which is ritually equivalent—they do so as a prolongation of *dhikr Allāh*, with no abatement of their aspiration to return to God. The doctrine of the Uncreatedness of the Revealed Book holds out a means of union which is not to be refused. Moreover the soul has need of the Qur'ān as a complement to the Name, being as it is by its very nature what might be called a multiple unity, and its God-given multiplicity demands a certain direct recognition which it is not the Name's function to accord. The following passage will find an echo in every reader of the Qur'ān. But it concerns the Sufis above all, for they alone are fully conscious of the problem it touches on:

> The Qur'ān is, like the world, at the same time one and multiple. The world is a multiplicity which disperses and divides; the Qur'ān is a multiplicity which draws together and leads to Unity. The multiplicity of the holy Book—the diversity of its words, sentences, pictures, and stories—fills the soul and then absorbs it and imperceptibly transposes it into the climate of serenity and immutability by a sort of divine "cunning". The soul, which is accustomed to the flux of phenomena, yields to this flux without resistance; it lives in phenomena and is by them divided and dispersed—even more than that, it actually becomes what it thinks and does. The revealed Discourse has the virtue that it accepts this tendency while at the same time reversing the movement thanks to the celestial nature of the content and the language, so that the fishes of the soul swim without distrust and with their habitual rhythm into the divine net.[2]

The Name and the Book are two poles between which lie a wealth of possibilities of invocation and litany, some being nearer to one pole and some to the other. The recitation of the two Shahādahs, for example and the invocation of the two Names of Mercy are nearer to the Supreme Name, whereas certain long and complex litanies are more comparable to the Qur'ān and as often as not they largely consist of extracts from it. But the Name may be said to have another complement which is very different from the Revealed Book though parallel to it in the sense that it directly recognizes the diffuse nature of the soul, and this is the individual prayer when the suppliant speaks directly to the Divinity as to another person, telling him of his difficulties and his needs, for himself and for those near to him, both

[2] Frithjof Schuon, *Understanding Islam*, p. 50.

living and dead, and asking for favors of various kinds—or not, as the case may be, for it is essential that this prayer should be a spontaneous laying bare of the individual, and no two individuals are alike.

In this connection it must be remembered that night is the symbol of the soul, and that even the unclouded shining of the full moon does not change night into day. Whatever faith the soul may be said to possess can only be very relative as compared with the certainty of the Heart, but it can be more or less a prolongation of that certainty. There is a significant passage in the Qur'ān where Abraham asks God to show him how He brings the dead to life. *Hast thou not faith?* is the divine rejoinder. *Yes, but (show me) so that my heart may be at rest* (2:260) is his answer. These last words could be glossed: So that the certainty in the depth of my being may be left in peace, untroubled by the surface waves of reason and imagination. The answer is accepted and followed by a miracle of vivification, which proves that the soul has a right to certain concessions. It could in fact be said that the purpose of a miracle is to enable the whole soul to partake supernaturally of an "absolute" certainty which is normally the prerogative of the Heart; but a small part of this effect can be produced through that most natural and human means, the individual prayer—not by any superimposition of faith but by the elimination of obstacles and distractions. This prayer, like the recitation of the Qur'ān, is shared by the whole community and is generally considered as an adjunct to the ritual prayer, which it normally follows, preceded by the words of the Qur'ān: *Your Lord hath said: Call upon Me and I will answer you* (40:60). But the majority are not concerned with method, whereas the Sufi Shaykhs insist on this prayer above all for its methodic value, not only as a means of regular communion for the soul but also as a means for it to unburden itself, that is, to unload some of its inevitable cares and anxieties so that it may be, at any rate in its higher reaches, a prolongation of the peace of the Heart rather than a discontinuity. Nor should the gestural value of this prayer be underrated, for the suppliant, head slightly bowed and hands held out with hollowed empty palms upturned, becomes a soul-penetrating incarnation of spiritual poverty.

It may be concluded from what is taught about human perfection that the primordial soul is a unified multiple harmony suspended as it were between the next world and this world, that is, between the Inward and the Outward, in such a way that there is a perfect balance between the pull of the Inward signs—the Heart and beyond it the Spirit—and the *signs on the horizons* (Qur'ān 41:53). This balance has moreover a dynamic aspect in that the Heart sends out through the soul a ray of recognition of the outer signs, the great phenomena of nature; and these by the impact they make on the senses, give rise to a vibration which traverses the soul in an inward direction, so that with man, the last created being, the outward movement of creation is reversed and everything flows back as it were through his Heart to its Eternal and Infinite Source. But in the fallen soul, where the attraction of the Heart is more or less imperceptible, the balance is broken and the scales are heavily weighted in favor of the outer world.

To ask how the true balance can be restored is one way of asking "What is Sufism?" And the first part of the answer is that the Divine Name must take the place of the veiled Heart, and a movement towards it must be set up in the soul to counteract the pull of the outer world so that the lost harmony can be regained.

THE GREAT NAME OF GOD

Leo Schaya

Leo Schaya *was born and raised within the Jewish tradition. He was particularly known for his writings on Jewish esoterism, with his book* The Universal Meaning of the Kabbalah *being one of the best known and often-quoted works in that field; however, he was also at home in the area of Sufi metaphysical interpretation. He lived most of his adult life in Nancy, France, where he shared his time between the elaboration of his metaphysical output and his interactions with spiritual seekers from various religious horizons. The following chapter concludes his aforementioned masterpiece on the Kabbalah.*

The Judaic confession of divine unity, the scriptural formula of which—the *Shema*—combines several names of God, represents for the Jew one of the most important "means of union"; another central or direct means of attaining union with God lies in the invocation of a single one of his names.

The tetragrammaton YHVH—the "lost word"—was above all others the "saving" name in the tradition of Israel; it is known as *shem hameforash*, the "explicit name," the one, that is, of which every consonant reveals and symbolizes one of the four aspects or fundamental degrees of divine all-reality. It is also called the "complete name" and the "synthesis of syntheses," because it includes all the other divine names, each of which, by itself, expresses only one or another particular aspect of the universal principle; it is also called the "unique name" because it is for the "unique people," and more especially because of its incomparable spiritual efficacy, in that it gives the possibility of direct actualization of the divine presence (*shekhinah*). It was exactly on account of the direct outpouring of divine grace brought about by the invocation of the name YHVH that the traditional authority in Israel found it necessary, even before the destruction of the second Temple, to forbid the spiritually fallen people to invoke, or even merely to pronounce the tetragrammaton. In his "Guide of the Perplexed," Maimonides says on this subject: "A priestly blessing has been prescribed for us, in which the name of the Eternal (YHVH) is pronounced as it is written (and not in the form of a substituted name) and that name is the 'explicit name.' It was not generally known how the name had to be pronounced, nor how it was proper to vocalize the separate letters, nor whether any of the letters which could be doubled should in fact be doubled. Men who had received special instruction transmitted this one to another (that is, the manner of pronouncing this name) and taught it to none but their chosen disciples, once a week. . . . There was also a name composed of twelve letters, which was holy to a lesser degree than the name of four letters; in my opinion it is most probable that this was not a single name but one composed of two or three names which, joined together, had twelve letters (representing their synthesis).[1] This was the name which was substituted for the name of four letters wherever the latter occurred in the reading (of the Torah), just as today we use the name beginning with the consonants *Alef, Daleth* (*ADoNaY*, 'My Lord'). Doubtless this twelve-letter name had originally a more special meaning than that conveyed by the name *Adonai*; it was not at all forbidden to teach it and no mystery was made of it in the case of any well-instructed person; on the contrary, it was taught to anyone who wished to learn it. This was not so in respect to the tetragrammaton; for those who knew it taught it only to their sons and disciples, once a week. However, as soon as undisciplined men, having learnt the twelve-letter name, began thereafter to profess erroneous beliefs— as always happens when an imperfect man is confronted by a thing which differs from his preconceived notion of it—they began to hide this name also and no longer taught it except to the most devout men of the priestly caste, for use when blessing the people in the sanctuary; it was indeed on account of the corruption of men that the pronunciation of the *shem hameforash* had already been abandoned, even in the sanctuary: 'After the death of Simeon the Just,' so say the Doctors, 'his brother priests ceased to bless by the name (YHVH) but blessed by the name of twelve letters.' They also say: 'At first it was transmitted to every man (in Israel), but after heedless men increased in number, it was no longer transmitted save to men of the priestly caste and the latter allowed (the sound) of it to be absorbed (during the priestly blessing) by the (liturgical) melodies intoned by their fellow-priests.'"

Even after the destruction of the second Temple, however, invocation of the "explicit name" appears to have continued as the sacred prerogative of a few initiates who were unknown to the outside world and who served as the spiritual poles of the esoteric "chain of tradition" (*shalsheleth hakabbalah*). The function of this chain is the initiatic transmission—uninterrupted through the ages—of the "mysteries of the Torah," which include, among others, the mystery of the invocation of the holy names; except for the extremely restricted "elect" who retain the high function of guarding and secretly invoking the

---

[1] Like the eight-letter name: YAHDVNHY, which is the synthesis of the two names YHVH and ADoNaY (My Lord).

"complete name,"[2] no one may know its exact pronunciation. Although today Hebrew scholars render the name YHVH by "Jehovah" on the strength of the Masoretic vocalization given in the Bibles and prayerbooks, or by "Yahveh," in an attempt to imagine some way to pronounce it, these introductions of vowels into the tetragrammaton certainly do not correspond to the authentic pronunciation, and that is why it is written here only in the form of the four consonants which are its known basis.

The prevailing ignorance as regards the pronunciation of the "explicit name" is certainly not the result of mere "forgetfulness" nor of a purely human decision arrived more than two thousand years ago. The suppression of the teaching and pronunciation of this name—by decree of the traditional authority—is so categorical and so radical in its consequences that it can be affirmed that God himself has withdrawn this name from the mass of the people of Israel. However, such intervention "from above" expresses not only the rigor, but also the mercy of God, who foresaw that the human recipients of "the last days," no longer possessing the requisite theomorphism, would be shattered by the weight of his lightning descent.

The "complete name," therefore, cannot be the medium for deifying invocation in our age, which in the prophecies is called the "end of time"; this being so, we must consider its fragmentary substitutes without particular reference to the "twelve-letter name," the ritual use of which lasted only a short time. As we have seen, it had to be replaced by the name *Adonai*, which has been pronounced, ever since the destruction of the Temple, every time the tetragrammaton occurs in the reading of the Torah and the daily prayers. It should be noted that the substitution of the name *Adonai* was decreed only in respect to the exoteric ritual, whether performed in the synagogue or in private, the aim of which is the salvation of the soul in a restricted sense, that is, within the confines of the ego; it does not have in view the invocation which is intended to raise man's being to the highest "place" (*hamakom*) which embraces all that is. The restriction does not apply to the "two-letter name," YH (יה) which is pronounced *Yah* and is nothing other than the first half of the "name of four letters," YHVH (יהוה); from the very fact that it is directly substituted for the *shem hameforash*, this name must have the same esoteric potentialities as the latter, without, however, involving the danger of

---

[2] According to the word of God addressed to Moses: "Thou shalt say unto the children of Israel: 'YHVH, the God of your fathers, the God of Abraham, the God of Isaac, and the God of Jacob hath sent me to you. This is my name for ever, and this is my memorial (*zikhri*, the invocation of God) unto all generations'" (Exodus 3:15).

a too sudden actualization of the divine.[3] This even appears obvious, firstly because the "name of two letters" has the same transcendent significance as the tetragrammaton, which includes it and further, in a more general way, because every divine name not referring to a particular quality to the exclusion of other qualities, refers to the being or essence of God.

*   *   *

Since the "complete name" was withdrawn from the Jewish people, they have used above all the following three names, which together replace the unity of the "four letters"; firstly the name *YaH* which integrates the two first letters—the "transcendental half"—of YHVH; secondly the name *Elohenu*, "Our God," which includes the six active causes of cosmic construction and represents divine immanence as first revealed in the subtle, celestial, and psychic world, symbolized by the *vav*; thirdly the name *Adonai*—an exoteric replacement for the name YHVH—designates *malkhuth*, the final *he*, representing divine immanence as manifested particularly in the corporeal world.

But the name which concerns us here is *Yah*, the transcendental nature of which leads, in principle, to the state of *Yobel* (Jubilee), final "deliverance" (in the same sense as the Hindus understand the word *moksha*). This name seems to represent not only the "means of grace" *par excellence* of the final cycle of Jewish history, but also that of its beginning. In fact, it can be deduced from Scripture that *Yah* was the divine name used particularly by Jacob and his people, whereas YHVH was the "name of Israel" so long as Israel represented the "portion of YHVH." In the Psalms (135:3-4) it is said: "Praise *Yah*, for he is good! YHVH, sing praises to his name, for it is pleasant! For *Yah* has chosen Jacob unto himself, and Israel for his costly possession," the possession, that is, of YHVH, according to Deuteronomy (32:9): "For the portion of YHVH is his people." And Isaiah (44:5) explicitly distinguishes between the "name of Jacob" and the "name of Israel": "One shall call himself by the name of Jacob (*Yah*) and another shall subscribe with his hand, unto YHVH and surname himself by the name of Israel." This distinction can be explained in

---

[3] In his commentary on the *Sefer Yetsirah* written in 931, Gaon Saadya de Fayyum says: "When it is said: 'YaH has two letters, YHVH has four letters,' what is meant is that YaH is one half of the name YHVH. Now, the half was said everywhere and at all times, but the whole was only said in the Sanctuary in a particular period and at the moment of the blessing of Israel." And the Talmud (*Erubin* 18b) states: "Since the destruction of the Sanctuary, the world need only use two letters (as a means of invocation, that is, the two first letters of YHVH, forming the name YaH)."

relation to the history of Israel, all the phases of which are contained in three fundamental cycles: the first, or "patriarchal" cycle, from Shem to Jacob's victorious struggle at Peniel with the divine manifestation; the second, or "Israelite," cycle, from Peniel, where Jacob and his people received the name of Israel, to the destruction of the second Temple; and the third, or "final," cycle, from the collapse of the priestly service and theocracy to the advent of the Messiah. Now Shem was the "seed" of the Jewish race; Abraham was the "father of many peoples" and Isaac the "sacrifice of oneself to God," while Jacob gave birth to the twelve tribes and the "mystical body" of Israel; so the latter is considered above all others as the patriarch of Israel and the people of God are called "Jacob" until the struggle at Peniel.

"Jacob was chosen to belong to *Yah*," that is, to be raised up in spirit to divine transcendence. But at Peniel there was a fundamental change in the mystical destiny of Jacob and his people, for it was said to him (Genesis 32:28): "Thy name shall be called no more Jacob, but Israel (he who struggles with God), for thou hast striven with God and with men and hast prevailed." In the language of the Kabbalah this means that after having "wrestled with God until victory"—absorption in the transcendence of *Yah*—Jacob prevailed also at Peniel over the divine manifestation called "man," that is, over the "descent" of God into humanity. This revelatory and redemptive "descent" is symbolized, in sacred ideography, by the *vav* (ו). According to the *Zohar* (*Terumah* 127a): "When the *vav* emerges mysteriously self-contained from the *yod-he* (*YaH*), then Israel attains to his costly possession," its *corpus mysticum*, which is identical with the *Sefirah malkhuth*, represented by the last *he* of the tetragrammaton. Thus, thanks to the sacred struggle of its patriarch, the people entered into possession of the reality hidden in the last two letters of the *shem hameforash*—the spiritual (V) and substantial (H) fullness of the divine immanence—and itself became, in its mystical body, the "final *He*," the "portion of YHVH."

It appears, therefore, that during the "Jacobite" phase the people were not yet the "possession of YHVH," just as YHVH—the "complete name" or actualized unity of divine transcendence (YH) and divine immanence (VH)—was not yet the "possession of Israel." The people of "Jacob" was centered on the transcendent aspect of God: *Yah*. In that cyclical moment and in that environment, spiritual realization must not necessarily have required initiation into the sacred sciences (symbolized by the *vav*), any more than it needed the priestly service in the sanctuary (represented by the last *he* of the tetragrammaton). It was only when YHVH established the roots of the earthly center of his presence in the midst of Jacob's family—which thereby became "Israel," or the Chosen People—that the *vav* or "mysteries of the faith" had to be communicated to it through the intermediary of its patriarch. These mysteries, transmitted from generation to generation to the "children of Israel," were lost at the time of their servitude in Egypt, but were reborn and permanently crystallized in the revelation on Sinai; and the "final *he*" of YHVH, the pure and imperceptible substance of the *shekhinah*, called the "Community of Israel," entered into the Holy Land and took up its abode in the Temple of Jerusalem, where the High Priest blessed all the people by the *shem hameforash*.

By the grace of the "complete name," the Chosen People long ago actualized the "kingdom of God" in the Holy Land, but on account of their sins the first Temple was destroyed and Israel had to suffer exile in Babylon: ". . . during the whole seventy years of exile," says the *Zohar* (*Shemoth* 9b), "Israel had no divine light to guide her and, truly, that was the essence of the exile. When, however, Babylon's power was taken away from her and Israel returned to the Holy Land, a light did shine for her, but it was not as bright as before (when Israel received the emanation of the 'complete name,' which was broken up by the sins which also caused the destruction of the first Temple), being only the emanation of the 'lower *he*' (the *shekhinah*, or 'mystical body' of Israel, identical with that of the second Temple), since the whole of Israel did not return to purity to be a 'peculiar people' as before. Therefore, the emanation of the supernal *yod* did not descend to illumine in the same measure as before, but only a little. Hence Israel was involved in many wars until 'the darkness covered the earth' and the 'lower *he*' was darkened and fell to the ground (so that Israel was forbidden to invoke the 'complete name') and the upper source was removed as before (as at the time of the destruction of the first Temple), and the second Temple was destroyed and all its twelve tribes went into exile in the kingdom of Edom.[4] The *he* also went into exile

---

[4] The name of the biblical kingdom of Edom (situated between the Dead Sea and the Gulf of Elath) is here used as a symbolic term of the whole Roman Empire. According to the Kabbalah, Edom symbolizes sometimes the imperfect or unbalanced state of creation preceding its present state—the latter being an ordered manifestation of the *Fiat Lux*—and sometimes the idolatrous world of antiquity and, by extension, every materialistic, profane, or atheistic civilization, such as our own. The Bible (Genesis 36) identifies Edom with Esau, who sold his birthright—implying the right of the first-born, the major patriarchal blessing—for "a mess of pottage." Therefore, in the Jewish tradition, Esau or Edom is opposed to Jacob or Israel, as the animal and materialistic tendency of man is opposed to his spiritual and theomorphic tendency.

there. . . ." the *shekhinah* was "decentralized," dispersed with Israel all over the world. It continued to radiate only through weak "reflections" wherever there was a community of orthodox Jews; nevertheless, its sacred "embers" have continued to flare up with an increased light and, sporadically, its true "grandeur" has been recaptured amidst the elect; these are the *Mekubbalim*, or initiated Kabbalists, who—with certain exceptions, such as the "false Messiahs"—formed the "pillars" of the exiled people; but they appear to have become a negligible minority in the era of the triumph of "Edomite" civilization, this modern world of ours which has even been transplanted to the Holy Land itself.

According to the *Zohar*, David, through the holy spirit, foresaw the end of the last exile of Israel—identifying it with the very "end of days" in accordance with the prophecies—and revealed it in Psalm 102:19:[5] "This shall be written for the future (or the last) generation and a people which shall be created (in the time of the 'end') shall praise *Yah*!" The same prophecy is hidden in the verse from Malachi (3:23): "Behold, I will send you Elijah (my God is *Yah*) the prophet (whose very name reveals which divine name was to be invoked during his pre-Messianic ministry and who represents, not only the type of the eternal master of masters, but also the type of all prophetic activity preceding and directly preparing the universal redemptive act of God's anointed), before the coming of the great and terrible day of YHVH." Finally, the *Zohar* shows the exact reason why the name *Yah*—as in the time of Jacob—represents the means above all others of salvation in the period from the destruction of the Temple to the advent of the Messiah; and this reason becomes fully apparent in our day, when even the believing Jews can no longer live in freedom from the materialistic and profane organization of the modern world and so are unable any longer perfectly to carry out the Mosaic law, which presupposes as its "sphere of activity" either a theocracy or a closed traditional world.[6] Now, the *Zohar* (*Terumah* 165b) says, referring to

---

[5] This Psalm is called the "prayer of the unhappy man" whose "days vanish into smoke" and "are like a shadow at its decline." These phrases refer to the end of time.

[6] That the "name of two letters" applies to the present time is made clear not only in the saying from the Talmud (*Erubin* 18b) which we have quoted, but also in the following formulation, amongst others, which was used in the school founded by the great master Isaac Luria (1534-72) and which shows that a spiritual method was based upon it as modern times approached: "For the sake of union of the Holy One, be he blessed, with his *shekhinah*, in fear and in love, that the name *YaH*, be blessed, may be unified in complete unification." It should be remembered that the phrase "to unify the name" has the meaning, from the point of view of method: to invoke the divine name.

the name *Yah*: "All is included in this name: those that are above (epitomized in the *yod*, the ideogram of pure transcendence, *kether-hokhmah*) and those that are below (hidden, in its principal and undifferentiated state, in the 'upper *he*,' *binah*, the archetype of immanence). In it the six hundred and thirteen commandments of the Torah, which are the essence of the supernal and terrestrial mysteries, are included." When this name is invoked sincerely, then it is as though one were carrying out all the commandments of the Jewish religion. This name compassionately forgives and compensates for the inadequacy of man in relation to the divine will; that is why the psalmist and "prophet of *Yah*" cried out: "In my anguish I called upon *Yah*; *Yah* heard my prayer and set me in a large place" (Psalm 118:5). "I shall not die, I shall live and declare the works of *Yah*. *Yah* has chastened me sorely, but he has not given me over to death. Open the gates of righteousness before me; I will enter into them, praising *Yah*!" (Psalms 118:17-19). God can and will save Zion, not by his rigor, but by his compassion, when "time shall have come to its end": "Thou wilt arise and have compassion upon Zion; for it is time to be gracious unto her, for the appointed time is come!" (Psalms 102:13).[7]

The name *Yah* does not have the "descending" efficacy of the *shem hameforash*; it lacks the direct influx of the *vav* or "living God," the spiritual brilliance of which cannot be borne without the presence of the "final *he*," represented at the same time by the Temple and its priestly service, the transmission and practice of the sacred sciences, the functioning of theocratic institutions, and the conformity of an entire people to the divine will. Yet the reasons for the substitution of the name *Yah* for that of YHVH are not only restrictive, for, since they are connected, from the cyclical point of view, with the "end of time," this end ceases also to be of a purely negative character; on the contrary, according to the prophets, it precedes a positive renewal, namely, the creation of "a new Heaven and a new earth"—more perfect than

---

[7] "For He hath looked down from the height of his sanctuary; from heaven did YHVH behold the earth to hear the groaning of the prisoner (of the civilization of 'Edom') and to loose those that are appointed to death (represented by the anti-spiritual life of the modem world)" (Psalms 102:19-20). "YHVH is full of compassion and gracious, slow to anger and plenteous in mercy. He will not always contend, neither will he keep his anger forever. He hath not dealt with us after our sins, nor requited us according to our iniquities, for as the heaven is high above the earth, so great is his goodness towards them that hear him. As far as the east is from the west, so far hath he removed us from our transgressions. Like a father hath compassion upon his children (and *Yah* is precisely the name of the divine 'father,' *hokhmah*) so hath YHVH compassion upon them that fear him. For he knoweth our frame; He remembereth that we are dust (and can in no way change the cyclical conditions in which we are born and have to live)" (Psalms 103:8-14).

those now existing—as well as the creation of a new Jerusalem, whose "places shall be sacred to YHVH and will never be laid waste nor destroyed." By the very fact that it is the name to be invoked by the "last generation," *Yah* is also the name for the return to the "beginning," to the perfect original of all things. It is different from the tetragrammaton, the efficacity of which is above all "descending," revelatory, and existential, for the name *Yah* is in fact the name of "ascent" and of redemption; it is exactly the name of the "beginning" and of the "end" of every ontological emanation and cosmic manifestation of God, while the name YHVH is the whole emanation, and the whole manifestation.

The "upper (or transcendent) YHVH" manifests through the "lower (or immanent)[8] YHVH"; in the same way, the "upper (or ontological) *Yah*" manifests through the "lower *Yah*" or cosmic principle, which retains its transcendent nature everywhere, even "below." Therefore, if the "lower YHVH" represents divine immanence, the "lower *Yah*" then represents "transcendent immanence." The *yod* which, in its pure transcendence "on high" is the unity of *kether* and *hokhmah*, signifies "below," in the metacosmic center of the cosmos, the unity of the *shekhinah* and its active aspect, *metatron*, the cosmic intellect, the inner regulator of creation, while the following *he* represents its passive aspect *avir*, "ether," the quintessence—the *he* having in fact the numerical value of five—of the four subtle and the four coarse elements; it is, as we have already seen, the undifferentiated principle of all subtle, celestial, or psychic substance and of all coarse or corporeal matter. If the *shekhinah*, in so far as it dwells in the prototypical and spiritual world (*olam haberiyah*), is the "transcendent immanence" of *kether*, then *metatron* is that of *hokhmah*, and *avir* that of *binah*; now just as the three highest *Sefiroth* cannot be separated one from another, since they represent the one infinite and indivisible principle, *Yah*, so also *metatron* and *avir* must not be separated from the *shekhinah*, of which they are respectively the active or regulating aspect and the receptive or generative aspect. These three immanent principles, undifferentiated, compose the "lower *Yah*," also called the "heaven of heavens," the inseparable unity of the tenth, ninth, and eighth heaven being "the one who rides in *Araboth*,[9] (the seventh heaven):

---

[8] These two aspects of YHVH are revealed to Moses in the Scriptures (Exodus 34:6) when God shows him His attributes (*Middoth*) beginning with the twice repeated: "YHVH, YHVH *El rahum wehanun*. . . ." (YHYH, YHVH, God merciful and compassionate. . . .)

[9] It should be remembered that the word *Araboth* for the seventh heaven, translated sometimes as "clouds," sometimes by "plains," "desert," or "heaven," is derived from the root ARB, which means something mixed. In fact, *avir*, the undifferentiated ether, that "pure and imperceptible

Yah is his name" (Psalms 68:5). The "heaven of heavens," identical with the prototypical "world of creation" (*olam haberiyah*) is the intermediary plane between the Sefirothic "meta-cosmos" and the created cosmos which begins in the seventh heaven, *Araboth*, the "surface of the lower waters." The "lower *Yah*" is therefore "transcendent immanence," the mediator between pure transcendence and immanence in that it penetrates that which is created and is called by the last two letters of the "lower YHVH."[10]

When YHVH comes down from the highest "place" to the center of this world, he brings the secrets of all the divine and cosmic degrees, the "mysteries of the Torah" with their various graces; thus his "four letters" form what is preeminently the revealing name, while *Yah* is enthroned on the "surface of the waters," where the "heavens and the earth" begin and end, that is to say the whole of the world "created in one single instant"; there it is that all creatures emerge from God and return to him, in a single "cry of joy" which is nothing other than the "primordial sound." The name *Yah* is the revealed utterance of this inarticulate and universal "cry" or "sound" which manifests and reabsorbs the entire cosmos; it is the name of creative and redemptive joy. Thus the Psalmist cries out: "Make way for him who rides in *Araboth*: *Yah* is his name. Rejoice before him!" "What the verse tells us," comments the *Zohar* (*Terumah* 165b), "is that the ancient of ancients (the supreme principle) rideth in the *Araboth* (that he is really present) in the sphere of *Yah*, which is the primordial mystery emanating from him, namely the ineffable name *Yah*, which is not identical with him (the absolute), but is a kind of veil emanating from him. This veil is his name, it is his chariot, and even that is not manifested (in the cosmos, but is enthroned on the 'surface of the waters'). It is his 'great name.' . . . For when all is well with this name, then harmony is complete, and all worlds rejoice in unison."

Yah, in its immanent aspect, is the immediate cause of the cosmos, the

air" of the eighth heaven, is manifested in *Araboth* in its first differentiation, subtle substance or "water" which reflects the uncreated light, or spiritual "fire" descending from the *shekhinah* or from its universal irradiation, *metatron*. Now the "surface of the waters" shines so brightly in the light of the divine "fire" that it seems to be utterly fused or "mixed" in it. This "mixture" or more precisely this "immanence" of the spirit in the subtle substance, which endures as long as the cosmos subsists, produces the whole of the seven "heavens," *shamaim*, this word being composed of *esh*, spiritual "fire" and of *maim*, substantial "waters."

[10] The *vav* of the "lower YHVH—having the numerical value of six—symbolizes the *shekhinah* which penetrates the first six of the seven heavens constituting the subtle "world of formation" (*olam hayetsirah*). The "final he of the lower YHVH"—having the numerical value of five—represents *avir*, the quintessence, in that it has descended into the lowest heaven, there to dwell as the ether or undifferentiated principle of the four elements constituting *olam haasiyah*, the sensory or corporeal "world of fact"; thus the "final *he*," dwelling in the lowest heaven, is the immediate and omnipresent center of our world.

cause that transcends all its effects: it remains hidden in the prototypical world, as uncreated and infinite light. But its irradiation transpierces its envelope, the ether, with a "sound" which is that of the revelatory, creative, and redemptive "word"; this is the "voice" of the Creator, the "primordial sound" which produces the two lower worlds, the world of subtle "formation" and the sensory world of "fact." It is the "inner voice" which sounds in the innermost depths of all things, so that it is said that "the heavens declare the glory of God, and the firmament showeth his handiwork. Day unto day uttereth speech and night unto night revealeth knowledge. There is no speech, no language where the sound is not heard: their voice resounds through all the earth and their words go out to the end of the world. . ." (Psalms 19:2-5).

The "inner" (divine) voice is in truth the very light of God, an infinite light which, by refraction in the ether, has been transformed into revelatory, creative, and redemptive "sound." That is the universal "name" of God, inwardly his light, outwardly his voice, emitted spontaneously and in innumerable modes—articulate or inarticulate—by "everything that has a soul." This is why the psalmist calls, not only to men, but to everything he sees as animated by the universal name, to invoke that name for the glory of the "named" and the salvation of the world; he even goes so far as to exhort the "heaven of heavens" to join in the invocation, because it is from there, from *Yah* itself, that the voice in effect descends and resounds on the "surface of the waters"—where the created heavens begin—and is thence transmitted throughout the whole of existence, even to the earthly "abysses." "Praise *Yah*! Praise YHVH from the height of the heavens! Praise him in the heights! Praise ye him, all his angels! All his hosts, praise ye him! Praise ye him, sun and moon! Praise him, all ye stars of light! Praise him, ye heavens of heavens and the waters that are above the heavens! . . . Praise YHVH from below on the earth, ye sea-monsters and all ye deeps; fire and hail, snow and vapors, stormy wind fulfilling his word, mountains and all hills; fruitful trees and all cedars; beasts and all cattle; creeping things and winged fowl! Kings of the earth and all peoples, princes and all judges of the earth; both young men and maidens, old men and children; let them praise the name of YHVH! For his name alone is exalted; his glory is above the earth and heaven. . ." (Psalms 148).

For the prophet-king, the synonym of this universal praise is either the call to the "great name," *Yah*, or the call to the "complete name," YHVH;[11] this

---

[11] The name *Yah* is the direct and synthetic articulation of the "primordial sound," whereas the name YHVH is the indirect and "explicit" articulation of the same; every holy name moreover represents a more or less explicit utterance of the divine voice, but to a lesser degree than the name YHVH.

is why his exhortation begins with the words: "Praise *Yah*! Praise YHVH! . . ." This universal invocation is made up of the indefinite multitude of modes in which the divine voice chooses to speak through his "organs" which are his creatures; however, where all worlds, all beings, all things emerge directly from their first and divine unity, that is, from *Yah* "who rides on *Araboth*," there is only one mode of invocation, a single sound, a single cry, which expresses the joy of myriads of creatures in union with the One, the Unique. For where all beings issue from God is the place where all return to him without delay; here, on the "surface of the waters," in the seventh heaven, *Araboth*, all that becomes separated from the Lord is separated only in order to be reunited with him. In effect, his creative act and his redemptive act are experienced there as one and the same thing: thanks to separation from him, union with him takes place.

Beings emerge like so many "sparks" from the irradiation of the *shekhinah*, that is to say of *metatron*, the divine "sun" which contains them all in so far as they are immanent and unseparated archetypes. On leaving this luminous world, where all is one with God, the sparks become enveloped in the differentiated manifestation of *avir*, that is, in the subtle "waters" of the seventh heaven, over the surface of which the "wind of *Elohim*" breathes and produces innumerable "waves." This wind is the cosmic spirit, *metatron*, which sets *avir*, the universal substance, in motion in order for it to produce subtle "waves," that is, souls each one of which is animated, illuminated, and inhabited by a spiritual "spark," a "living being." Each "wave" appearing on the "surface of the waters," whether issuing from God or returning from the depths of the cosmic "ocean," bursts into a single cry of joy and expands over the whole extent of the existential sea, the whole of *Araboth*. Over this hovers the eighth heaven, *avir*, the undifferentiated and translucid ether, which is wholly penetrated by the spiritual sun, *metatron*, so that the whole firmament itself appears like a sun, illuminating the "surface of the waters" from one end to the other. As we have said, each "wave" produced on this surface instantly expands in the supreme invocation and becomes the whole of the indefinite expanse, the immense "mirror," which is so filled with divine light that it mingles—in essential "fusion" and not in qualitative "confusion"—with the "radiant face" of *Yah* inclined towards it. Thus each being is simultaneously united with the whole of existence and with the infinite source of existence.

But if it is said that this integral union takes place at the very instant when the created being issues from uncreated being, one may wonder how the being then descends to the lower heavens and down to this earth in the form of a separate individual or separate "world." This descent takes place as follows: The "fine upper point" of the created being, which is its spiritual or divine "spark," remains in the seventh heaven in constant fusion with the infinite light of God, whilst its extension downwards—inwardly a spiritual vibration, outwardly a subtle "wave"—begins to expand on the "surface of the waters" and descend into the midst of the cosmic "ocean," there to follow its predestined path. The created being is similar in this way to a letter of the Hebrew alphabet, which, starting from its upper point, opens out first in the form of a horizontal stroke and is prolonged in one fashion or another in the direction of its lower limit. Just as letters, when pronounced, return to their origin—the silent world of the uncreated and creative Word—so do animate beings or subtle "waves," having issued with the "primordial sound" from the divine silence and having vibrated through the heavens as far as here below, then return from their terrestrial end-point towards their celestial point of departure, from which they have never been separated and which is itself in permanent union with God.

We have seen that all created beings without exception issue through the same invocation—the "primordial sound"—from their divine origin and return to it through this same "cry for joy." This simultaneously creative and redemptive sound is heard when the vibration of the divine light falls on the first subtle and cosmic expanse of the ether, on the "surface of the waters." Each of the waves formed therein truly "bursts" with joy and is nothing but an exclamation of gladness which expands over the whole of *Araboth*; each being there is just a "voice" vibrating with bliss, joined with all the other "cries" in the one "voice of YHVH" which "resounds over the waters" (Psalms 29:3). This "voice," this first and universal sound, expressed simultaneously by the Creator and by all his creatures, is symbolized in sacred ideophony by the vowel *a*; this issues from the *y* (*yod*)—from the unity of *shekhinah-metatron*—and spreads out indefinitely to the confines of the existential "ocean," through the *h* (*he*) or *avir*, that "very pure and imperceptible air" coming from the mouth of God. Such is the genesis of the divine great name, *Yah*, of which it is said (Psalms 150:6): "Let everything that hath breath praise *Yah*! *Halaluyah*! (praised be *Yah*)."[12]

---

[12] In the Apocalypse (19:6-7) there is also an allusion to the invocation of *Yah* by the "waters" of the cosmic ocean; St. John speaks of their "voice" which says *Hallelujah*! and of the redemptive joy which goes with the invocation: "And I heard as it were the voice of a great multitude and as the voice of many waters, and as the voice of mighty thunderings, saying: Hallelujah: for the Lord God omnipotent reigneth!"

Let us remember that "Hallelujah" represents not only a form of invocation of *Yah* in Judaism, but also became, by way of the Psalms, a praise of God in the Christian tradition.

God, by invoking his creative and redemptive name, causes everything that exists to issue from him and to return into him; by invoking his name with him, every being is born from him, lives by him, and is united with him.

NEMBUTSU AS REMEMBRANCE[1]

Marco Pallis

Marco Pallis *was born of Greek parents in Liverpool in 1895, received his education at Harrow and Liverpool University, and served in the British army during the First World War. He wrote two books,* Peaks and Lamas, *which was reprinted several times and became a bestseller, and* The Way and the Mountain. *The first derived from his experiences traveling in the Eastern Himalaya region prior to the Communist Chinese invasion, and the second is primarily on Tibetan Buddhism. Pallis also wrote many articles for the journal* Studies in Comparative Religion, *some of which are included in his last publication,* A Buddhist Spectrum, *from which the following chapter is excerpted.*

Were one to put the question wherein consist the differences between Theravāda, the Buddhism of the Pali Canon, and the Mahāyāna with its vast variety of schools and methods, one might for a start mention the particular emphasis laid, in the Mahāyāna teachings, upon the cosmic function of the Bodhisattva: saying this does not mean that in relation to the Theravāda the Bodhisattvic ideal constitutes some kind of innovation; it suffices to read the Jātakas or stories about the Buddha Shakyamuni's previous births in order to find those characteristic postures which the word "Bodhisattva" came to imply in subsequent centuries here prefigured in mythological mode.[2] These stories

---

[1] The word *nembutsu* is a compressed form of the phrase *namu amida butsu*, itself a Japanese reduction of the Sanskrit formula *namo'mitābhaya buddhaya*. The literal meaning is "praise to Amitabha Buddha"; here *namo* must be taken as comprising the faith, veneration, and gratitude which suffering beings owe to the Buddha as dispenser of light; the name "Amitabha" itself means "infinite light." This formula has provided its invocatory *mantram* for the Pure Land school of Buddhism; this "buddha-field" is named after Amitabha's paradise, symbolically situated in the West. The Pure Land teachings, first enunciated by the Indian masters Nagarjuna and Vasubhandu, reached Japan via China and became widely diffused thanks to the example of two great saints, Honen (1133-1212) and his preeminent disciple Shinran (1173-1262), who gave its present form to the tradition under the name of Jōdo-Shinshū (= Pure Land true sect): with us, "sect" has an unhappy sound, but it has become conventional to use it in this context without any opprobrious implications. These elementary facts should be sufficient to prepare readers unacquainted with Japanese Buddhism for what is to follow.

[2] The epithet "mythological" has been introduced here advisedly, in order to draw attention to an important feature of traditional communication which modern terminological usage has tended to debase. The Greek word *mythos*, from which our word derives, originally just meant

were current long before the distinction between Theravāda and Mahāyāna came in vogue; since then they have remained as common means of popular instruction extending to every corner of the Buddhist world. Nevertheless it is fair to say that, with the Mahāyāna, the Bodhisattva as a type steps right into the center of the world-picture, so much so that "the Bodhisattva's Vow" to devote himself consciously to the salvation of all beings without exception might well be considered as marking a man's entry into the Mahāyāna as such; viewed in this light, whatever occurs at a time prior to his taking this decisive step must be accounted an aspiration only, one waiting to be given its formal expression through the pronouncing of the vow, when the hour for this shall have struck.

By its root meaning the word "Bodhisattva" denotes one who displays an unmistakable affinity for enlightenment, one who tends in that direction both deliberately and instinctively. In the context of the Buddhist path it indicates one who has reached an advanced stage;[3] such a man is the dedicated follower of the Buddha in principle and in fact. If all this is commonly known, what we are particularly concerned with here, however, is to extract from the Bodhisattvic vocation its most characteristic trait, as expressed in the words of the Vow which run as follows: "I, so and so, in the presence of my Master, so and so, in the presence of the Buddhas, do call forth the idea of Enlightenment. . . . I adopt all creatures as mother, father, brothers, sons, sisters, and kinsmen. Henceforth . . . for the benefit of creatures I shall practice charity, discipline, patience, energy, meditation, wisdom,[4] and the means of application. . . . Let my Master accept me as a future Buddha."

---

a story and not a particular kind of story, supposedly fictitious, as nowadays. It was taken for granted that such a story was a carrier of truth, if only because, for the unsophisticated mentality of people brought up on the great myths, anything different would have seemed pointless; the idea of a fictional literature intended as a passing means of entertainment was quite alien to that mentality, and so was allegory of a contrived kind, however elevated its purpose. As a factor in human intelligence a "mythological sense" corresponds to a whole dimension of reality which, failing that sense, would remain inaccessible. Essentially, myths belong to no particular time; there is an ever-present urgency about the events they relate which is the secret of their power to influence the souls of mankind century after century.

[3] In Tibet the word for Bodhisattva, side by side with its more technical uses, is often loosely applied where, in English, we would use the word "saintly"; this is not surprising really, since a saintly person evidently exhibits traits appropriate to an incipient Bodhisattvahood.

[4] The six *pāramitās* or Transcendent Virtues: according to Mahāyāna convention *dāna*, the readiness to give oneself up to the service of others, charity in the broadest sense, heads the list as being the "note" whereby a Bodhisattva can be recognized. It is, however, unlikely that a man would have reached such a pitch of self-abnegation without previously espousing a

Marco Pallis

It can be seen at a glance that this profession of intent anticipates, by implication, the vow taken by the Bodhisattva Dharmakara from which the Pure Land teaching and practice stem. He who first had vowed to dedicate himself wholeheartedly to the good of his fellow creatures, "down to the last blade of grass" as the saying goes, after treading the Path from life to life or else, in an exceptional case like that of Tibet's poet-saint Milarepa, in the course of a single life, finds himself clearly set for the great awakening; his unremitting efforts, canalized thanks to the proper *upāyas* (means) matching each successive need, have placed him in possession of *prajñā*, that wisdom whereby all things in a formerly opaque world have been rendered transparent to the light of *bodhi*—it is at this crucial point that the Bodhisattva renews his vow to succor all beings. This time, however, he gives to his vow a negative as well as a more intensive turn by saying that "I shall *not* enter *nirvāna* unless I be assured that I can draw after me all the other creatures now steeped in ignorance and consequent suffering": through this vow the Bodhisattva's compassion becomes endowed with irresistible force; aeons of well-doing pass as in a flash; countless creatures are lifted out of their misery, until one day the cup of Dharmakara's merit overflows, and lo! we find ourselves face to face with Amitabha radiating in all directions his saving light. By this token we are given to understand that the vow has not failed in its object; the Buddha himself stands before us offering tangible proof of the vow's efficacy through the communication of his Name under cover of the *nembutsu*; henceforth this will suffice to ferry across the troubled waters of *samsāra* any being who will confidently trust his sin-weighted body to this single vehicle, even as Zen's stern patriarch Bodhidharma once trusted the reed he picked up on the water's edge and was borne safely upon its slender stalk across to the other shore. Such is the story of the providential birth of Jōdo-shin.

* * *

religiously inspired life of discipline, *shīla*, under its double heading of conscious abstention from sin and positive conformity with the ritual, doctrinal, and other prescriptions of the religion in question; such conformity does not go without effort, *vīrya*, the combative spirit. As complement to the above outgoing virtues, *shanti*, contentment, repose in one's own being, follows naturally. It is after a certain blending of these three virtues that the urge into *dāna* may be expected to be felt strongly, thus pointing the way to a Bodhisattva's vocation. The last two *pāramitās*, namely *dhyāna*, contemplation, itself implying discernment between what is real and what is illusory, and *prajñā*, that transcendent wisdom which is a synthesis of all other virtues, completes their scheme of life for followers of the Mahāyāna: obviously this general pattern is applicable in other religions besides Buddhism.

103

Reduced to bare essentials *nembutsu* is first of all an act of remembrance, whence attention follows naturally[5] thus giving rise to faith in, and thankfulness for, the Vow. From these elementary attitudes a whole program of life can be deduced.

Given these properties comprised by the *nembutsu* as providential reminder and catalyst of the essential knowledge, it should cause no one any surprise to hear that comparable examples of the linking of a divine Name with an invocatory *upāya* are to be found elsewhere than in China and Japan; details will of course be different, but the same operative principle holds good nevertheless. To point this out is in no wise to impugn the spiritual originality of the message delivered by the agency of the two great patriarchs, Honen and Shinran Shonin, within the framework of Japanese Buddhism with effects lasting even to this day; on the contrary, this is but further proof of the universal applicability of this method to the needs of mankind, and more especially during a phase of the world-cycle when the hold of religion on human minds seems to be weakening in the face of a vast and still growing apparatus of distraction such as history has never recorded before. The fact that the obvious accessibility of such a method does not exclude the most profound insights—indeed the contrary is true—has turned *nembutsu* and kindred methods to be found elsewhere into potent instruments of regeneration even under the most unfavorable circumstances: this gives the measure of their timeliness as well as of their intrinsic importance.

As an example of mutual corroboration between traditions, I have chosen a form of invocation current in the Tibetan-cum-Mongolian world where however, it is not, as in Japan, associated with any particular school but is in fact widely used by adherents of all schools without distinction. Other examples might also have been chosen belonging to non-Buddhist traditions, but it has seemed best to confine one's choice to places nearer home both because one can continue to use a common terminology and also, more especially, because in the Tibetan version the Buddha Amitabha figures in a manner which makes this tradition's kinship with Jōdo-shin clearly apparent.

The operative formula in this case is the six-syllable phrase *Om mani padme Hum* of which the acknowledged revealer is the Bodhisattva Chenrezig (Avalokiteshvara in Sanskrit, Kwannon in Japanese). It is his intimate

---

[5] In the Islamic world the word *dhikr*, remembrance, is used of the invocation practiced by members of the Sufi confraternities with the Divine Name as its operative formula; the Buddhist term *smrti* and the Sufic *dhikr* bear an identical meaning.

relationship with the Buddha Amitabha which provides the mythological link between the two traditions in question. In order to illustrate this point it will be necessary to hark back to the moment when the Bodhisattva Dharmakara became transfigured into the Buddha of Infinite Light; what we shall have to say now will be something of a sequel to the history of Dharmakara's ascent to Buddhahood as previously related.

If one stops to examine that history somewhat more closely one will become aware of a fact replete with meaning, namely that it would be possible without the least inconsistency to reverse the emphasis by saying that it is an Amitabha about to be who has been replaced by a Dharmakara fulfilled. In other words, if Buddhahood as such represents a state of awareness or knowledge, Bodhisattvahood when fully realized, as in this case, represents the dynamic dimension of that same awareness; *it is* that awareness in dynamic mode. It is moreover evident that this latter mode of awareness can only be realized in relation to an object in view; if the rescue of suffering beings be its ostensible motive, then this dynamic quality will necessarily take on the character of *compassion*, the Bodhisattvic virtue already specified in the elementary version of the vow; such a virtue moreover postulates a given world for its exercise, apart from which compassion would not even be a possible concept.

As the dynamic expression of *that* which Buddhahood is statically, Bodhisattvahood belongs to this world; it is with perfect logic that the Mahāyāna teachings have traditionally identified compassion with "method." Method is the dynamic counterpart of "wisdom," the quality of awareness: try to separate these two ideas and they will forfeit all practical applicability, hence the Mahāyāna dictum that Wisdom and Method form an eternal syzygy excluding any possibility of divorce. The Bodhisattva incarnates method as exercisable in *samsāra*; the Buddha personifies wisdom as ever present in *nirvāna*: this leaves us with two complementary triads, namely "Bodhisattva–this world–method" and "Buddha–Buddha-field (= Pure Land)– wisdom." "Human life hard of obtaining" is the opportunity to realize these complementary possibilities; if the saying be true that at the heart of each grain of sand a Buddha is to be found, it is no less true to say that in every being a potential Bodhisattva is recognizable, in active mode in the case of a man, in relatively passive mode in the case of other beings but nonetheless realizable by them via the prior attainment of a human birth.[6]

[6] For an unusually illuminating commentary on the relationship Bodhisattva-Buddha the reader is referred to Part III of *In the Tracks of Buddhism* by Frithjof Schuon, published by Allen

From all the above it follows that a Bodhisattva's activity on behalf of beings does not lose its necessity once Buddhahood is attained; the ascending course from Dharmakara to Amitabha, as confirmed by the Vow, must needs have its counterpart in a descending course under a fresh name. This name in fact is Chenrezig or Kwannon who, as the story tells us, took birth from the head of Amitabha himself, thus becoming the appointed dispenser of a mercy which is none other than a function of the nirvanic Light; in Chenrezig we see a Dharmakara as it were nirvanically reborn, if such an expression be permissible. Here again the story of this celestial event is illuminating, since we are told that Chenrezig, in his exercise of the merciful task laid upon him by his originator and teacher Amitabha, began by leading so many beings towards the promised Buddha-land that the very hells became emptied. However, when this Bodhisattva looked back upon the world, just as his predecessor Dharmakara had done prior to taking his Vow, he perceived the horrifying fact that as quickly as one lot of beings climbed out of the infernal round of birth and death following in his wake, another lot of beings, in apparent unconcern, hastened to fill the vacant places, so that the mass of samsaric suffering remained virtually as bad as ever. The Bodhisattva was so overcome by disappointment and pity that his head split in fragments, whereupon the Buddha came to the rescue with a fresh head for his representative. This same thing happened no less than ten times until, with the bestowing by Amitabha of an eleventh head, the Bodhisattva was enabled to resume his mission without further hindrance.

In the Tibetan iconography Chenrezig is frequently portrayed under his eleven-headed form, appropriately known as the "Great Compassionate One"; multiple arms go with this portrait, as showing the endless ways in which the Bodhisattva can exercise his function as helper of beings. The most usual portrait of Chenrezig, however, is one with four arms, the whole figure being colored white; in one hand he holds a rosary and it is this object which symbolizes his communication of the *mani* as invocatory means. Some details of how the invocation with *mani* is carried out by the Tibetans will serve to relate the practice to other similar methods found in Japan and elsewhere.

First, about the formula itself: the most usual translation into English has been "Om, jewel in the lotus, Hum." Obviously, such words do not immediately lend themselves to logical paraphrase; one can reasonably assume, however,

---

& Unwin, a work to which the present writer gratefully acknowledges his own indebtedness.
[Editor's Note: An augmented edition of this work is published by World Wisdom, entitled *Treasures of Buddhism* (1993). See especially the chapter, "Mystery of the Bodhisattva."]

that since in the traditional iconography Buddhas are normally shown as seated upon a lotus, that serene flower resting on the waters of possibility and thereby evocative of the nature of things, the jewel must for its part represent the presence of the Buddha and the treasure of his teaching inviting discovery, but this by itself does not get one very far. As for the initial and concluding syllables, these belong to the category of metaphysically potent ejaculations whereof many figure in the Tantric initiations: one can safely say, with this kind of formula, that it is not intended for analytical dissection, but rather that its intrinsic message will spontaneously dawn upon a mind poised in one-pointed concentration. This view, moreover, was confirmed by the Dalai Lama when I put to him the question of whether the *mani* would by itself suffice to take a man all the way to Deliverance. His Holiness replied that it would indeed suffice for one who had penetrated to the heart of its meaning, a ruling which itself bears out the saying that the *Om mani padme Hum* contains "the quintessence of the teaching of all the Buddhas." The fact that the Dalai Lama specifically exercises an "activity of presence" in this world in the name of the Bodhisattva Chenrezig, revealer of *mani*, renders his comment in this instance all the more authoritative.

As in all similar cases an initiatory *lung* (authorization) must be sought by whoever wishes to invoke with *mani*, failing which the practice would remain irregular and correspondingly inefficacious. Once the *lung* has been conferred it is possible to invoke in a number of ways, either under one's breath or, more often, in an audible murmur for which the Tibetan word is the same as for the purring of a cat. It is recommended, for one invoking regularly, that he precede each invoking session by a special poem of four lines and likewise repeat a similar quatrain by way of conclusion. Here is the text:

I

Unstained by sin and white of hue
Born from the head of the perfect Buddha
Look down in mercy upon beings
To Chenrezig let worship be offered.

II

By the merit of this [invocation] may I soon
Become endowed with Chenrezig's power.
Let all beings without even one omission
In his [Chenrezig's] land established be.

No need to underline the reference to Amitabha in the first verse and the reference to the Buddha-land in the second in order to show how close to one another *mani* and *nembutsu* stand as regards their basic purpose.

Mention should also be made here of the standard treatise on the *mani* invocation, in which are outlined the various symbolical correspondences to which the six syllables lend themselves, each of which can become a theme for meditation. These sixfold schemes range over a wide field, starting with deliverance from each in turn of the possible states of sentient existence and the realization one by one of the six *pāramitās* or Transcendent Virtues; the latter parts of this treatise lead the mind into still deeper waters which it is beyond the scope of this essay to explore.

To turn to more external features of the *mani* invocation, it is common practice to use some kind of rhythmical support while repeating the words of the mantra, which can be either a rosary or else an appliance peculiar to Tibet which foreign travelers have rather inappropriately (since no idea of petition enters in) labeled as a "prayer-wheel." This wheel consists of a rotating box fixed on the end of a wooden handle and containing a tightly rolled cylinder of paper inscribed all over with the *mani* formula. A small weight attached by a chain to the box enables the invoking person to maintain an even swing while repeating the words; sometimes, especially with elderly people, the practice becomes reduced to a silent rotatory motion, with the invocation itself taken for granted.

Very large *mani*-wheels are commonly to be found at the doors of temples, so that people as they enter may set them in motion; likewise, rows of smaller wheels are often disposed along the outside walls so that those who carry out the *pradak-shinam* or clockwise circuit of the sacred edifice may set them revolving as they pass. But remembrance of the *mani* does not stop there; immense *mani*-wheels ceaselessly kept going by waterfalls exist in many places, while flags bearing the sacred words float from the corners of every homestead. Lastly, flat stones carved with the formula and dedicated as offerings by the pious are to be found laid in rows on raised parapets at the edge of highroads or along the approaches to monasteries. These "*mani*-walls" are so disposed as to allow a passage on either side, since reverence requires that a man turn his right side towards any sacred object he happens to pass, be it a *stupa* or one of these *mani*-walls; being on horseback is no excuse for doing otherwise. The popular dictum "beware of the devils on the left-hand side" refers to this practice.

If it be asked what effect all this can amount to, the answer is that it serves to keep people constantly reminded of what a human life is for; reminiscence is the key to a religiously directed life at all levels, from the most external and popular to the most interior and intellectual; "popular" may often be allied with deep insights, of course, for the above distinctions are not intended in a social sense. Certainly in the Tibet we visited while the traditional order there was still intact the whole landscape was as if suffused by the message of the Buddha's Dharma; it came to one with the air one breathed, birds seemed to sing of it, mountain streams hummed its refrain as they bubbled across the stones, a dharmic perfume seemed to rise from every flower, at once a reminder and a pointer to what still needed doing. The absence of fear on the part of wild creatures at the approach of man was in itself a witness to this same truth; there were times when a man might have been forgiven for supposing himself already present in the Pure Land. The India of King Ashoka's time must have been something like this; to find it in mid-twentieth-century anywhere was something of a wonder.

Moreover a situation like this was bound to be reflected in the lives of individuals, despite inevitable human failings; piety was refreshingly spontaneous, it did not need dramatizing attitudes to bolster it up nor any rationalized justifications. Each man was enabled to find his own level without difficulty according to capacity and even a quite modest qualification could carry him far. Among the many people using the *mani* one can say that a large proportion stopped short at the idea of gathering merit with a view to a favorable rebirth; the finality in view, though not entirely negligible in itself remained essentially samsaric: it did not look far beyond the limits of the cosmos. More perceptive practitioners would resort to the same invocation for the general purpose of nourishing and deepening their own piety; the finality here was "devotional," in the sense of the Indian word *bhakti*, implying a comparatively intense degree of participation; such a way of invoking represents an intermediate position in the scale of spiritual values. Rarer by comparison is the kind of person whose intelligence, matured in the course of the practice, is able to envisage that truth for which the invocation provides both a means of recollection and an incentive to realize it fully; this is the case to which the Dalai Lama was referring when he spoke of penetrating to the heart of the teaching which the six syllables between them enshrine.

In a more general connection, the question often arises as to how much importance should be attached to the frequent repetition of a formula like the *mani* or the *nembutsu* compared with a sparser use of it; here one can recall the fact that in the period when Honen was preaching the Pure Land doctrine in Japan many persons, carried away by their enthusiasm, vied with one another as to the number of times they were able to repeat the formula, as if this were the thing that mattered. In the face of such extravagances Shinran Shonin applied a wholesome corrective by showing that the value of *nembutsu* is primarily a qualitative one, with number counting for nothing in itself as a criterion of effectiveness. The essence of a thing, that which makes it to be what it is and not something else, is not susceptible of multiplication: one can for instance count one, two or a hundred sheep, but the quality of "sheepness" becomes neither increased nor subdivided thereby. The same applies to *nembutsu* or *mani*; each represents a unique and total presence carrying within itself its own finality irrespective of number, situation, or timing. This is an important principle to grasp; were one able to penetrate as far as the very heart of the sacred formula a single mention of it would be sufficient to bring one home to the Pure Land; the various steps that have led one as far as the threshold become merged in fulfillment.

At the same time, on the basis of an empirical judgment, one is not justified in despising the man who finds frequent repetition of an invocatory formula helpful; to estimate the value of such repetition in purely quantitative terms is certainly an error, but to feel an urge to fill one's life with the formula because one values it above everything else and feels lonely and lost without it is another thing. To rise of a morning with *nembutsu*, to retire to bed at night with its words on one's lips, to live with it and by it, to die with its last echo in one's ear, what could in fact be better or more humanly appropriate? Between one who invokes very often and another who does so with less frequency there is little to choose provided attention is focused on the essential. It is the effects on the soul which will count in the long run, its alchemical transmutation in witness of the Vow's power, thanks to which the lead of our existential ignorance is enabled to reveal its essential identity with the Bodhic gold, even as Dharmakara's identity with Amitabha is revealed in the Vow itself.

There is one more question of practical importance for all who would follow a contemplative discipline outside the monastic order which here does not concern us, namely the question of how one may regard the interruptions imposed by the need to transfer attention, during one's working hours, to external matters either of a professional kind or else, in the majority of cases, as means of earning a livelihood. Does not this, some may well ask, render the idea of a lifelong concentration on *nembutsu* virtually unrealizable? And, if so, what result will this have in regard to the essential awakening of faith? Some such question has in fact always worried mankind in one form or another, but has become more pressing than ever as a result of the breakdown of traditional societies formerly structured according to religiously linked vocations. The individual is now left in so-called freedom to make choices which his ancestors were mercifully spared. Nevertheless, there is sufficient precedent to enable one to answer this question in a way that all may understand.

The criterion which applies in such cases is this, namely that so long as a man's work is not obviously dishonest, cruel, or otherwise reprehensible, that is to say as long as it conforms, broadly speaking,[7] to the definitions of the Noble Eightfold Path under the headings of Proper Ordering of Work and Proper Livelihood, the time and attention this demands from a man will not *per se* constitute a distraction in the technical sense of the word; rather will the stream of contemplation continue to flow quietly like an underground river, ready to surface again with more animated current once the necessary tasks have been accomplished for the time being. Here "necessary" is the operative word: activities undertaken needlessly, from frivolous or luxurious motives such as a wish to kill time because one expects to feel bored when not actually working, cannot on any showing be ranked as work in the proper sense. A vast number of so-called "leisure activities" fall under this condemnable heading: these do, on any logical showing, constitute distractions in the strict sense of the word. One would have thought that the briefest portion of a "human life hard of obtaining" could have been put to better uses; yet nowadays such abuse of the human privilege is not only tolerated but even encouraged on the vastest scale by way of tribute to the great god of Economics, Mara's fashionable alias in the contemporary world. By rights most of these time-wasting practices belong to the category of noxious drugs, addiction to which comes only too easily.

Apart from this question of man's occupational calls and how these properly fit in, the invocation with *nembutsu* or its equivalents in other

---

[7] "Broadly speaking": this reservation was necessary, inasmuch as no person is in a position to assess all the repercussions of his work or his livelihood in an ever-changing world. All he can do is to avoid practices of a self-evidently wicked kind, while conforming to a reasonable degree with the circumstances in which his karma has placed him. In earlier times, when vocations were more clear-cut and also religiously guaranteed, discrimination was relatively easy though by no means infallible in practice. Nowadays, with the bewildering complications which beset almost everybody's life in the modern world a man can but do his limited best to conform to the ideal prescriptions of the Eightfold Path under the two headings in question; there is no call for him to scrape his conscience by looking far beyond what lies obviously within reach of a human choice. This does not mean, of course, that one need have no scruples as to what one does or does not undertake; where discernment is still possible, it should be exercised in the light of the Buddha's teachings.

traditions will always offer a most potent protection against distractions of whatever kind. A life filled with this numinous influence leaves little chance for Mara's attendant demons to gain a footing. I remember one lama's advice when he said, "Finish the work in hand and after that fill the remaining time with *mani* invocation." This sets the pattern of a life's program, details of which can be left to settle themselves in the light of particular needs.

*   *   *

The heart-moving tale of Dharmakara's journey to enlightenment, on which our own participation in the teachings of Jōdo-shin depends, may at first sight appear to record events dating from long, long ago. It is well to remember, however, what has already been said about the timeless nature of mythological happenings, whereby they are rendered applicable again and again, across the changing circumstances of mankind, as means of human illumination. There are certain truths which are best able to communicate themselves in this form without any danger of entanglement in the alternative of belief versus disbelief which, in the case of historical claims, is all too likely to be raised by the very nature of the evidence on which those claims rest: question the factual evidence, and the truths themselves become vulnerable, as has been shown in the case of Western Christianity during recent times where the attempt to "demythologize" its sacred lore, including the Scriptures, has only made the situation worse for present-day believers. Historical evidence of course has its own importance—no need to deny this fact. In relation to history a traditional mythology provides a factor of equilibrium not easily dispensed with if a given religion is to retain its hold over the minds of men.

As it stands, the old story of Dharmakara represents the Wisdom aspect of a teaching whereof the Method aspect is to be found when this same story comes to be reenacted in a human life, be it our own life or another's, thanks to the evocative power released by the original Vow, following its confirmation in the person of Amitabha Buddha. Hence the injunction to place all our faith in the Other Power, eschewing self. The consequences of so doing will affect both our thinking and feeling and all we do or avoid doing in this life.

Here it is well to remind ourselves of what was said at the outset, namely that the Bodhisattva's compassion, his dynamic virtue, needs a field for its exercise as well as suffering beings for its objects, failing which it would be meaningless. For a field one can also say "a world" either in the sense of a particular world (the world familiar to us, for example) or in the sense of *samsāra* as such, comprising all possible forms of existence, including many we can never know. A world, by definition, is a field of contrasts, an orchard of karma replete with its fruit, black or white, which we ourselves, in our dual capacity of creators and partakers of these fruits, are called upon to harvest in season, be they bitter or sweet. This experiencing of the world, moreover, also comes to us in a dual way, at once external and internal: for us, the external world is composed of all beings and things which fall into the category of "other," while to the internal world there belong all such experiences as concern what we call "I" or "mine," the ego-consciousness at every level. One can go further and say that man, in this respect, himself constitutes something like a self-contained world; it is not for nothing that the human state has been described, by analogy with the Cosmos at large, as a "microcosm," a little world. It is in fact within this little estate of ours that the drama of Dharmakara and Amitabha has to be played out if we are truly to understand it, this being in fact the Method aspect of the story which thus, through its concrete experiencing, will reveal itself as Wisdom to our intelligence. It is with this, for us, most vital matter that the present essay may fittingly be concluded.

The three principal factors in our symbolical play are, first, the psychophysical vehicle of our earthly existence which provides the moving stage and, second, the faculty of attention under its various aspects including the senses, reason, imagination, and above all our active remembrance or mindfulness. These between them represent the Bodhisattvic dynamism in relation to our vocational history; third and last, there is the illuminative power of Amitabha as represented by the unembodied Intelligence dwelling at that secret spot in the center of each being where *samsāra* as such is inoperative[8] or, to put the point still more precisely, where *samsāra* reveals

---

[8] By way of concordant testimony one can profitably recall the teaching of the great medieval sage of Western Christendom, Meister Eckhart, when he said that in the human soul "is to be found something uncreated and uncreatable and this is the Intellect"; to which he adds that were it entirely such, it too would be uncreate and uncreatable. Substitute "Bodhic Eye" for the word "Intellect" and you have there a statement any Buddhist might understand. In the traditions issuing from the Semitic stem, where the idea of "creation" plays a dominant part, to say of anything that it is "uncreate" is the equivalent of "beyond the scope of samsaric change." It should be added that, at the time when Meister Eckhart was writing, the word "intellect" always bore the above meaning, as distinct from "reason" which, as its Latin name of *ratio* shows, was a faculty enabling one to relate things to one another apart from any possibility of perceiving their intrinsic suchness, which only the Intellect is able to do. The modern confusion between intellect, reason, and mind, to the practical emasculation of the former, has spelt a disaster for human thinking.

its own essential identity with *nirvāna*; but for this Bodhic Eye enshrined within us, able to read the Bodhic message all things display to him who knows where to look, human liberation through enlightenment, and the liberation from suffering of other beings via a human birth, would not be a possibility; the door to the Pure Land would remain forever closed. Thanks to Dharmakara's example, culminating in his Vow, we know that this Pure Land is open, however; herein consists our hope and our incentive. What more can one ask of existence than this supreme opportunity the human state comprises so long as that state prevails?

Before quitting this discussion one other question calls for passing consideration, affecting the manner of presenting Jōdo-shin ideas in popular form today. Writers on the subject seem much given to stressing the "easy" nature of the Jōdo-shin way; faith, so they say, is all we really need inasmuch as Amitabha, Dharmakara that was, has done our work for us already, thus rendering entry into the Pure Land as good as assured, with the corollary that any suggestion of responsibility or conscious effort on our part would savor of a dangerous concession to Own Power and is in any case redundant. In voicing such ideas a sentimentally angled vocabulary is used without apparently taking into account the effect this is likely to have on uncritical minds. Though this kind of language is doubtless not actually intended to minimize the normal teachings of Buddhism, it does nevertheless betray a pathetically artless trend in the thinking of authors who resort to it. Some will doubtless seek to defend themselves by saying that the writings of Shinran and other Jōdo-shin luminaries also contain phrases having a somewhat similar ring; those who quote thus out of context are apt to ignore the fact that a teaching sage, one who is out to win hearts but not to destroy intelligences (this should not need saying), may sometimes resort to a schematic phraseology never meant to be taken literally. Lesser persons should show prudence in how they quote from, and especially in how they themselves embroider upon, such statements of the great.

When, for example, Nichiren, that militant saint, declared that a single pronouncing of the *nembutsu* was enough to send a man to hell, he was obviously exaggerating for the purpose of goading his own audience in a

---

The above example can be paralleled by another, taken this time from Eastern Christianity, where it is said that the crowns of the perfected saints are made of "Uncreated Light," or, as we might also say, the diadems of the perfected Bodhisattvas are made from Amitabha's own halo.

predetermined direction; religious history offers many such examples of rhetorical excess, albeit spiritually motivated. The proper reply to such a diatribe would be to say, in the tone of respect due to a great Master, "Thanks Reverend Sir, your warning brings great comfort; for me Hell with *nembutsu* will be as good as Heaven; without *nembutsu* paradise would be a hell indeed!"[9]

Let us, however, for a moment, as an *upāya* nicely matched to the occasion, carry the argument of the very people we had been criticizing a little further by putting the following question: if Dharmakara's compassionate initiative, culminating in the Vow, has come to the aid of our weakness by completing the most essential part of our task for us, leaving it to us to take subsequent advantage of this favor, how best can we repay our debt of gratitude for the mercy shown us? Surely an elementary gratitude requires, on the part of a beneficiary, that he should try and please his benefactor by doing as he has advised and not the contrary. The Eightfold Path is what the Buddha left for our life's program; in following this way, whether we are motivated by regard for our own highest interest or by simple thankfulness for Amitabha's mercy makes little odds in practice, though this second attitude may commend itself to our mentality for contingent reasons. To bring all this into proper perspective in the context of Jōdo-shin one has to bear in mind its operative principle, namely that the *nembutsu* itself comprises all possible teachings, all methods, all merits "eminently," requiring nothing else of us except our faith, which must be freely given. A genuine faith, however one may regard it, does not go without its heroic overtones; how then are we to understand it in relation to the finality of Jōdo-shin, as symbolized by the Pure Land? Surely, in this same perspective, faith is there to act as catalyst of all the other virtues, whether we list them separately or not. In this way an attitude that may sometimes seem one-sidedly devotional can still rejoin Buddhism's profoundest insights; for one who does so, the way may well be described as "easy."

What is certain, however, is that no Buddhist, whatever his own personal affiliations may happen to be, can reasonably claim exclusive authority for the teachings he follows; as between an Own Power (*jiriki*) and an Other Power (*tariki*) approach to salvation we can perhaps say that if the latter

---

[9] My friend Dr. Inagaki Hisao has supplied a quotation from Shinran's teachings as embodied in the *Tannishō* (Chapter II) where the same sentiment is expressed consonantly with Jōdo tradition and using its typical dialect: "I would not regret even if I were deceived by Honen and thus, by uttering the *nembutsu*, fell into hell. . . . Since I am incapable of any practice whatsoever, hell would definitely be my dwelling anyway."

may sometimes take on a too passive appearance as in the cases previously mentioned, the former type of method, if improperly conceived, can easily imprison one in a state of self-centered consciousness of a most cramping kind. The best defense against either of the above errors is to remember that, between two indubitably orthodox but formally contrasted teachings, where one of them is deliberately stressed the other must always be recognized as latent, and vice versa. This excludes moreover any temptation to indulge in sectarian excesses. No spiritual method can be totally self-contained; by definition every *upāya* is provisionally deployed in view of the known needs of a given mentality; there its authority stops: to say so of any particular teachings implies no disrespect.

The stress laid on Other Power in Jōdo-shin provides a salutary counterblast to any form of self-esteem, a fact which makes its teachings peculiarly apt in our own time when deification of the human animal as confined to this world and a wholesale pandering to his ever-expanding appetites is being preached on every side. In the presence of Amitabha the achievements of individual mankind become reduced to their proper unimportance; it is in intelligent humility that a truly human greatness is to be found.

One important thing to bear in mind, in all this, is that the Buddha's mercy is providential, but does not, for this very reason, suspend the Law of Karma: if beings will persist in ignoring that law while coveting the things mercy might have granted them, that mercy itself will reach them in the guise of severity; severity is merciful when this is the only means of provoking a radical *metanoia* (change of outlook), failing which wandering in *samsāra* must needs continue indefinitely. The *nembutsu* is our ever-present reminder of this truth; if, in reliance on the Vow, we abandon all wish to attribute victory to ourselves, the unfed ego will surely waste away, leaving us in peace.

Apart from all else, reliance on Other Power will remain unrealizable so long as the egocentric consciousness is being mistaken for the real person; it is this confusion of identity which the great *upāya* propounded by Honen and Shinran Shonin was providentially designed to dispel. Let *nembutsu* serve as our perpetual defense against this fatal error, through the remembrance it keeps alive in human hearts. Where that remembrance has been raised to its highest power, there is to be found the Pure Land.

THE SHIN TEACHING OF BUDDHISM

D. T. Suzuki

Daisetz Teitaro Suzuki *(1870-1966) was a prominent Japanese Buddhist scholar, educated at Tokyo University. After studying in the United States from 1897-1909, he became a lecturer at Tokyo University; he later taught at leading universities in Japan, Europe, and the United States. In his day, Suzuki was a leading authority on Buddhism and is known for his introduction of Zen Buddhism to the West. Among his many works are* Essays in Zen Buddhism *(3 vols.),* The Training of the Buddhist Monk, Zen Buddhism and Its Influence on Japanese Culture, An Introduction to Zen Buddhism, Mysticism: Christian and Buddhist, Outlines of Mahayana Buddhism, *and* Shin Buddhism.

Both Jōdo and Shin belong to the Pure Land school. *Jōdo* means the "Pure Land" and the official title of the Shin is Jōdo Shin and not just Shin. *Shin* means "true" and its devotees claim that their teaching is truly *tariki* whereas the Jōdo is not quite so, being mixed with the *jiriki* idea: hence *Shin* "true" added to *Jōdo*.

The main points of difference between the Jōdo and the Shin teaching are essentially two: 1. Jōdo fully believes with Shin in the efficacy of Amida's Vow but thinks that Amida's Name is to be repeatedly recited; whereas Shin places its emphasis upon faith and not necessarily upon the *nembutsu*, which is the repeated recitation of the Name. 2. Jōdo encourages good works as helpful for the devotee being born in the Pure Land; whereas Shin finds here a residue of the *jiriki* ("self-power") and insists that as long as the devotee awakens his wholehearted faith in Amida, Amida will take care of him unconditionally, absolutely assuring his entrance into the Pure Land. Whatever *nembutsu* he may offer to Amida it is no more than the grateful appreciation of the favor of the Buddha.

The fundamental idea underlying the Shin faith is that we as individual existences are karma-bound and therefore sinful, for karma is inevitably connected with sin; that as no karma-bound beings are capable of effecting their own emancipation, they have to take refuge in Amida who out of his infinite love for all beings is ever extending his helping arms; and that all that is needed of us is to remain altogether passive towards Amida, for he awakens in our hearts, when they are thoroughly purged of all the ideas of self and self-reliance a faith which at once joins us to Amida and makes us entirely his. This being so, we as creatures subject to the law of moral causation can accomplish nothing worthy of the Pure Land; all good works so called are not all good from the viewpoint of absolute value, for they are always found deeply tinged with the idea of selfhood which no relatively-conditioned beings are able to shake off. Amida, in his capacity of Infinite Light and Eternal Life, stands against us ever beckoning us to cross the stream of birth-and-death. Faith is the act of response on our part, and its practical result is our crossing the stream.

One difference at least between Jōdo and Shin or between *jiriki* and *tariki* as regards their attitude towards the *nembutsu* is, according to the author of the *Anjin-ketsujō-shō*, that:

> The *nembutsu* as practiced by the *jiriki* followers puts the Buddha away from themselves far in the West, and thinking that they are worthless beings they would now and then recollect the Original Vow of the Buddha and pronounce his Name (*shōmyō*). This being so the most intimate relationship between the Buddha and all beings fails to establish itself here. When a pious feeling however slight moves in their hearts, they may be persuaded to think that their rebirth is approaching. But when they are not too anxious to say the *nembutsu* and whatever pious feeling they have grows weaker, the assurance of their rebirth wavers. Inasmuch as they are common mortals, it is only on exceptional occasions that they cherish pious feelings; and they thus naturally have an uncertain outlook in regard to their rebirth [in the Pure Land]. They may have to wait in this uncertain state of mind until the time actually comes for them to depart from this life. While they occasionally pronounce the Name with their mouth, they have no definite assurance for the Pure Land. This position is like that of a feudal retainer who only occasionally comes out in the presence of the lord. [His relationship with the latter can never be intimate and trustful.] Such a devotee is all the time in an unsettled state of mind as to how to court the favor of the Buddha, how to be reconciled to him, how to win his loving consideration, and this very fact of his uncertainties alienates him from Buddha, resulting in the unharmonious relationship between the devotee's unsettled mind and Buddha's great compassionate heart. The [*jiriki*] devotee thus puts himself at a distance from Buddha. As long as he keeps up this attitude of mind his rebirth in the Pure Land is indeed extremely uncertain.

From this, we see that the *jiriki* followers' relation to Buddha is not so intimate and trustful as that of the *tariki*. They endeavor to court the favor of Amida by doing something meritorious, including the recitation of his Name, but this attitude indicates a certain fundamental separation and irreconcilability as existing between Buddha and his devotees. The *jiriki* thus tends to create an unnecessary gap where according to the *tariki* there has never been any from the very first. The being conscious of a gap interferes with the assurance of rebirth and peace of mind is lost. The *tariki* on the other hand places great stress on the significance of the eighteenth vow made by Amida, and teaches that when the significance of this vow is fully realized, rebirth is assured and the devotee is released from all worries arising from the sense of separation.

What, then, is the significance of Amida's Vow?

According to the *Anjin-ketsujō-shō* it is this:

The purport of all the three sūtras of the Jōdo school is to manifest the significance of the Original Vow. To understand the Vow means to understand the Name, and to understand the Name is to understand that Amida, by bringing to maturity his Vow and Virtue (or Deed) in the stead of all beings, effected their rebirth even prior to their actual attainment. What made up the substance of his Enlightenment was no other than the rebirth of all beings in the ten quarters of the world. For this reason, devotees of the *nembutsu*, that is, of the *tariki*, are to realize this truth each time they hear Amida's Name pronounced that their rebirth is indeed already effected, because the Name stands for the Enlightenment attained by Hōzō the Bodhisattva who vowed that he would not attain enlightenment until all beings in the ten quarters of the world were assured of their rebirth in his Pure Land. The same realization must also be awakened in the minds of the *tariki* devotees when they bow before the holy statue of Amida Buddha, for it represents him in the state of Enlightenment which he attained by vowing that he would not have it until all beings were assured of the rebirth. When any reference is made to the Pure Land, they should cherish the thought that it is the realm established by Hōzō the Bodhisattva for the sake of all beings whose rebirth there was assured by his Vow and Enlightenment. As far as the devotees themselves are concerned they have nothing in their nature which will enable them to practice any form of good either worldly, or unworldly since they only know how to commit evil deeds; but because of Amida's having completed an immeasurable amount of meritorious deeds which constitutes the substance of Buddhahood, even we who are ignorant and addicted to wrong views are now destined for the Land of Purity and Happiness. What a blessing it is then for us all! We may believe in Amida's Original Vow and pronounce his Name; but if we, failing to perceive that Amida's meritorious deeds are our own, stress the merit of the Name in order to assure ourselves of rebirth, we would indeed be committing a grievous fault.

When the belief is once definitely awakened that *Namu-amida-butsu* symbolizes the truth of our rebirth assured by Amida's Enlightenment, we see that the substance of Buddhahood is the act [or fact] of our rebirth, and consequently that one utterance of the Name means the assurance of rebirth. When, again, the Name, *Namu-amida-butsu*, is heard, we see that the time is come for our rebirth and that our rebirth is no other than the Enlightenment attained by Amida. We may cherish a doubt, if we choose, whether Amida already attained his Enlightenment or whether he has not yet attained it; but we should never have a doubt as to our rebirth being an accomplished fact. Amida has vowed not to attain his Enlightenment as long as there is one single being whose rebirth has not yet been assured. To understand all this is said to understand what is meant by Amida's Original Vow.

While the *jiriki* teaches us that it is on our side to make vows and to practice good deeds if we wish to be assured of our rebirth, the *tariki* teaches just the reverse: it is on the side of Amida who makes vows and practices good deeds while the effect of all this is matured on our side—the fact which altogether goes beyond the reason of causation as we see in this world or anywhere else.

It is thus evident that for the *tariki* devotees the Buddha is not very far away from them, indeed that they are living with him, in him, "rising with him in the morning and retiring at night again with him." Amida to them is not an object of worship or thought which stands against them, although as far as logical knowledge goes which is good for the world of karma and birth-and-death, Amida is a being quite apart from us who are nothing but ignorant and sinful beings. It is by faith that we transcend the logic of dualism, and then, in Shin terminology, we are assured of our rebirth in the Pure Land of Amida. Faith is an eternal mystery, and the truth and vitality of Shin faith is rooted in this mystery.

To quote further the author of the *Anjin-ketsujō-shō*:

Generally speaking, the *nembutsu* means to think of the Buddha, and to think of the Buddha means that the Buddha has by the karmic power inherent in his Great Vow cut asunder for all beings the bonds whereby they are tied to birth-and-death, and that he has thus matured the condition for their rebirth in the Land of Recompense where once entered they would never retrograde, and further that when thinking of this merit accomplished by the Buddha they take advantage of his Original Vow and give themselves up to it, their threefold activity [of body, mouth, and mind] is supported by the Buddha-substance and raised up to the state of enlightenment which constitutes Buddhahood. For this reason, by being thorough in the *nembutsu* we are to understand that our pronouncing the Buddha's Name, or our paying him homage, or our thinking of him is not an act originating in ourselves but doing the act of Amida Buddha himself. (Or shall we say "living the life of Amida," or "living in Christ and not in Adam"?)

What the Shin devotees object to in the way cherished by their fellow-believers of the Jōdo teaching is that the latter are a mixture of *jiriki* and *tariki* and not *tariki* pure and simple, that if one at all advocates *tariki*, this must be thoroughly purged of the *jiriki* element, and that *tariki* even to the slightest degree tainted with *jiriki* is not only logically untenable but is a revolt against the universal love of Amida which he entertains for all sentient beings. As long as one puts a wholehearted trust in the Original Vow of Amida, one ought not to harbor even an iota of *jiriki* idea against it; when this is done the entire scheme collapses. *Jiriki* means literally "self-power," that is, self-will, and what self-will is needed in the work of transcending the karmic law of causation which binds us to this world of relativity? The self-will is useful and means something while we stay in the realm of birth-and-death, but what is to be achieved by the Buddhists is the realization of things of eternal value. The self-will is called *hakarai* by Shinran, founder of the Shin school of the Jōdo (Pure Land) teaching. *Hakarai* is "to contrive," "to calculate," "to lay down a plan," "to have an intention," for one's rebirth in the Land of Amida. Shinran has consistently disavowed this *hakarai* as the essence of *jiriki* lying in the way of absolute faith in which all the Jōdo followers are to accept the Original Vow of Amida. So we have the following in one of his epistles given to his disciples:

By *jiriki* is meant that the devotees, each according to his karmic condition, think of a Buddha other [than Amida], recite his Name, and practice good deeds relying on their own judgments, that they plan out their own ideas as regards how properly and felicitously to adjust their activities of the body, mouth, and mind for the rebirth in the Pure Land. By *tariki* is meant wholeheartedly to accept and believe the Original Vow of Amida whereby he assures those who pronounce his Name that they will be reborn in his Pure Land. As this is the Vow made by Amida, it has a sense which cannot be prescribed by any common measure of judgment—a sense which is beyond sense, as has been taught by my holy master. Sense is contrivance, that is, intention. The devotees have an intention to move in accordance with their own ideas, and thus their doings have sense.

The *tariki* devotees, however, have placed their faith whole-heartedly in Amida's Original Vow and are assured of their rebirth in the Pure Land—hence they are free from sense [or from intention of their own]. This being so, you are not to imagine that you would not be greeted by Amida in his Land because of your sinfulness. As ordinary beings you are endowed with all kinds of evil passions and destined to be sinful. Nor are you to imagine that you are assured of rebirth in the Pure Land because of your goodness. As long as your *jiriki* sense is holding you, you would never be welcomed to Amida's True Land of Recompense.

To begin with, according to Shinran, Amida's Original Vow is a mysterious deed altogether beyond human comprehension, and now that you have awakened faith in it, what worries could ever harass you? What contrivances could ever save you from sinfulness so completely that you would be worthy residents of the Pure Land? You just give yourselves up absolutely to the mysterious workings of the Original Vow and, instead of growing anxious about or being vexed by anything of this world, be satisfied with yourselves, be free as the wind blows, as the flowers blossom, in the unimpeded light of Amida. Shinran frequently advises not to think of good, nor of evil, but just to give oneself up into the mysterious Original Vow and be "natural."

To be "natural" (*jinen*) means to be free from self-willed intention, to be altogether trusting in the Original Vow, to be absolutely passive in the hands of Amida who has prepared for you the way to his Pure Land. We humans are supposed to be intelligent beings but when we reflect at all on things claiming our attention and try to carry out the thinking to the furthest end, we find that our intelligence is not adequate for the task and that we are surrounded on all sides by thick clouds of mysteries. It makes no difference in which direction our thinking turns, inwardly or outwardly, it always confronts a mystery, for it is in its nature that it can never solve the questions it raises for itself. We have thus no other way but to give ourselves up to this mystery, which, from the Shin point of view, is known as the mystery of the Original Vow or the mystery of the Name. When this mystery is reached which is the limit of intellectual reflection, it is comprehended, not indeed intellectually but intuitively, that is to say, it is accepted unconditionally—which is another way of describing faith. In terms of the Shin teaching, the faith thus awakened is the assurance of rebirth in Amida's Pure Land, and those who have this faith are said to be already walking in the Pure Land in company with all the Tathāgatas. That the Shin devotees of true and never-relapsing faith are the equals of Maitreya Bodhisattva is a most significant declaration on the part of the Shin teachers. It is evident that the faith advocated by them is an identical state of mind with Enlightenment realized by all the Buddhas. As for the real Supreme Enlightenment the devotees are to wait until they reach the Pure Land itself. In so far as they still belong to this world, the body may commit acts of impurity, but the mind is already where all the Tathāgatas are, that is, in the Pure Land. To live this mystery is known as being "natural," following the course of things, especially of things of the spirit, as arranged by the Original Vow of Amida.

To have the body in this world of time and space with the mind somewhere else, to let the body live a life of evils since it cannot do anything different and yet to keep the mind in the Land of Purity in the most friendly relationship with all the Buddhas—how can this be possible? Apart from the psychological and philosophical question of body and mind, how can one individual totality be at two points at the same time? Logically stated, the Shin expressions such as above referred to are full of difficulties, in fact impossible for intellectual solution. But one thing we can say about the statements made by the Shin teachers is that, generally speaking, religious intuition consists in consciously coming into contact with a realm of absolute values, which stands in no spatial or temporal relationship to this world of senses and ratiocination, but which forms the basis of it, gives it its meaning, and without which it is like a dream, like a dew-drop, like a flash of lightning. The relation of the body and the mind, of this world and the Pure Land, of sinfulness and enlightenment, and of many other forms of opposition is an inscrutable mystery so long as it is viewed from this world, but it becomes at once natural and acceptable when we become conscious of another world which Christians may call supernatural, and the truth thus dawned upon one is "revealed" truth. Here also lies the mystery of the Original Vow and of the Name, which is indeed the mystery of *tariki*.

ON THE PRACTICAL USE OF THE JESUS PRAYER

Archimandrite Lev Gillet

Lev Gillet was a monk of both the Western Church's Benedictine order and of the Eastern Church, although he was actually resident in a monastic community for a relatively brief time of his long life. Born on August 6, 1893, in Isère, France, his early life saw service in combat in World War I, and university studies in philosophy and psychology. After the war he entered the Benedictine Order at Clervaux abbey in Luxembourg. Later in life, his work as a priest and scholar would take him across Europe and to the Near East. He would be a member, albeit briefly, of a fledgling monastic community in the Ukraine, and also a priest on a mission near Nice. After entering the Orthodox Church, he was rector of the first French language Orthodox parish in Paris. Fr. Lev died in 1980 and was buried at the Greek Orthodox cathedral in London by his friend and younger colleague, Metropolitan Anthony (Bloom) of the Russian Patriarchal diocese of Sourozh.

1. THE FORM OF THE PRAYER

The Byzantine East has somewhat inadequately designated by the term "Jesus Prayer" every kind of invocation centering upon the actual name of the Savior. This invocation has assumed various specific forms according to whether the name was used alone or inserted into more or less developed formulas. It rests, however, with each individual to determine his or her own form of the invocation of the name. In the East the invocation became crystallized in the formula "Lord Jesus Christ, Son of God, have mercy on me a sinner," but this formula has never been and is not the only one. Every *repeated* invocation, in which the name of Jesus forms the core and motive force, is authentically the "Jesus Prayer" in the Byzantine sense. One may say, for example, "Jesus Christ" or "Lord Jesus." The oldest, the simplest, and in our opinion the easiest formula is the word "Jesus" used alone. It is with this last possibility in mind that we shall speak here of the "Jesus Prayer."

This type of prayer may be pronounced or thought. Its place is thus on the boundary between vocal and mental prayer, between prayer of meditation and prayer of contemplation. It may be practiced at all times and in any place: church, bedroom, street, office, workshop, and so on. We can repeat the name while walking. Beginners, however, will do well to bind themselves to a certain regularity in their practice of the prayer, choosing fixed times and solitary places. Yet this systematic training does not exclude a parallel and entirely free use of the invocation of the name.

Before beginning to pronounce the name of Jesus, we should try first of all to put ourselves in a state of peace and recollection, and then implore the help of the Holy Spirit in whom alone we can "say that Jesus is the Lord" (1 Cor. 12:3). Every other preliminary is superfluous. In order to swim one must first throw oneself into the water; similarly we must in one leap cast ourselves into the name of Jesus. Having begun to pronounce the name with loving adoration, all that we have to do is to attach ourselves to it, cling to it, and to repeat it slowly, gently, and quietly. It would be a mistake to "force" this prayer, to raise our voice inwardly, to try to induce intensity and emotion. When God manifested himself to the prophet Elijah, it was not in a strong wind, nor in an earthquake, nor in a fire, but in the gentle, whispering breeze that followed them (1 Kings 19:11-12). Little by little we are to concentrate our whole being around the name, allowing it like a drop of oil silently to penetrate and impregnate our soul. When invoking the name, it is not necessary to repeat it continually. Once spoken, the name then may be "prolonged" for several minutes of repose, of silence, of purely interior attention, much as a bird alternates between the flapping of its wings and gliding flight.

All tension and haste are to be avoided. If fatigue comes upon us, the invocation should be interrupted and taken up again simply when one feels drawn towards it. Our aim is not a constant, literal repetition but a kind of latent and quiescent presence of the name of Jesus in our heart. "I sleep, but my heart keeps vigil" (Song of Songs 5:2). Let us banish all spiritual sensuality, all pursuit of emotion. No doubt it is natural to hope to obtain results that are in some measure tangible, to want to touch the hem of the Savior's garment and not to give up until he has blessed us (cf. Matt. 9:21; Gen. 32:26). But let us not think that an hour during which we have invoked the name without "feeling" anything, remaining apparently cold and arid, has been wasted and unfruitful. This invocation that we thought sterile will be, on the contrary, highly acceptable to God, since it is chemically pure, if we may put it that way, because stripped of all preoccupation with spiritual delights and reduced to an offering of the naked will. At other times in his generous mercy the Savior often enfolds his name in an atmosphere of joy, warmth, and light: "Thy name is as oil poured forth. . . . draw me" (Song of Songs 1:3-4).

2. EPISODE OR METHOD?

For some the invocation of the name will be an episode on their spiritual journey; for others it will be more than an episode, it will be one of the methods they habitually use, yet without being *the* method; for yet others it will be *the* method around which their whole interior life is organized. To decide by arbitrary choice, by some whim, that this last case will be ours, would be like constructing a building which then collapses wretchedly. We do not choose the "Jesus Prayer." We are called to it, led to it by God, if he thinks it right. We devote ourselves to it out of obedience to a very special vocation, provided that other obediences do not have prior right. If this form of prayer does not stand in the way of the other forms to which we are committed by virtue of our state in life, if it is accompanied by a pressing attraction, if it produces in us fruits of purity, charity, and peace, if our appointed spiritual guides encourage us to practice it, there is in all this, if not the infallible signs of a vocation, then at least indications which deserve to be humbly and attentively considered.

The "way of the name" has been approved by many Eastern monastic Fathers and also by several saints of the West. It is therefore legitimate and remains open as a possibility for all. But we should avoid all indiscreet zeal, all untimely propaganda. We should not cry out with an ill-informed fervor, "It is the best prayer," much less, "It is the only prayer." We should keep hidden in their secret place the mysteries of the King. Those who are bound to a community or to a rule will discern to what extent the way of the name is compatible with the methods to which they owe obedience; the appropriate authorities will help them in this task of discernment. We are not referring here to liturgical prayer; for this could not enter into conflict with the kind of inner prayer that we are discussing. In particular we would not wish to suggest to those whose existing prayer is an authentic dialogue with the Lord, nor to those who are established in the deep silence of the contemplative life, that they should abandon their way of prayer in order to practice the "Jesus Prayer." We do not depreciate the value of any form of prayer. For in the final analysis the best prayer for each person is the one, whichever it may be, to which each is drawn by the Holy Spirit, by particular circumstances, and by properly appointed spiritual direction.

What we may say with soberness and truth on behalf of the "Jesus Prayer" is that it helps to simplify and unify our spiritual life. When complicated methods dissipate and weary the attention, this "one-word prayer" possesses the power of unification and integration, assisting the fragmented soul that finds its name and its sin to be "legion" (Mark 5:9). The name of Jesus, once it has become the center of our life, brings everything together. But let us not imagine that the invocation of the name is a "short-cut" that dispenses us from ascetic purification. The name of Jesus is itself an instrument of asceticism, a filter through which should pass only thoughts, words, and acts compatible with the divine and living reality which this name symbolizes. The growth of the name in our soul implies a corresponding diminution of our separated self, a daily death to the self-centeredness from which all sin is derived.

3. THE FIRST STEPS: ADORATION AND SALVATION

There are many levels in the "Jesus Prayer." It grows deeper and broader as we discover each new level in the name. It should begin as adoration and a sense of presence. Then, this presence is experienced specifically as that of a Savior (for such is the meaning of the word "Jesus"). The invocation of the name is a mystery of salvation in the sense that it brings with it deliverance. In uttering the name, we already receive what we need. We receive it here and now in Jesus who is not only the giver but the gift; not only the purifier, but all purity; not only the one who feeds the hungry and gives drink to the thirsty, but who is himself our food and drink. He is the substance of all good things (if we do not use this term in a strictly metaphysical sense).

His name gives peace to those who are tempted: instead of arguing with the temptation, instead of thinking about the raging storm—that was Peter's mistake on the lake after his good beginning—why not look at Jesus alone and go to him walking on the waves, taking refuge in his name? Let the person tempted gather himself together gently and pronounce the name without anxiety, without feverishness; then his heart will be filled by the name and in this way protected against violent winds. If a sin has been committed, let the name serve as a means of immediate reconciliation. Without hesitation or delay, let it be pronounced with repentance and perfect charity, and it will become at once a token of pardon. In an altogether natural way Jesus will take his place again in the life of the sinner, just as after his Resurrection he came back and sat in such a simple manner at table with the disciples who had deserted him, and then offered him fish and honey (Luke 24:41-42). Of course we do not intend to reject or underestimate the objective means of repentance and absolution which the Church offers to the sinner; we are speaking here only of what happens in the hidden places of the soul.

4. INCARNATION

The name of Jesus is more than a mystery of salvation, more than help in time of need, more than pardon after sin. It is a means by which we can apply to ourselves the mystery of the Incarnation. Beyond his presence, it brings union. By pronouncing the name, we enthrone Jesus in our hearts, we put on Christ; we offer our flesh to the Word so that he may assume it into his Mystical Body; we cause the interior reality and the power of the word "Jesus" to overflow into our members that are subject to the law of sin. In this way we are purified and consecrated. "Set me as a seal upon thy heart, as a seal upon thy arm" (Song of Songs 8:6). But the invocation of the name of Jesus does more than enable us to appreciate the meaning of the mystery of the Incarnation for ourselves personally. Through this prayer we also catch a glimpse of the "fullness of him who fills all in all" (Eph. 1:23).

5. TRANSFIGURATION

The name of Jesus is an instrument and method of transfiguration. When we utter it, it helps us to transfigure—without any pantheistic confusion—the whole world into Jesus Christ.

This is true even of inanimate nature. The material universe, which is not only the visible symbol of the invisible divine beauty, but which turns with "groaning" toward Christ (Rom. 8:22), and whose mysterious movement elevates all that comes into being towards the Bread and Wine of salvation, this universe murmurs secretly the name of Jesus: ". . . even the stones will cry out . . ." (Luke 19:40). It belongs to the priestly ministry of each Christian to give a voice to this aspiration, to pronounce the name of Jesus upon the elements of nature, stones and trees, flowers and fruit, mountains and sea, and so to bring to fulfillment the secret of things, to provide an answer to that long, silent, and unconscious expectation.

We can also transfigure the animal world. Jesus, who declared that not a sparrow is forgotten by his Father (Luke 12:6) and who dwelt in the desert "with the wild beasts" (Mark 1:13), did not leave the beasts outside the sphere of his goodness and influence. Like Adam in Paradise we are to give a name to all the animals. Whatever the name that science gives to them, we shall invoke upon each one of them the name of Jesus, thereby giving back to them their primitive dignity which we so often forget, and remembering that they are created and loved by the Father in Jesus and for Jesus.

But it is especially in relation to our fellow humans that the name of Jesus helps us to exercise a ministry of transfiguration. Jesus, who after his Resurrection chose several times to appear to his disciples "in another form" (Mark 16:12)—the unknown traveler on the road to Emmaus, the gardener near the tomb, the stranger standing on the shore of the lake—continues to meet us in our daily life in a veiled way and to confront us with this all-important aspect of his presence: his presence in man. What we do to the *least* of our brethren, we do to him. Under the faces of men and women we are able, with our eyes of faith and love, to see the face of the Lord; by attending to the distress of the poor, of the sick, of sinners, of all men, we put our finger on the place of the nails, thrust our hands into his pierced side, and experience personally the Resurrection and the real presence (without any confusion of essence) of Jesus Christ in his Mystical Body; and so we can say with St. Thomas, "My Lord and my God" (John 20:28).

The name of Jesus is a concrete and powerful means of transfiguring men into their most profound and divine reality. Let us reach out toward the men and women whom we pass in the street, the factory, or the office—and especially toward those who seem to us irritating or antipathetic—with the name of Jesus in our heart and on our lips. Let us pronounce silently over them his name, which is their very own name; let us call them by this name in a spirit of adoration and service. Let us devote ourselves to them in a practical way, if that is possible, or at all events by an interior aspiration, for in them we are really devoting ourselves to Jesus Christ. By recognizing and silently adoring Jesus imprisoned in the sinner, in the criminal, in the prostitute, we release in some way both these poor jailers and our Master. If we see Jesus in everyone, if we say "Jesus" over everyone, we will go through the world with a new vision and a new gift in our own heart. In this way, as far as lies in our power, we can transform the world and make our own the words that Jacob spoke to his brother: "I have seen thy face, and it is as though I had seen the face of God" (Gen. 33:10).

6. THE BODY OF CHRIST

The invocation of the name of Jesus has an ecclesial aspect. In this name we meet all those who are united with the Lord and in the midst of whom he stands. In this name we can embrace all those who are enclosed within the Divine Heart. To intercede for another is not so much to plead on his behalf before God, but rather to apply to his name the name of Jesus and to unite ourselves to the intercession of our Lord himself for his loved ones.

Here we touch upon the mystery of the Church. Where Jesus Christ is, there is the Church. The name of Jesus is a means of uniting us to the Church, for the Church is in Christ. In him the Church is unsullied. It is not that we seek to dissociate ourselves from the existence and the problems of the Church on earth, or to close our eyes to the imperfections and disunity of Christians. We do not wish to separate or oppose the visible and invisible aspects of the Church. But we know that what is implied in the name of Jesus is the spotless, spiritual, and eternal aspect of the Church which transcends every earthly manifestation and which no schism can destroy. When Jesus speaks to the Samaritan woman about the hour that "comes and now is" (John 4:23) in which the true worshipers will worship the Father, no longer in Jerusalem or on Garizim, but in spirit and truth, there is an apparent contradiction in his words. How can the hour already have come and yet still be coming? The paradox is explained by the fact that the Samaritan woman was standing at that moment before Jesus. Certainly the opposition between Jerusalem and Garizim still existed, and Jesus, far from minimizing it, had declared that salvation comes from the Jews: therefore the hour was still to come. But, because Jesus was there and in his person Jerusalem and Garizim are infinitely transcended, the hour had already come. When we invoke the name of the Savior we are in an analogous situation. We cannot believe that divergent interpretations of the Gospel are all equally true or that divided Christians all possess the same measure of light; but we do believe that those who, in pronouncing the name of Jesus, try to unite themselves to their Lord by an act of unconditional obedience and perfect charity, transcend human divisions, participate in some way in the supernatural unity of the Mystical Body of Christ and are, if not visible and explicit, at least invisible and implicit members of the Church. And thus the invocation of the name of Jesus, made with an upright heart, is a way towards Christian unity.

It also helps us meet again, in Jesus, the faithful departed. To Martha who professed her faith in the future Resurrection, Jesus replied: "I *am* the Resurrection and the Life" (John 11:25). This means that the resurrection of the dead is not merely a future event; that the person of the risen Christ is already the resurrection and the life of all the redeemed; and that instead of seeking, either through prayer or by the memory and the imagination, to establish a direct spiritual contact between our departed and ourselves, we should try to reach them in Jesus, where their true life now is, linking the name of Jesus to their own names. These departed, whose life is hidden in Christ, are within the heavenly Church that forms the most numerous part of the eternal and total Church.

In the name of Jesus we meet the saints who bear "his name on their foreheads" (Rev. 22:4), and also the angels, one of whom said to Mary, "Thou shalt call his name Jesus" (Luke 1:31), as well as Mary herself. Let us in the Spirit seek to hear and to repeat the name of Jesus as Mary heard it and repeated it!

7. THE SUPPER OF THE LORD

The name of Jesus can become for us a kind of Eucharist. Just as the mystery of the Upper Room was a summing up of the Lord's whole life and mission, so also a certain "Eucharistic" use of the name of Jesus brings together and unites all the aspects of the name considered thus far.

The sacramental Eucharist does not fall within the limits of our theme. But our soul is also an upper room where Jesus desires to eat the Passover with his disciples, and where the Lord's Supper can be celebrated at any moment whatever in an invisible way. In this purely spiritual Last Supper, the name of the Savior can take the place of the bread and wine of the sacrament. We can make of the name of Jesus an offering of thanksgiving—and this is the original meaning of the word "eucharist"—the support and substance of a sacrifice of praise rendered to the Father. In this interior and invisible offering, we present to the Father, by pronouncing the name of Jesus, a lamb sacrificed, a life given, a body broken, blood poured out. The sacred name, when used in this sacrificial way, becomes a means of applying to ourselves here and now the fruits of the perfect oblation offered once for all on Golgotha.

There is no Lord's Supper without communion. Our invisible Eucharist implies what tradition has called "spiritual communion," that is, the act of faith and desire by which the soul is nourished on the Body and Blood of Christ without making use of the visible elements of bread and wine. Nothing could be further from our mind than to diminish or underestimate the sacrament of the Eucharist, as practiced by the Church, which we cannot simply identify with spiritual communion. But we believe that we are within the Church's authentic tradition in affirming the reality of a constant, invisible, purely spiritual approach to the Body and Blood of Christ, an approach which is distinct from the general drawing-near to his person, for it implies a special kind of relation between ourselves and the Savior, who is considered in this instance as both the feeder and the food of our souls. The name of Jesus can be used as the form, support, and expression of this approach. It can be for us a spiritual food, a sharing in the Bread of Life. "Lord, give us always of this bread" (John 6:34). In his name, in this bread we are united to all the members of the Mystical Body of Christ, to all those who sit down at the banquet of the Messiah, we who "being many, are one bread, one body" (1 Cor. 10:17).

And since the Eucharist proclaims "the death of the Lord, until he come" (1 Cor. 11:26), since it is an anticipation of the eternal kingdom, the "eucharistic" use of the name of Jesus also possesses an "eschatological" meaning. It proclaims the "end" and the Second Coming, it is an ardent yearning, not only for the occasional "breakings-in" of Christ into our earthly life, but for that definitive coming of Christ to us which will be the moment of our death. There is a certain way of saying the name of Jesus which constitutes a preparation for death, a leaping of our heart beyond the barrier, a last general appeal to the Bridegroom "whom, without having seen, you love" (1 Pet. 1:8). To say "Jesus" is therefore to repeat the cry of the Apocalypse: "Come, Lord Jesus" (Rev. 22:20).

8. THE NAME AND THE SPIRIT

When we read the Acts of the Apostles, we see what a central place the name of Jesus occupied in the message and action of the apostles. Through them "the name of the Lord Jesus was magnified" (Acts 19:17); in this name miraculous signs were performed and lives were changed. After Pentecost the apostles became capable of proclaiming the name "with power." Here we have a "pentecostal" use of the name of Jesus, a use which is not the monopoly of the apostles, but which remains open to all believers. Only the weakness of our faith and charity prevents us from renewing in the name of Jesus the fruits of Pentecost, from driving out devils, from laying hands on the sick and curing them. Saints continue to act in this way. The Spirit writes the name of Jesus in fiery letters upon the hearts of his elect. This name is a burning flame within them.

But there also exists, between the Holy Spirit and the invocation of the name of Jesus, another link more interior than the "pentecostal" ministry of the Christian. By pronouncing the name of our Savior, we can obtain a certain "experience"—this word being used with all the necessary reservations—of the relation between the Son and the Spirit. We can make ourselves coincide with the descent of the dove upon our Lord; we can unite our heart—in so far as a creature can unite itself to a divine activity—to the eternal movement of the Spirit towards Jesus. "Oh that I had wings like a dove" (Psalm 55:6), not only to take flight far from earthly cares but to alight upon him who is all my good! Oh if only I knew how to hear the "voice of the turtledove" (Song of Songs 2:12), as she speaks with "sighs too deep for words" (Rom. 8:26) the name of the Beloved! Then the invocation of the name of Jesus would be an initiation into the mystery of the relationship of love between Christ and the Spirit.

Conversely, we may strive to coincide—always respecting the proper limits—with the reverse relationship, Jesus' attitude towards the Holy Spirit. Conceived by the Spirit, led by the Spirit, Jesus showed the most humble docility towards the Breath of the Father. While pronouncing the name of Jesus let us unite ourselves, in so far as this is given to humans, to the complete surrender that Jesus made of his life to this divine Breath.

Let us also see in the name of Jesus a hearth whence the Spirit radiates, let us see in Jesus the point of departure whence the Spirit is sent to men, the mouth whence the Spirit is breathed upon us. The invocation of the name of Jesus, uniting us with these various moments—Jesus being filled by the Spirit, the sending of the Spirit to men by Jesus, and also Jesus' yearning for the Father—will make us grow in knowledge of, and union with, the one whom Paul calls "the Spirit of his Son" (Gal. 4:6).

9. TOWARDS THE FATHER

There is the Son. And there is the Father. Our reading of the Gospel will remain superficial as long as we see in it only a life and a message directed to men. The heart of the Gospel, the mystery of Jesus, is the relationship between the Father and the only-begotten Son.

To utter the name of Jesus is to utter the Word which "was in the beginning" (John 1:1), the Word which the Father utters from all eternity. The name of Jesus, we might even say with a certain anthropomorphism (easily corrected), is the only human word which the Father utters as he begets the Son and gives himself to him. To utter the name of Jesus is to draw near the Father, to contemplate the love and the gift of the Father which is concentrated upon Jesus; it is to feel, to a limited extent, something of that love and to unite ourselves to it from afar; it is to hear the Father's voice declaring, "Thou art my beloved Son" (Luke 3:22), and humbly to respond "yes" to this declaration.

To utter the name of Jesus is, on the other hand, to enter, as much as a creature is able, into Christ's filial consciousness. After finding in the word "Jesus" the Father's tender appeal "My Son!", it is also to find in it the Son's tender response, "My Father!" It is to recognize in Jesus the perfect expression of the Father, to unite ourselves to the eternal orientation of the Son towards the Father, to the total offering of the Son to his Father. To utter the name of Jesus—if it is permissible to speak in this way—is in a certain fashion to join the Son to the Father and to glimpse some reflection of the mystery of their unity. It is to find the best approach to the Father's heart.

SOME IMPORTANT *DHIKRS*

Mir Valiuddin

Mir Valiuddin *was a professor of philosophy at the Osmania University in Hyderabad, India, for many years, specializing in Sufism, but also focusing on Islamic mysticism in a wider metaphysical and comparative perspective. He was a scholarly expositor of the mystic Islamic heritage, and his work has contributed to demonstrating the extent to which this heritage has shaped Muslim thought and civilization through the centuries. One of the foremost academic scholars of Sufism in the East, he is the author of* Quranic Sufism, Contemplative Disciplines in Sufism—*from which the following pages are excerpted—and* Love of God: A Sufic Approach.

Dhikr or the remembrance of God is enjoined by clear and categorical verses of the Koran. What is enjoined is *dhikr* as such, and this is opposed to *ghaflah* ("forgetfulness"). It follows that whatever may remind us of God's Essence, attributes, or perfections is in reality *dhikr* or "remembrance." Keeping this in view, *salāt* ("ritual prayer"), reading the Holy Koran, uttering the ninety-nine Names of God, saying *tahlīl* (there is no object worthy of worship except God), *takbīr* (God is great), uttering the *shahāda*, *istighfār* (asking forgiveness of God), *isti'ādha* (seeking refuge in God from the promptings of the evil forces), and prayers for the Prophet Muhammad or *durūd* are all included in remembrance.

Of all these *dhikr*s, the shaykhs of the *tarīqa*s have especially chosen the name of the Essence of God, i.e. *Allāh*, and the *dhikr* of *nafy wa ithbāt*, i.e. the *dhikr* of negation and affirmation or *Lā ilāha illā Allāh*. They have chosen this latter because the Prophet himself has regarded it as superior to all *dhikr*s.

There are a number of *hadīth*s describing its advantages. It is the very essence of all *dhikr*s. It is the hub of the Unity of God, *tawhīd*, and is a resplendent light. The entire Koran explains in detail its meaning and significance. It negates all false deities and affirms the One Reality. Not only does it negate false gods, but it also negates all ephemeral objects, and forms a close connection with the One Object, the *desideratum*, i.e. it is concerned with the remembrance of God and frees one from all confusion and discomfiture.

The Name of the Essence or *dhāt*, of God, i.e. *Allāh*, has been chosen as supreme for the remembrance of God, because while all the ninety-nine Names of God are the names of His attributes, which signify particular qualities, *Allāh* is the proper Name of God, which indicates the Essence of

God, to which all His attributes relate. To remember God by this short name is, as it were, to recollect His Essence together with all Names and Attributes. Besides, the ease and limitlessness with which the remembrance of the *dhikr* of *Allāh* is possible, is not possible with any other name. If all the ninety-nine names are uttered, the uttering of them cannot be regarded equal to it from the point of view of comprehensiveness, as *Allāh* is the very Essence together with all Names and Attributes. . . . Every name has a special light, and has a particular effect. The Name of the Essence (*Allāh*) is the source of all lights, and of the properties of all Names. As it is the proper Name of God, it establishes a direct connection with the Absolute Essence. It is also worthy of note that *Allāh* is the Name of the Lord and cherisher of all human beings. Consequently, every individual has a firm connection with this Holy Name; he is benefited by it in all circumstances, and it is a cure for all his ills. That is why the Name of *Allāh* is spoken of as the Great Name. This comprehensiveness is not found in any other Name. For these reasons, the shaykhs of the *tarīqa*s have preferred the remembrance of the name of the Essence.

The emphasis laid by the great Sufis on the repetition of the Name of the Essence has created a doubt as to whether the mere repetition of His Name can help us in winning His grace, especially in the mind of the Imām Ibn Taimiyya. But the repetition of the Name of the Essence without joining anything to it can be justified from many verses of the Koran:

1. "Remember Me and I will remember you" (2:152);
2. "Call upon *Allāh* or call upon *ar-Rahmān*, by whatever name ye call upon Him (it is well); for to Him belong the Most Beautiful Names" (17:110);
3. "Remember the Name of Thy Lord at dawn and dusk" (76:25);
4. "So remember the name of Thy Lord and devote thyself with complete devotion" (73:8).

And the Prophet's *hadīth* tells us:

1. "Doomsday will be held when *Allāh Allāh* will not be uttered on earth";
2. "Doom will not overtake him who says *Allāh, Allāh.*"

Objections have been raised by Muslim scholars regarding the special methods of *dhikr* or the postures for remembrance chosen by the shaykhs of the *tarīqa*s as being unauthenticated by the *sharī'a*. They have called these methods *bid'a*, or "innovation."

Our answer is that the different methods of *dhikr*, i.e. the repetition of the Name of the Essence, or of the *shahāda* by restraining breath etc. are like the rules of syntax, for understanding the language of the Koran and the Prophet's *hadīths*; these are the necessary tools. No one has regarded them as leading to the proximity of God in themselves. If anyone has regarded these instrumental devices as ends in themselves, then of course, they must be regarded as innovations for him alone.

But experience bears witness to the fact that the presence of the mind with God, which is the real goal, cannot be attained unless the methods and procedures suggested by the great Sufis are adopted; they seem to be indispensable, especially for the novice. That is the reason why among the shaykhs of the *tarīqas*, those who are the interpreters of the law, and are divine contemplatives, in the true sense of the word, have prescribed them, by way of treatment for inward maladies, and they are fully competent to prescribe them. The instructions of Junayd of Baghdād, Bāyazīd Bīstāmī, Shaykh 'Abd al-Qādir Jīlānī, Shaykh Shihāb ad-Dīn Sūhrawardī, Khwāja Bāhā ad-Dīn Naqshband, Khwāja Mu'in ad-Dīn Chishtī, Shaykh Ahmad Mujaddid Alf-e-thani etc. are worthy of being carried into effect. The reason for following their instructions is that these great Muslim saints hold the rank of *mujtahid-i muntasb*, or *mujtahid fī'l-madhhab*, or *ahl-i tarjīh* (authority in the science of interpretation in the juridical schools of Islam), and all of them (and other saints of their rank) are regarded as spiritual guides and leaders of the Muslims.

One's leisure is precious and should not be wasted, but rather it should be spent in performing the *dhikr* of *Lā ilāha illa Allāh*.

Attach no value to anything that thou hast lost,
But thou shouldst never lose thy time.

To begin with, one should dispel from one's heart all distractions, like listening to people's idle talk, or taking interest in mundane things.

If thou desirest to cleanse thy heart, close thy eyes to the world,
This is the hole through which comes dust.

The *dhākir* should also free his heart from all things that may cause internal perplexities, for instance anger, hunger, gluttony, or anguish of any kind.

He should then recollect his death, and keep it in view. He should ask forgiveness of God with humility, for his sins of commission and omission; and then he should roll his tongue towards his palate. Shutting his lips and eyes, he should retain his breath in his abdomen, he should utter the word *Lā*, drawing it from the navel to the heart, and take it to the brain. Then while saying the word *ilāha*, he should move his head to his left shoulder and from there apply the *darb*, i.e. impress the words *illā Allāh* vigorously on the heart in such a manner that the effects of the *darb* may manifest themselves in all the limbs. The form of *dhikr* in this case is like the inverted letter *Lam-alif*.

BRAIN

HEART   NAVEL

The *dhākir* should negate his own ego and instead posit the Being of God, and say with all sincerity:

O Allāh! Thou art my ultimate End and it is Thy pleasure that I seek.

There should be no movement of the body. He should be mindful of the odd number every time he restrains his breath; he should say: "Muhammad is the Apostle of God" when he exhales and while holding the breath, he should recite this *dhikr* first once, then three times (thus keeping in view the odd number). After a few days' practice he should be able to repeat it twenty-one times. If, after repeating the *dhikr* twenty-one times the heart is not turned towards God, and is not attracted by His love, the *dhākir* should begin it over again, carefully observing the conditions mentioned above, and gradually advance to repeating it twenty-one times. In the *dhikr* of *Lā ilāha illā Allāh* the most important condition is the negation of the idea that there is any object worthy of worship except God, or any object which may be regarded as the ultimate goal and object of life except God, or any object possessing real existence or being except God. These should be affirmed for God alone.

It is the experience of the Naqshbandiyya shaykhs that the holding of the breath has wonderful properties of dispelling the affectations of the heart, kindling the fire of love, developing singleness of purpose, and creating internal warmth. Restraining the breath should be practiced gradually, so that it may not prove too much for the *dhākir*, and cause dryness of the brain. In restraining the breath, moderation is always recommended. Shāh Waliallāh has explained that we should not think that the Naqshbandiyya method of restraining the breath is necessarily adopted from the yoga system. The yogi restrains his breath for long periods, while the Sufis' restraining of breath is done in moderation.

Similarly, in their experience, regard for odd numbers (which is called *wuqūf al-'adudī* or "numerical awareness") has also wonderful properties.

Every *dhākir* will experience it one day, but it requires patience and perseverance.

In the Naqshbandiyya Order, the two-*darb* (strokes) and the four-*darb* *dhikr*s of *Lā ilāha illā Allāh* are also practiced. While practicing them, the *dhākir* of this Order should conceive the Prophet on his right side and his preceptor or Sufi shaykh on his left; and facing the heart is the Almighty God alone, the Absolute Being.

How else can I keep my heart and eyes busy!
The heart seeks Thee and the eye wants Thee alone!

Another *dhikr* of the Naqshbandī Sufis is called *dhikr al-mashīy al-aqdām*, i.e. "recollecting God while walking." According to it, if the devotee is walking with a medium pace, he should say "*Allāh*," "*Allāh*" at every step; if he is walking fast, he should say *illā Allāh*. If his pace is slow, he should say *Lā* when on his right step, and when on his left step *ilāha*; again *illā* on the right step, and *Allāh* on the left step. Some hold that it is better that he should say only "*Allāh*," "*Allāh*" every time, so that he may be accustomed to one *dhikr* only and his mind may not be confused.

One of the *dhikr*s of the Naqshbandī shaykhs is the *dhikr al-ithbāt al-mujarrad* or *dhikr* of "mere affirmation," that is, the *dhikr* of the name *Allāh*, without affirmation or negation. It is said that the early Naqshbandī theologians did not practice this *dhikr*. It has been the practice of Khwāja Bāqī-billāh, or the great shaykhs who preceded him. It is agreed that the *dhikr* of affirmation and negation is good for devotion, *sulūk*, and that of mere affirmation is more conducive to absorption in God (*jazb*).

According to some Sufis the method of *dhikr al-ithbāt al-mujarrad* is this: the devotee should pull the word *Allāh* from his navel and should draw it up to the brain with all his strength, all the while restraining his breath; he should gradually extend the time of restraining the breath and meanwhile increase the repetition of the *dhikr*. Some repeat the *dhikr* a thousand times in one breath.

One of the great disciples of the Naqshbandiyya Order is Shaykh Ahmad of Sirhind, the *mujaddid alf ath-thānī*, or "renewer of Islam at the beginning of the second millennium of the Islamic era." After him, this Order became known as the Naqshbandiyya Mujaddidiyya Order. As Shāh Walīallāh says of Ahmad Sirhindi: "He is the founder of the second millennium of the Islamic era, and he has put the Muslims under a debt which cannot be repaid. He who denies his saintship is wicked." . . .

The early Sufis had informed us of the *latīfas* ("subtle faculties") of *qalb* or "heart" and *rūh* or "soul" only, and some of them had told us of *latīfa-i-sirr*. Ahmad Sirhindi informed us of the five *latīfas* in the human breast which are: *qalb* (heart), *rūh* (soul), *sirr* (secret), *khafī* (the hidden or mysterious) and the *akhfā* (the deeply hidden); and he has drawn attention to the lights they shed and the stages they are capable of. A letter of Khwāja 'Abdul Ahad, grandson of the Mujaddid, which Shāh Walīallāh has cited in his book, *Intibāh fi-Salāsil-i-Auliyā Allāh* (pp. 61-64), explains them briefly but clearly.

According to the findings of the Mujaddid, a man has ten *latīfas*; out of these, five are concerned with the *'ālam-i-amr* or "the world of command," and five of them are concerned with the *'ālam-i-khalq* or "the world of creation." By the former he means the world of existence which has been brought into existence by God directly by His word of command, *Kun* or "Be," while the latter means that which is created gradually. . . . The former is not material, but the latter is material. The place of the *'ālam-i-amr* is above the *'Arsh* (Throne of God), and that of the *'ālam-i-khalq* is below the Throne. The faculties or *latīfas* of the *'ālam-i-amr* are: *qalb*, *rūh*, *sirr*, *khafī*, *akhfā*; and the faculties of the *'ālam-i-khalq* are the *nafs* and the four elements: earth, water, air and fire. By the sphere of possibility, *daira-i-imkān*, is meant these two worlds. The upper half of this sphere is above the Throne of God and the lower half is below the Throne. The form of the sphere will be as follows:

Akhfā

Khafī

Sirr

Rūh

Qalb

The Throne (*'Arsh*)

Nafs

Fire

Air

Water

Earth

The *latīfas* of the *'ālam-i-amr* are connected with the inner life of an individual, and as such are located in the body. Their exact location, including that of the *nafs* (ego) which also belongs to the physical aspect of man, is: the *nafs* is under the navel, *qalb* on the left side, *rūh* on the right side of the chest, and the *sirr* is exactly between the *qalb* and the *rūh*. *Khafī* is said by some

Sufis to be in the forehead, and *akhfā* in the brain; while others locate *akhfā* in the middle of the chest, *sirr* between the *qalb* and the *akhfā*, and *khafī* between *rūh* and *akhfā*.

The procedure of *dhikr* of *ism-a-dhāt* (the name of the Essence) is that one should touch the palate with the tongue, and keep in mind the meaning of the blessed name *Allāh* (who does not resemble any entity and no entity resembles Him; who is not like anything and nothing is like Him; whom measures do not contain and boundaries do not confine, whom directions do not surround; who does not resemble bodies; who is single without any similar; who is separate without any like) and should turn the heart to Almighty God and be engrossed in the *dhikr* of *ism-a-dhāt*.

> Do not apply musk to the body, rub it on the heart.
> What is musk? The sacred name of Him who is full of Majesty.
>
> (Rūmī)

Before commencing the *dhikr*, the following words should be said, and their meaning, which really is the meaning of the name of God, should be borne in mind:

> Spiritual grace is overflowing from the Being—who is single without any similar, separate without any like, who is attributed with all qualities and perfections, and is exempt from all defects and blemishes—onto my heart

while concentrating on a particular *latīfa*.

When the *dhākir* repeats the *ism-a-dhāt* a hundred times, he should say the following words with humility and faith, by way of loving converse with God:

> O Allāh, Thou and Thy satisfaction alone are my sole objective; vouchsafe unto me Thy love and gnosis.

These words should be said from the heart. In the terminology of the Naqshbandiyya Order, this is called *bāz-gasht* or "returning." They negate the affectations of the heart. The *dhākir* becomes pure and uncontaminated and the heart is disengaged from all else save God. Khwāja Mīr Dard says that before commencing *dhikr*, the *dhākir* should with all humility and faith, keeping in view his own shortcomings, turning his face towards God and anticipating that his *dhikr* would be accepted, choose the name of God as the means of approach and fix his attention on the *dhikr* of the heart and say:

Though the heart did not know the reality,
Yet the steps of quest continue treading the path;
O Lord! whether Thou dost give us Thy Grace or not,
We would repeat Thy name, *Allāh, Allāh*!

During the *dhikr*, *wuqūf-i qalbī* (the alertness of the heart) should be of such a degree, and so much *dhikr* should be done, that the awareness of God, which is the very essence of human reality, may manifest itself to the heart; i.e. the *dhikr* should be repeated so often that its fruit, which is remembrance and awareness of God, and the sensing of His Presence inwardly and outwardly, may be reaped. The faculty of awareness, or the sensing of the Presence of God, is bestowed on man, and is found in every human being potentially, so it should be realized and made an actuality.

III.

CONTEMPORARY TESTIMONIES

*In this Kali Age salvation is not gained by
knowledge, karma, and worship,
but only by taking shelter in the Name.*

TULSĪDĀS

ALWAYS PRAYING AND THINKING OF GOD

Thomas Yellowtail

Thomas Yellowtail *was medicine man and Sun Dance priest of the Crow tribe. As the chief figure of the Crow-Shoshone Sun religion, he preserved the traditional and sacred ways that he had inherited from the "old timers" of pre-reservation days. His autobiography, as told to Michael Oren Fitzgerald, was published under the title* Yellowtail: Crow Medicine Man and Sun Dance Chief, *from which this short extract is taken.*

While the prayer with the pipe will start and end the day, it is also important to pray during the day. Each day, whatever I am doing, I am always praying and thinking of God. As I work along, whether I am out in the field or wherever, I am always praying right along when I am alone. Even when I am driving down the highway, like today; I am alone nowadays in most of my travels. If I am going to town or somewhere and driving, I say prayers as I drive along. Or in my work, anywhere; all the time I am praying. Acbadadea knows that I pray to Him, and He hears me. I am always praying, no matter what I am doing. I am so used to it that I just can't stop, and I think that it is the best thing a person can do. I say that if you look for them, then you will find many parts of the day that could be spent in praying. I am sure that there are a lot of people who are that way, continually praying to God, remembering the name of God. For a Crow Indian, "Acbadadea" is probably the best short prayer during the day. This does great honor to God. Praying for people is also good. Once you get used to that, why, you just can't get away from it. You can't forget your day-to-day prayers. People think other things are more important than prayer, but they are mistaken. A person may have plenty of money but doesn't take that along with him. It is good to share what little we have and pray. A person should measure his wealth in terms of the knowledge and love of God.

PRAY TO GOD WITH A YEARNING HEART

Sri Ramakrishna

Ramakrishna Paramahamsa *is the best known saint of nineteenth century India. He was born into a poor* brahmin *(priestly) family in 1836, in a small town near Calcutta, West Bengal. Ramakrishna had little interest in school or the world. In 1866, he became a priest at a temple to the Goddess Kāli, located near Calcutta on the Ganges River. He meditated in a sacred grove on the edge of the temple grounds seeking a vision of the Goddess Kāli. Ramakrishna's spiritual plasticity was such that he would take on ritual and mythical roles, identifying with the Gods from Indian holy books. His intuition of the validity of different approaches to the worship of God and the religious paths, led him to practice both Christianity and Islam during periods of his life. Ramakrishna died of cancer of the throat in 1886.*

Devotee: "How can I develop love for God?"
Master: "Repeat His name, and sins will disappear. Thus you will destroy lust, anger, the desire for creature comforts, and so on."
Devotee: "How can I take delight in God's name?"
Master: "Pray to God with a yearning heart that you may take delight in His name. He will certainly fulfill your heart's desire.

"As is a man's feeling, so is his gain. Once two friends were going along the street, when they saw some people listening to a reading of the *Bhāgavata*. 'Come, friend,' said the one to the other. 'Let us hear the sacred book.' So saying he went in and sat down. The second man peeped in and went away. He entered a house of ill fame. But very soon he felt disgusted with the place. 'Shame on me!' he said to himself. 'My friend has been listening to the sacred words about Hari; and see where I am!' But the friend who had been listening to the *Bhāgavata* also became disgusted. 'What a fool I am!' he said. 'I have been listening to this fellow's blah-blah, and my friend is having a grand time.' In course of time they both died. The messenger of Death came for the soul of the one who had listened to the *Bhāgavata* and dragged it off to hell. The messenger of God came for the soul of the other, who had been to the house of prostitution, and led it up to heaven.

"Verily, the Lord looks into a man's heart and does not judge him by what he does or where he lives.

"Everyone can attain Knowledge. There are two entities: *jivātmā*, the individual soul, and *Paramātmā*, the Supreme Soul. Through prayer all individual souls can be united to the Supreme Soul. Every house has a connection for gas, by which gas can be obtained from the main storage tank of the gas company. Apply to the company and it will arrange for your supply of gas. Then your house will be lighted.

"In some people spiritual consciousness has already been awakened; but they have special marks. They do not enjoy hearing or talking about anything but God. They are like the chātak bird, which prays for rainwater though the seven oceans, the Ganges, the Jamunā, and other rivers nearby are filled with water. The bird won't drink anything but rainwater, even though its throat is burning with thirst.

"Bound souls, worldly people, are like silkworms. The worms can cut through their cocoons if they want, but having woven the cocoons themselves, they are too much attached to them to leave them. And so they die there."

CONSTANT REPETITION OF THE DIVINE NAME

Swami Ramdas

Swami Ramdas *was born in Kerala in 1884. Having been inspired by the teachings of Ramakrishna, and then initiated into the* Rām-mantra *(Om Srī Rām Jai Rām Jai Jai Rām) by his father, his life's spiritual trajectory shifted in 1921. He left the world and gave himself entirely into the hands of Rām. In 1931, after years of living on the road as a pilgrim, he accepted his devotees' invitation to come to Anandashram, an ashram (retreat) established for him by them, in Kanhangad, Kerala, where he lived with Mother Krishnabai. Together, they did extensive tours in India, and a world tour in 1954-55. Swami Ramdas was one of the most inspiring advocates and embodiments of* japa-yoga *in the twentieth century. His enthusiasm for devotion was extraordinarily vibrant, joyful, and communicative. His utter childlikeness as a confirmed master beautifully contrasted with his early ascetic style. Swami Ramdas died in 1963. The following excerpts are taken mainly from his spiritual journal published under the title,* In the Vision of God.

The supreme Lord is seated in the hearts of all beings and creatures. He is absolute existence, consciousness, and bliss—*Sat-chit-ānanda*. You can realize Him through one-pointed devotion and complete self-surrender. The initial step on the path to this goal is purity and control of mind which is acquired through concentration. An easy method for concentration is constant repetition of the divine Name and performance of all actions as a sacrifice to the Lord. You may call God by any name—Rāma, Krishna, Shiva or any other you hold dear. The Name Himself is *Brahman*. The reiteration of the Name coupled with the meditation on the attributes of God purifies the mind. Prayers, hymns, and fasting are necessary aids. You must develop the divine qualities of compassion, peace, and forgiveness. God reveals Himself in that heart in which these ennobling virtues reside. Now the divine light shining within you dissolves the ego-sense, and your identity with the Godhead is realized. This experience grants you the knowledge of immortality. Thereafter, you dwell in a divine consciousness and your vision becomes universalized, bringing you supreme peace and ecstasy. Now it is that you behold the whole universe as the very expression of God, whom you have discovered within you. Now God is everywhere for you—in everybody and everything. This transcendent vision unlocks the infinite fountain of love in your heart—a love that fills and embraces the entire cosmos. All distinctions now disappear in the equality of this vision. This supreme state of beatitude bestows on you liberation and immortal joy. Believe that incarnations or divine teachers like Jesus Christ, Muhammad, Zoroaster, and others are also manifestations of the same great Truth. Verily, all the different religions are so many paths that lead mankind to the one universal God.

* * *

Ramdas and Ramcharandas, on arrival at Mangalore, were put up at Sitaramrao's house. An invitation came from Kasaragod to attend the closing day of a *nama-saptah* (seven-day recitation of God's names) held in the house of T. Bhavanishankarrao, a relation of Ramdas' old life. He and his house people had undertaken to repeat the *Rām-mantram* thirteen *lakh*s of times within a week, and in the *japa* children and servants had also joined.

About this time Ramdas had a visit at Mangalore from Savoor Shankarrao, who held English degrees and was then a professor in the Presidency College, Madras. In spite of his great learning and attainments, Ramdas found him to be a simple, humble, and pious soul. He conceived a great love for Ramdas at first sight and frequently courted his company. The very talk of God would work on his emotions and bring tears into his eyes. He joined Ramdas at the *nama-saptah*. Ramdas spent a most blissful time for about two or three days on this occasion. The *japa* had exceeded fifteen *lakh*s. The zeal, even of the youngsters, to make up the highest possible number of *japa* as their quota was admirable.

* * *

God and His Name are not distinct from one another. The Name is God Himself. God the absolute is the nameless Name.

There is no easier way of focusing our thought upon God than taking constantly His Name. When we repeat the Name aloud, we feel our heart flooded with the ecstasy of love because the sound of the divine Name awakes the heart to the bliss and love of God. Though the mental repetition of the Name is held to be far more efficacious than the verbal repetition, still the rare experience of the sweetness and joy derived by uttering the Name aloud is incomparable. When the entire being of the devotee thrills with rapture to the music of the Name, he realizes that the Name is Brahman.

There is no *sādhanā* that can be universally adopted by all people and is at the same time as simple for realizing God as the Divine Name. . . . He who has God's Name always on his tongue is a *jīvana mukta*—a liberated soul.

. . . The Power of the Name is invincible—a mind that is deemed uncon-querable becomes docile, yielding, and submissive, by the soothing influence of the Name. The mind itself is transformed into God by the power of the Name.

He who takes refuge in the Name can work wonders. Death itself will stand in awe of him. He can command all the forces of nature and direct them to bring about a spiritual awakening in the hearts of men. . . . The Name can free the soul from bondage. The Name can grant a blind soul divine sight. . . . The Name lifts the soul to inconceivable heights of God-realization.

So friends, to whatever race, caste, creed, or color you may belong, take up the Name of God and feel the sweet communion with it, and you may depend on it, your soul through constant bathing in the nectar of the Name will not only be purified but will also be illumined by an omnipresent and omniscient light and love of God. This practice to taking the Name will lead the unyielding spirit of man to complete surrender to the omnipotent power and will of God. In the early stages, if the Name is repeated with earnestness, faith, and concentration the face and body of the devotee will shine with a peculiar luster, his mind will be filled with wisdom, and his heart with love. This is due to the predominance of *sattva guna* in the devotee. Later, if the repetition is continued with the same zeal, he will behold the universe before him as the very expression of God. He will have the vision of God everywhere—verily the Name is God Himself.

PRAYER

Mahatma Gandhi

Mohandas K. Gandhi *was born in India in 1869. His family sent him to London to study law, and in 1891 he was called to the bar. His early career took him to Southern Africa where he worked unceasingly to improve the rights of the immigrant Indians. It was there that he developed his notion of non-violent resistance against injustice, and he was frequently jailed as a result of the protests he led. Back in India, it was not long before he was taking the lead in the long struggle for independence from Britain. When Muslim and Hindu compatriots committed acts of violence, he fasted until the fighting ceased. In 1947, at the time of its independence, the country was partitioned into Hindu India and Muslim Pakistan, much to Gandhi's despair. The last two months of his life were spent trying to end the violence which ensued, leading him to fast to the brink of death, an act which finally put an end to the riots. In 1948, at the age of 79, he was killed as he walked through a crowded garden in New Delhi to take evening prayers. He died with the name of Rāma on his lips. The following is an excerpt from a conversation between Gandhi and the Swiss pacifist Pierre Ceresole, the founder of Service Civil.*

"This repetition of one and the same thing over and over again jars on me. It may be the defect of my rationalist mathematical temperament. But somehow I cannot like the repetition. For instance, even Bach's wonderful music fails to appeal to me when the text 'Father forgive them, they know not what they do' is repeated over and over again."

"But even in mathematics you have your recurring decimals," said Gandhiji smiling.

"But each recurs with a definite new fact," said the mathematician.

"Even so," said Gandhiji, "each repetition or *japa*, as it is called, has a new meaning; each repetition carried you nearer and nearer to God. This is a concrete fact and I may tell you that you are here talking to no theorist, but to one who has experienced what he says every minute of his life, so much so that it is easier for the life to stop than for this incessant process to stop. It is a definite need of the soul."

"I quite see it, but for the average man it becomes an empty formula."

"I agree, but the best thing is liable to be abused. There is room for any amount of hypocrisy, but even hypocrisy is an ode to virtue. And I know that for ten thousand hypocrites, you would find millions of simple souls who find their solace from it. It is like scaffolding quite essential to a building."

"But," said Pierre Ceresole, "if I may carry the simile a little further, you agree that the scaffolding has to be removed, when the building is complete?"

"Yes, it would be removed when this body is removed."

"Why?"

"Because," said Wilkinson who was closely following the discourse, "we are eternally building."

"Because," said Gandhiji, "we are eternally striving after perfection. God alone is perfect. Man is never perfect."

JAPA-SĀDHANĀ

Vandana Mataji

Vandana Mataji *is a nun who heads the Christian ashram Jiva Dhara, in Rishikesh, at the foothills of the Himalayas. She studied history, politics, and Indian classical music, but her main objective as a teacher in Bombay was to promote an integration of Hinduism into Christian spirituality. She regularly spent six months of the year in the Himalayas for her spiritual exercises, and has emphasized the role of* japa-yoga *as a spiritual bridge between Hinduism and Christianity.*

The recitation of the Divine Name is known as *japa*. There is, however, a distinction between calling out the name of a particular individual and invoking the Name of the Almighty, the difference being that in ordinary parlance the object or the person whose name is called is outside the mind of the one who takes the name, but in the case of calling to one's mind the Name of God, the mind which performs this function is mysteriously involved in the holy act, inasmuch as God is not an external object somewhere in space and time, but an all-pervading Presence, inclusive even of the devotee himself or herself. There is a mysterious or rather miraculous alchemical transmutation spontaneously taking place within the mind of the devotee when the Name of God is chanted with sincerity and love from the bottom of one's heart. Thus, *japa* or the holy chanting of the Divine Name is a kind of mystical process of divine communion established by the devotees with the Divine Parent in humble submission and surrender of the individual personality at the altar of the All-Consuming Almighty presence.

In a very important sense, *japa* is inseparable from meditation. While it is commonly believed that meditation is an abstract occupation of the mind with the object of meditation, and *japa* is the concrete conceptualization of God by connecting His Presence with His Name, nevertheless, there is in the end no substantial difference between *japa* and meditation. This, because if *japa* has to be understood in the sense we have described above, viz. an inward communion with the Divine Presence by means of the summoning or invoking of God's Name, we would observe that there is hardly any distinction that can be drawn between *japa* and meditation. This is precisely so because both in *japa* and meditation, it is the mind that operates and it is not proper to imagine that *japa* is distinguishable from meditation because of the verbal utterance involved in the former. The utterance assumes significance only when the mind is attached to it and the value of *japa* consists in the extent to which the mental consciousness of devotion to God is associated with it. This has to be accepted irrespective of the common belief, which is widely held, that the recitation of a *mantra* has its own value and produces its own effect even if the mind is not to be consciously operating simultaneously with it.

In this age, when people are over-busy with activities and varieties of business, it is too much to expect the human mind to be able to directly absorb itself in meditation on the Universal Almighty. Just as one is able to recall to one's mind the form of an object or a person by remembering the name, its qualities, and its definitions, so also it is easier to entertain in the mind the holy presence of God by mentally defining His Form in the characterization of His Name which actually describes His might and glory. In this age of modernity in everything and weakness of will, generally speaking, *japa* or the constant taking of the Divine Name may be regarded as the best and perhaps the only means of maintaining a spiritual awareness in one's daily life.

ADVAITA AND JAPA

Ramana Maharshi

Ramana Maharshi was born in 1879 near Madurai in Southern India. In his early years, Ramana was uninterested in school and little interested in anything else than play and physical activities. In the summer of 1896, upon a sudden outburst of fear of death, he experienced a spiritual awakening that made him realize that he was none other than Ātman. Soon thereafter, he left for the sacred mountain of Arunachala, in the vicinity of which he spent ten years living in temples and caves, meditating and pursuing spiritual purification, and maintaining the disciplines of silence and non-attachment. At this point, his reputation as a serious teacher (he was called Brahma Swami) began to grow and other seekers began to visit him, even though he was at that time conveying his teachings exclusively in silence. A few years later, Ramana's devotees constructed an ashram and temple to accommodate the many visitors. Ramana laid emphasis on the method of inquiry into the nature of the Self, best expressed by the question "who am I?" Ramana developed cancer and when his devotees voiced concern about losing him, he responded with the statement, "I am not going anywhere, where shall I go? I shall be there where I am always." He died in April 1950. Even though the Maharshi primarily stressed Self-inquiry, he was far from rejecting the method of japa-yoga as a means to that end, as indicated in the following excerpts from his teachings.

A King visited his premier in his residence. There he was told the premier was engaged in repetition of sacred syllables (*japa*). The King waited for him and, on meeting him, asked what the *japa* was. The premier said that it was the holiest of all, *gāyatrī*. The King desired to be initiated by the premier, but the latter confessed his inability to initiate him. Therefore, the King learnt it from someone else, and meeting the minister later he repeated the *gāyatrī* and wanted to know if it was right. The minister said the *mantra* was correct, but it was not proper for him to say it. When pressed to explain, the minister called to a page close by and ordered him to take hold of the King. The order was however not obeyed. It was repeated several times, but still not obeyed. The King flew into a rage and ordered the same man to hold the minister, and it was done immediately. The minister laughed and said the incident was the explanation required by the King. "How?" asked the King. The minister replied, "The order was the same and the executor also, but the authority was different. When I ordered it, the effect was nil, whereas, when you ordered, there was an immediate effect. Similarly with *mantras*."

* * *

Advaita *and* Japa

Devotee: Can *advaita* be realized by *japa* of holy names; say Rāma, Krishna, etc.?
Maharshi: Yes.
Devotee: Is it not a means of an inferior order?
Maharshi: Have you been told to make *japa* or to discuss its order in the scheme of things?

* * *

The utterance and then remembrance and later meditation are the successive stages, finally ending in involuntary and eternal *japa*. The *japakarta* (doer of *japa*) of that kind is the Self. Of all the *japa*s, "Who am I" is the best.

* * *

These people want some *japa*, *dhyāna*, or *yoga* or something similar. Without their saying what they have been doing so far, what more can be said to them? Again, why *japa*, its *phalasruti* (description of the results of an act), etc.? Who is it that makes the *japa*? Who gets the fruits thereof? Can they not look to the Self? Or again, even if instructed by others to do *japa* or *dhyāna*, they do it for some time, but are always looking for some results, e.g., visions, dreams, or thaumaturgic powers. If they do not find them, they say they are not progressing or the *tapas* is not effective. Visions, etc., are no signs of progress. Mere performance of *tapas* is its progress also. Steadiness is what is required. Moreover, they must entrust themselves to their *mantra* or their God and wait for Grace. They don't do so. *Japa* uttered even once has its own good effect, whether the individual is aware or not.

* * *

You are always repeating the *mantra* automatically. If you are not aware of the *ajapa* (unspoken chant) which is eternally going on, you should take to *japa*. *Japa* is made with an effort. The effort is meant to ward off other thoughts. Then the *japa* becomes mental and internal. Finally, its *ajapa* and eternal nature will be realized, for it will be found to be going on even without your effort. The effortless state is the state of realization.

THE PRAYER OF THE NAME

Swami Abhishiktananda (Henri Le Saux)

Henri Le Saux was born in 1910, in Brittany, France. In 1929 he decided to become a monk and entered the Benedictine Monastery of St. Anne de Kergonan. His attraction to India and her spiritual riches started as early as 1934. He came in contact with Fr. Jules Monchanin, who was then working as a village priest in Tamil Nadu, and who was longing for a contemplative life in the way of Indian asceticism or sannyāsa. *Fr. Le Saux was finally given permission by his abbot to go to India in 1948. A profoundly decisive event in his life was his meeting with Sri Ramana Maharshi. Swami Abhishiktananda spent several weeks and months in the caves of the Arunachala between 1950 and 1955 in deep meditation. He then made several pilgrimages to the Himalayas, to which he was strongly attracted. In 1971 a French seminarian, Marc Chaduc, came to meet him after a long correspondence, and Abhishiktananda found in him a disciple. In 1973 Abhishiktananda suffered a heart attack on the road in Rishikesh, which he survived for only six months. He described this experience as a great "spiritual adventure," a "state beyond life and death," an "awakening." Fr. Le Saux had come to experience Christ within the context of* advaita, *the* Vedānta *of non-duality, and, after overcoming the tensions brought about in him by the differences between the two traditions, he found an inner integration.*

There are indeed no methods, yet there is something which can help us and lead us further and further into the sanctuary of the soul, something which can bring us to the summit of Mount Horeb (cf. 1 Kings 19:8). We refer here to an age-long tradition both of India and of the Christian East.

In India this is called the *namajapa*, the prayer of the Name. It consists of repeating continuously the name of the Lord, either alone or enshrined in a formula of praise, for instance: "Rāma, Rāma"—"*Hare* Krishna"—"*Namah* Shivaya." Often the devotee counts his *mantras* on a sort of rosary, or else he may assign to himself some period of time in which he will repeat the name without ceasing. Some aim at achieving a given number of invocations every day. Some go on repeating endlessly the holy Name: they continue repeating it during the time they are working or walking about, whispering it even when they converse with others, interrupting it only when obliged to give an answer. As far as possible the Name is given by a *guru*. Then it is either an initiation into a particular name of the Lord given by the *guru* to any worthy disciple who applies to him, or it is a special *mantra* conferred by the *guru* on a given man, in accordance, at least theoretically, with the disciple's needs and aspirations.

The best counterpart in Christianity of the Hindu *namajapa* is what is called in Russia and in the Near East the Jesus Prayer. It is the endless repetition of the holy Name of the Savior. Here again it is either the mere utterance of the name of Jesus, or it is a more complex invocation in which the name of Jesus is inserted. The most common formula, in recent centuries, is the following: "Lord Jesus, Son of the living God, have mercy on me, a sinner."

One immediately notices the stress on sin and forgiveness found in the Christian prayer of the Name. But asking for forgiveness is not a sign of an unhealthy concern with oneself, as is sometimes asserted. It rather arises from, and leads to, the discovery that God is love, and that it is by forgiving that he manifests most fully both his love and his omnipotence. In the last analysis, to pray for forgiveness is to become aware of the deepest mystery of the Godhead.

On the other hand, the Hindu, for his part, is content simply to praise the Lord: "Glory to Shiva," "*Namah* Shivaya!" Here the simple stress on praise and adoration has nothing to do with the confidence of the Pharisee in his own righteousness which feels no need for the divine mercy. At least in those who are really spiritual, it is rather the sign of a complete self-forgetfulness and lack of concern with oneself. Once God has been realized, who could even think of himself in the presence of the Almighty?

The Christian prayer of the Name comes from a very ancient tradition. It originated among the monks of Egypt and St. John Climacus recommends it in his *Scale of Perfection*. Later on it was widely practiced in the monasteries of Mount Athos. It was the soul of the Hesychast movement, and among its protagonists it is sufficient to mention Simeon the New Theologian and Gregory Palamas. In recent centuries it has spread more and more widely among the Orthodox Churches, especially in Russia, which is the source of that gem of a book, *The Way of a Pilgrim*.

The forms of the Christian *japa* varied very much, especially in its beginnings, until it became a formula centered on the name of Jesus, as quoted above. It was perhaps the finest flower of the practice of brief ejaculatory prayers which were so warmly recommended by the Desert Fathers. Some of them spent their time crying to Heaven the *Miserere* ("Have mercy on me, O Lord"; Psalm 51:1). Some made constant use of the first verse of Psalm 70: "Be pleased, O God, to deliver me! O Lord, make haste to help me!" For others the common invocation was the *Trisagion*, in either of its forms: the "Holy, holy, holy is the Lord" of the vision of Isaiah (6:3), or the "Holy is God! Holy and Almighty! Holy and Immortal!" of the oriental liturgical tradition.

But all these prayers were fundamentally the same: a short appeal or a short act of praise to God, which a man repeats continuously, to fix his mind on the Lord and to offer him the homage of his love.

In India, as well as in the Christian Near East, the prayer of the Name is of different kinds and degrees uttered either by the lips, or in the mind, or in the heart. No one of these ways excludes the others; yet the "place" in which a devotee habitually whispers this prayer can normally be taken as an indication of the depth at which he is aware of the divine Presence.

The first step is to pray with the lips, to repeat the name of the Lord loudly, or at least audibly. The mind may be distracted and may move at its own pace; the heart may be full of desires, which are far from consistent with the prayer uttered by the tongue. It does not matter. The utterance of the holy Name will do its work by itself in its own time. The only important thing is that the devotee should repeat the Name with respect and a real longing for the grace of the Lord.

In the second step the lips remain closed. It is in the mind, in the head, as it were, that the prayer is whispered. The prayer has now become a thoughtful attention to the Name which is now being repeated. However, it is not so much a mental consideration of the meaning of the Name as a simple awareness of it. Sometimes to help his concentration the devotee will imagine either the chosen words in written form or a picture corresponding to them.

Then there is the third stage, when the prayer, or rather the Name, is placed in the heart. There is no longer any movement of the lips or of the vocal cords, or even at its best any movement of the mind. The prayer is lodged there in the very center of the being. Not only is the mind now completely quiet, but all desires too have been transformed and have passed into the sole desire for the Lord, the desire to contemplate his glory, to merge into it. To help place the Name in the heart, saints who have practiced it recommend that it be uttered (though inaudibly) according to the rhythm of the respiration or of the beating of the heart. Thus it is the whole being—body and soul, senses and mind as well—which is taken up into the prayer, and through the body, the whole universe also, of which the body is a part.

The mystery and virtue of the prayer of the heart can be conveyed only through images, for concepts would be even more misleading. The underlying idea is evidently that we must never be contented with living, even less with praying to and meeting God, on the surface of our being, at the level merely of our senses and minds. The real place of the divine Encounter is in the very center of our being, the place of our origin, from which all that we are is constantly welling up. Physically this is symbolized by the heart. Thus to direct the attention towards the heart, even in a physical way, is symbolically to turn all our activities towards the very center of ourselves. This center is really the point of which of course we can form no image, in which the soul is, as it were, coming from the hands of God and waking up to itself.

India too, from the beginning of her spiritual meditations, has been alive to the mystery of the heart, the *guha*, the "cave" within, as it is called in her scriptures. That *guha* is what is beyond the reach of sense or thought. It is the "abode of *Brahman*," the very place of the *atman* itself, the truest self of man. It is the source of everything in the *macrocosmos*, which is the whole universe, and in the *microcosmos*, which is man himself. In it is the Life from which has issued every manifestation of life. In it is the Fire from which all things get warmth and are kindled. In it is the Light by which everything shines and becomes visible.

Indian tradition has given even more precise details about the place in which the *mantra* may or must be recited. There is the theory of *cakra*s or centers through which the divine power or *shakti* is supposed to develop and to rise progressively up the body. The last center, or *cakra*, according to tantric tradition, is situated between the two eyes at the base of the nose. Here is placed the "third eye" of Shiva, his spiritual eye, the one which opens inside and sees everything in the light of the brightness within. There is also a supreme *cakra*, but this is not counted with the others. It is situated at the very top of the cranium, just below the opening point through which the spirit (*purusha*) entered the body (*Aitareya Upanishad*, 1, 3. 12) and through which the soul is supposed to flee at the time of release. The *guru*'s teaching and even more one's own personal experience alone can unveil the spiritual truth hidden behind this imagery. It is enough to have mentioned it here.

The fruits of the prayer of the Name differ according to the degree of the prayer and the "place" in which it is uttered; but at all levels they are infinitely precious. In the first place, it helps beginners to fix their wandering attention; it also leads advanced souls up to "the experience of the Holy Spirit," as the Russian mystics are accustomed to say.

If worthily practiced, the repetition of God's name is certainly a wonderful help in concentrating the attention and deepening the mind. We are creatures with fickle minds and are constantly liable to distraction. To live on the spiritual plane means to resist and to fight this weakness; such is the goal of any ascetic life. We can carry on this struggle through contrary mental processes, as was mentioned above, when speaking of "meditation."

But while doing so, we still remain on the level of the mind and run the risk of never "taking off."

The prayer of the Name, for its part, gives the mind just the kind of food it needs, and keeps it busy enough not to look for other outlets, without at the same time impeding the quest within. By repeating the Name, the mind becomes more and more one-pointed, *ekagra*. Distractions vanish, or, if images keep on recurring in our thoughts, they are rather like passing dreams with little effect on our actual concentration. The mind, once stabilized, plunges spontaneously within itself, towards its center. The wording of the *mantra* will then probably convey less and less of its original meaning. That does not matter at all. From the external meaning of the word the soul is now reaching up to its essential meaning, from the form conveyed by a particular name, to the mystery beyond all forms, whose sign indeed the name is. At long last, through the grace of the Holy Spirit, the mind goes to sleep, as it were, and all memory of itself disappears. Then it attains the true prayer, of which Antony the Great used to say: "The only real prayer is the one in which we are no longer aware that we are praying."

The prayer of the Name is therefore the best way to enter into meditation, in those periods which may be devoted to that exercise. It is also the best way to remain at all times aware of the presence of God. Such prayer indeed should always be on our lips, in our minds, in our hearts, during all occupations which do not require special attention on our part. There are so many hours in the day in which it is quite immaterial in itself whether we think of one thing or another; times when we are walking or traveling, times immediately before and after sleep, times of manual occupations like gardening, sewing, cleaning, times devoted to the needs of the body, etc. We could transform into conscious prayer all those times of our lives when our minds are not fully engaged. Thus we would also avoid the many distracting thoughts which continuously enter our minds and trouble us so much at the times specially assigned to prayer. So many useless or harmful desires would then be stifled at their very conception. As soon indeed as they appear, the recollection of the Name will confront them and they will be dashed on it as on the rock which is Christ, as St. Benedict explains in commenting on Psalm 137 (*Rule*, ch. 7).

Of course the prayer of the Name must not impair the application of the mind to its necessary duties. It is evident that the prayer of the Name cannot continue at such times at least on the tongue or in the thinking intellect, and it is just here that we find the marvels of the prayer of the heart. It can go on at all times even when the mind is consciously at work, or even when it is lost in sleep: "I slept, but my heart was awake . . ." was said by the bride in the Song of Solomon (5:2). Even when the mind is not aware of it, the prayer of the heart remains as a kind of background or substratum which underlies everything. It is like the rocky bed of a river which itself never moves, but over which the waters flow without ceasing. For some people the continuous flow of the *mantra* is so intense that they "hear" it, as it were, through all their mental processes.

Psychologically, there is no doubt that the prayer of the Name possesses an incomparable value. But its value is not merely practical. If it were, it would fall short of the praises given to it by the saints, and would be unable to produce the marvelous results described above. The Name is like an icon. Icons are signs and, as such, possess something of the reality they are intended to signify and represent. Of course they can become idols, when one stops at them. Yet they are a wonderful aid granted to us by the Lord, to help our feeble and fickle intellects in their groping towards him and in their longing to get at least some glimpse of his glory.

The Name is the supreme mental icon. That is specially true when the Name has been directly revealed by God, like the name of Yahweh in the Old Covenant and the name of Jesus in the Gospel. Yet we can hardly imagine that those who have not had direct access to the riches of evangelical revelation have been completely forsaken by their Father in heaven. We cannot otherwise understand how God so often made use of the *namajapa* to bestow on Hindus, for instance, some of his most precious spiritual favors. The names of God rose in the heart of sages and *rishis* from their deep experience of the Spirit. They tried to express in them something of their inner vision. They called God "Shiva," the Benevolent One, the Auspicious One; "Rāma," the Lovely One. They charged those syllables with all the spiritual power of their love and of their adoration. Others after them continued repeating those names and they also enriched them with their own faith and inner experiences. Disciples received them from their *gurus* in the sacred rites of initiation, or *dikshā*. Successive generations of men were called to draw out spiritual energy from them and to make them in return more and more expressive of the highest Mystery.

The name indeed is believed to contain in itself as in a nutshell the whole divine Mystery, to carry, as it were, in a concentrated form, everything that man can say or think of that Mystery, in the same way as a pearl, small though its volume is, is worth a large quantity of gold or other precious material. For the man who has tasted the prayer of the Name, the Name will mean all that theologians try to develop in countless volumes. But it will convey it no longer in a diluted and derived form. It will satisfy his thirst with water from the very fountainhead.

That is the reason why the *namajapa* is of itself so powerful. Of all *mantras* and prayers, the invocation of the Name is the most efficient. Psychologically it concentrates and deepens the mind. Furthermore, by the very power it enfolds within itself, it leads the soul towards the very center, the origin, the unique Source. It endows her with a spiritual energy which will never stop short of divine union. To come back now to biblical ways of speaking, is not the power of the Name the very power of the Holy Spirit present in us? It is in the Spirit alone that we are able to utter the name of Jesus.

SAYINGS ON *TARIKI*

Gōjun Shichiri

Gōjun Shichiri *was born in 1836. He lived at Hakata, in southwestern Japan. Shichiri was a very influential and popular propagator of the* Tariki *way (the way of the "Other") of Amidism. D.T. Suzuki tells the story of Shichiri's house being burgled: the thief, upon being arrested, later converted because of the deep impression left upon him by the saintly man. Shichiri was also a scholar and a prolific writer. The following excerpts, translated by D.T. Suzuki, are taken from "Sayings of Reverend Shichiri," compiled by Chizen Akanuma. Gōjun Shichiri died in 1900.*

1. According to the other schools of Buddhism, good is practicable only after the eradication of evil. This is like trying to dispel darkness first in order to let the light in. It is not so with us, followers of Tariki: if you have some worldly occupations such as shopkeeping, etc., just begin saying the Nembutsu even with your mind busily engaged in the work. It is said that where the dragon goes there follow clouds. With faith, with your thought directed towards the (Paradise of the) West, invoke the name of Amida with your mouth, and good actions will follow of themselves. You fail to hit the mark just because you try to catch the clouds instead of looking for the dragon itself.

2. You cannot stop evil thoughts asserting themselves because they belong to the nature of common mortals. In the "Sayings of Yokawa" we read that if we recite the Nembutsu we shall be quite certain of our rebirth in the Pure Land like the lotus blooming above the muddy water. The founder of our sect preaches that if we, instead of waiting vainly for water to recede, start at once to wade through it, the water will recede by itself from under our own feet. Now when the heart is gladdened in the faith of Tariki, there are in it no waters of greed, anger, etc.

3. Dedicate your mouth to the Nembutsu. When you regard the mouth as belonging to yourself, it always tends to foster the cause of your fall into Naraka.

4. [After enumerating the sins of common mortals, the reverend master said:] It is thus that, in spite of our wish to attain the Pure Land, we find ourselves destined for Naraka. Therefore, let us realize that Naraka is, after all our efforts, our destination. As far as our ignorant past is concerned there is no help for it; but as we have now come to the realization of our own situation,

nothing is left for us but to embrace the way of salvation; for herein lies the purport of the Original Vows.

5. There are some people who think that they understand what is meant by absolute devotion to the Nembutsu, but who are still doubtful as to their possession of the faith and inquire within themselves whether they are really all right. To such I would say: Give up your self-inquisition and have your minds made up as to the inevitableness of your fates for Naraka. When you come to this decision, you will be serener in mind ready to submit yourselves to the savior's will. To express the idea in a popular way, such people are like those wives whom their husbands do not seem to care for; they are in constant fear of being divorced. Being uncertain about Amida's love, they are anxious to court his favor. This is because they have not yet altogether given up their selves. When we know that Naraka is inevitable for common mortals filled with evil thoughts and passions—and in fact we all are such mortals—there is nothing left for us but to be cheerfully grateful for Amida's promise of salvation. Whether we should be saved after or before our sins are expiated is the business of The Other and not ours.

6. What? Is it so hard for you to surrender yourself? For, you say, when my advice is literally observed, you cannot carry on your business. Well, if you cannot, why would you keep it up? "If I don't I shall starve to death," you may say: Well, but is it after all such a bad thing as you think, this dying? When I say this you may regard me as inhuman and heartless, but is not your real aim to be reborn in the Pure Land of Amida? If so, when you die your wish is fulfilled. If this was not your original wish, what was it? What made you come here to listen to my sermons? You are inconsistent.

7. Some people are not quite sure of their state of faith. They seem to put their faith on the scale against Amida's miraculous way of salvation, and try to weigh the latter with their own understanding; while salvation is altogether in the hands of The Other. To think that our attainment of the Pure Land is conditioned by our understanding of Amida's plans so that we cease to harbor any doubt as to the wonderful wisdom of the Buddha—this is relying on the strength of our faith and setting Amida's mercy away from us. When his mercy is not taken into our own hearts and we only ask whether our doubt is cleared and faith is gained, this faith becomes a thing apart from mercy and the one is set against the other. This we call a state of confusion.

8. The great Original Vows of Amida are his Will, and the ten powers and four fearlessnesses are his Virtues. Both cause and effect are sealed up in the

one name of Amida. A paper parcel superscribed as containing one thousand yen may consist, when counted in detail, of so many ten-sen notes and so many fifty-sen notes, but all the same the total is one thousand yen. Whether we know the contents in detail or not, we are the owner of the one thousand yen as we have the parcel in our hands. Similarly, in whichever way we may embrace Amida, whether knowingly or unknowingly as to his Original Vows and manifold Virtues, we are, as soon as we accept him, the master of *Namu-amida-butsu*. So says Rennyo, "One is the master of *Namu-amida-butsu* when one accepts Amida." When his name resounds in your mind you have faith; and when it is expressed on your lips it is the Nembutsu. Oh, how grateful I feel for the grace of Amida! the Pure Land is drawing nigh day by day!

9. In case we are depending on others, for instance, if we are working as servants we must first win the confidence of the master by showing our loyalty; for otherwise we can never serve him for any length of time. When a poor man wants to borrow money from a rich man he must prove first how honest he is; for otherwise the latter will never have enough confidence in the debtor. The faithfulness of the debtor must be recognized by the creditor. So in the other sects of Buddhism people are encouraged to rely on their own sincere desire to be saved, which they would have Amida accept for the price of his grace. But "reliance" or "dependence" is differently understood in the teaching of Tariki. The feeling of dependence the child has for its mother has not been bought by its own filiality. When the sincerely-loving heart of the parents is taken into its own little heart and when these hearts are made into one heart, the child is truly said to be filial. "Think of your parents with even half as much of the love as is entertained for yourself by the parental hearts"—so goes the old saying. If you had even one-tenth of such love, you would be the most filial child in the world. In like manner we can't come to Amida and ask him to accept us as the reward of our sincere desire to be saved. [From Amida's infinite point of view our sincerity is not worth being taken notice of by him.] What we can do is to accept his own sincere desire to save us and rest assured of the fulfillment of his Vows. This is the adamantine faith of Tariki.

10. You say that you never count on the Nembutsu as the efficient cause of your rebirth in the Pure Land because it is only the expression of your grateful heart, but you feel uneasy when you find that you do not say it well. As long as an old lady has a stick in her hand she may not be conscious of its utility, but she would feel unsteady with her feet if she should leave it altogether. In like manner while you can say the Nembutsu you feel all right, but as soon as

your Nembutsu becomes rarer you are uneasy. Then you come to think that the Nembutsu has nothing to do with your rebirth in the Pure Land. So far so good, but still feeling that faith is somehow necessary you try firmly to take hold of it after all. While getting out of a boat one sometimes falls into water because one kicks off the boat in the effort to jump over to the bank. You fall into the fault of self-power because you jump at faith just as you let go the Nembutsu. Viewed in this light, this is also a sort of self-power, a self-power of mind if not of mouth. If you say that the Nembutsu is not the efficient cause of rebirth in the Pure Land, why should you not advance another step in your way and also quit the faith itself? Then there will be but one mercy of the Buddha that works, and indeed there is nothing to surpass this state of mind.

11. [Referring to children the reverend master said,] "Carried on the back of Amida as they are on the mother's, even the wanton, capricious ones will attain the Pure Land."

12. "To hear" is the whole thing in the teaching of Tariki. Says the sūtra, "Hear the name of Amida!" The Buddha, let us observe, does not tell us to *think*, for hearing is believing and not thinking. How do we hear then? No special contrivance is needed; in thinking we may need some method to go along, but hearing is just to receive what is given, and there is no deliberation here.

13. We should live in this world as in a branch office of the Pure Land.

14. We feel serene in mind not because we are assured of attaining the Pure Land, but because we believe the words of Amida who promises to embrace us, to save us in his love.

15. When holes are stopped in the broken paper-screen, no draught will pass through: when we say the Nembutsu continually with our mouth, no evil language will have a chance to be uttered. Be therefore watchful.

16. We read in the sūtra, "It is ten *kalpa*s now since the Enlightenment of Bhiksu Dharmākara," this means that family-fortune of father and children is merged in one; that is to say, the merits of Amida are now those of all sentient beings and the sins of all sentient beings are those of Amida. Here lies the uniqueness of the Enlightenment of Amida which distinguishes itself from Enlightenment attained by other Buddhas. According to the latter, thousands of virtues and merits are the sole possessions of the Buddhas themselves, whereas we poor creatures are altogether meritless. There are therefore in this

case two independent family legacies; the one rich in endowments and the other next to nothing: while in the Enlightenment of Amida all is merged in one, for in him there is the virtue of perfect interpenetration. When bundles of hemp are burned, not only their original shape is transformed, but they all turn into fire. In like manner, when the merits of Amida enter into our hearts and fill them up, not only the evil passions we have are consumed like bundles of hemp, but they themselves turn into merits. We read in the *Wasan*: "The greater the obstacles the greater the merits, just as there is more water in more ice. The merits of Amida know no boundaries."

17. The lamp itself has no light until it is lighted, it shines out only when a light is put in. As Amida is in possession of this light of virtue, eighty-four thousand rays shine out of him; broadly speaking, his light knows no impediments and fills all the ten quarters. "Long have I been in possession in myself of the Original Vows made by the Other-power and also their fulfillment! and yet how vainly I have wandered about deceived by the self-power's tenacious hold on me!" Again, "There is in the light of the Buddha of Unimpeded Light the light of purity, joy, and wisdom, and its miraculous virtues are benefiting all beings in the ten quarters." Again, "As this is the teaching of Amida who turns all his merits towards the salvation of all beings, his virtues fill the ten quarters." It is thus evident that Amida is surcharging us with his merits.

18. Certain Tariki followers imagine that as Amida attained his Enlightenment ten *kalpa*s ago which determined the status of sentient beings as ultimately destined for the Pure Land, all that they have to do on their part for salvation is but to remember the fact of Amida's Enlightenment, and that as to their understanding of the meaning of Tariki nothing is needed, for the remembrance is enough. This however is not the orthodox teaching. If we have no inner sense of acceptance as to Amida's infinite grace, it is like listening to the sound of rice-pounding at the next-door neighbor's which will never appease our own feeling of hunger. The ancient saying is, "A distant water cannot put out a near fire." A man comes into town from a faraway frontier district; while staying in an inn, fire breaks out in the neighborhood and confusion ensues. The traveler quietly remarks, "In my country there is a big river running in front of my house, and there is a great waterfall behind, besides the canals are open on all sides—you need not be afraid of the fire's getting ahead of you." But all the waters thousands of miles away will not extinguish the fire at hand. The inn is reduced to ashes in no time. You may imagine that in your native country of Amida's Enlightenment there securely lies the assurance of your rebirth in the Pure Land ten *kalpa*s ago and also

that there runs the great river of oneness in which are merged subject and object, Buddha and sentient beings; and you may nonchalantly say that you have no fear for hell-fire: but inasmuch as you have no inner sense of absolute dependence, your house is sure to be consumed by the flames.

19. Such old Chinese remedies as *kakkontō* (arrowroot infusion) may do us neither harm nor good, but with a strong effective medicine there is something we may call toxic after-effect. The grace of Amida as is taught by the Other-power school is so vast and overwhelming that its recipients may turn into antinomians. This is the danger one has to be on guard against. Such Tariki followers are inferior to the Jiriki, who cherish a feeling of compunction even in innocently destroying the life of an ant. Whatever the Buddha-Dharma may teach, we as human beings ought to have a certain amount of conscience and the feeling of compassion; when these are missing, there will be no choice between ourselves and the lower animals.

20. Some say that Buddhism is pessimism and does not produce beneficial results on our lives. But could Buddhists be induced to love this world so full of evils? If they were addicted to saké-drinking, a life of wanton pleasures, an insatiable thirst for fame and gain, how would they ever be expected to see into the true signification of this life? As they are detached from all these evils, they really know how to benefit the world. Since olden days there has been no one who truly worked for our welfare by leading a life of dissipation.

21. The lower grow the mountains the further we recede from them, but the nearer we approach the higher they are; so with the grace of Amida.

22. When they are told this: "If you are going to take refuge in the teaching of Tariki, you must refrain from committing evil deeds such as drinking, smoking, etc.," they are apt to hesitate. Well, let them drink then, let them wander away from the ordinary moral walks, if they are positively so inclined—but let them at the same time only believe in Amida, believe in the Original Vows of the Buddha. When the faith gradually takes possession of their hearts, they will naturally cease from evil doings. Through the grace of Amida their lives will be made easier and happier.

23. Knowledge is good, its spread is something we have to be grateful for. But it is like fire or water without which we cannot live even for a day. But what a terrible thing fire is and water too, when we fail to make good use of them! How many human lives and how much property, we cannot begin to estimate, were lost in fire and flood! In proportion to its importance to life,

knowledge is to be most cautiously handled. Especially in the understanding of Tariki faith, knowledge proves to be a great hindrance.

24. Knowledge is the outcome of reasoning and knows no limits: faith is the truth of personality. Faith and knowledge are not to be confused.

25. Knowledge grows as we reason, but love stands outside of reasoning. In the education of children the mother ought to know how to reason about their future welfare and not to give way to her momentary sentiment. Love is the string that binds the two.

26. Amida holds in his hands both love and knowledge for the salvation of sentient beings. So we read: "In the depths of Amida's love there lies his wisdom beyond calculation." *Namu-amida-butsu* signifies the union of love and wisdom and is the free gift of Amida to us sentient beings.

27. Doubt is impossible when our salvation by Amida is so positive; and when salvation is so positive we cannot but help saying the Nembutsu.

28. According to the Tariki teaching, all that we sentient beings have to do in the way of salvation is to accept and believe. Have you ever seen a puppet-show? The marionettes are worked from behind, somebody is pulling the strings. We are all likewise moving through the absolute power of Amida.

29. While Amida's Original Vows are meant universally for the salvation of all sentient beings in the ten quarters, we may not experience real joy if we are to receive only portions of Amida's grace as our shares. According to Shinran, Amida's meditation for five *kalpa*s was only for his own sake, for himself alone; why then should not each of us take the whole share of Amida's grace upon himself? There is but one sun in the world, yet wherever we move does it not follow each of us?

30. "To return to the great treasure-ocean of merits" means throwing oneself into it, that is, throwing oneself into a mass of wisdom, into the midst of Light.

I read somewhere a fine story about a rabbit. As it ran into a heath of scouring rush (*tokusa*), the hunter followed it but could not find any trace of the animal. When he closely searched for it, he noticed that it had been rubbed off by the rush into a nonentity. In a similar way when we throw ourselves into the Light of Amida, all the evil karma and evil thoughts we may be in possession of altogether disappear. When flakes of snow fall into the boiling water they all at once melt away. When we have returned into the great ocean of Merits, that is, when we have thrown ourselves into the midst of Light and Wisdom, nothing of evil deeds and thoughts will be left behind. Think of it, O you, my brethren in faith, while enlightenment is impossible for us unless we reach the forty-first stage, we common mortals possessed of ignorance are now firmly established in the faith that we are to be born in the Pure Land of Amida when we have thrown ourselves into his Light where the boiling water of Wisdom melts all our evil karma and evil thought without even leaving a trace of them. This being proved, have we not every cause to be joyous?

31. We are told to believe deeply in the mercy of Amida, but if you are too concerned with your state of mind the very mercy of Amida may prove to be a hindrance to the growth of your faith. If you strive to grow in faith thinking this must be accomplished for your salvation, the very effort will smother it. For faith means unconditionally to submit oneself to The Other, and the straining is the outcome of self-power; the heavier you step the deeper you go into the mud of self-power, and the further you stand away from Other-power. In this case a step forward means a step backward, and when you think you are deep in it, that is the very time you are receding from Amida.

32. "To have faith" means not to have any doubt about the Original Vows of Amida; when there is not the least shadow of doubt about the Vows, other things will take care of themselves.

33. The principle of the Tariki teaching is: "Just ask and you will be saved," and not "You do this and salvation will be its reward." Nothing is imposed upon you as the price of salvation. When you give sweets to your children you do not tell them to do this or that, you simply give them away; nothing is expected of them, for it is a free gift. With Amida, his gift has no conditions attached to it. Let your mortal weaknesses remain what they are, and be absorbed in the infinite grace of Amida.

34. Saké cannot be poured into an overturned cup, but when it stands in its natural position, anybody can pour saké into it and as fully as it can hold. Therefore, have the cup of your heart upright ready to receive, and hear; it will surely be filled with Amida's mercy.

35. There are some people who have heard of the Original Vows and say that they believe in them, but somehow they feel uneasy when they think of their last moments. They are like those who, feeling dizzy at the surging billows, are not at all sure of their safely sailing over the ocean. If they are too frightened at the evil passions that are stirring in their hearts, which they

think will assuredly interfere with their ultimate salvation, there will be no end to their vexations. Look at the spacious boat instead of the billows; for the boat is large enough and safe enough for every one of us, however sinful and numerous we are, and there will be no feeling of uneasiness left in us. When you think of the mighty power of Amida, you cannot have any fear as to your salvation.

36. We must pay fair prices for things that belong to others. But when they are our own parents' they are justly ours too and we do not have to pay for them. This is because of the parental love that we are allowed to inherit all that belongs to him regardless of our mental capacities. So with Amida, he bestows upon us freely all that he has—and here is the secret of the Tariki teaching.

37. There are two ways to get rid of illusions and be enlightened. The one way is to accumulate our own merits and thereby aid in gaining enlightenment. The other way is to gain enlightenment depending upon the promise of the Original Vows of Amida; we are then admitted to the Pure Land, not indeed on account of our own wisdom or merit, but solely through the grace of The Other, who is the father of all beings. When we seek the Pure Land, we feel uneasy reflecting on our moral imperfections and the lack of a yielding, believing heart. But this is a state of mind not in accord with the spirit of Tariki, for our attitude here is that of the one who would receive things from strangers and not from his own parent. As we followers of Tariki are all naked with no outward vestments such as virtues or merits, we jump right into the water of the Original Vows of Amida where good men do not stand out any higher than wicked ones; for Amida's grace makes no preference between the two sets of beings.

38. According to the old Chinese legend, the jellyfish has no eye and relies upon the crab for its sight. Supposing this true, we are all like the jellyfish, for we have no wisdom-eye to see through the triple world; and it is only when we are given Amida's own Light of Wisdom that we are really relieved of worry and can see the truth as the one who is destined for the Pure Land.

NAMO AMITOFU

Gao Xingjian

Gao Xingjian *was the first Chinese recipient of the Nobel Prize for Literature in 2000. Born in 1940 in Jiangxi province in eastern China, he earned a university degree in French at Beijing, and decided to become a writer. Choosing exile in 1987, he settled in Paris, where he completed* The Soul Mountain *two years later. He is a playwright and painter as well as a fiction writer and critic. At the time of his first successes as a playwright, Gao was falsely diagnosed with lung cancer. The narrator of* The Soul Mountain *shares these circumstances with the author as he leaves Beijing to explore various rural regions of China. Ostensibly undertaken to collect folk songs and legends, the trip is a means of reconnecting with traditional China, particularly Taoism and shamanism, beyond the Cultural Revolution. The book itself is narrated in two voices: a "rational" "I" and a "mystical" "you." The "you" wanders through an otherworldly Chinese landscape looking for Lingshan, the "Soul Mountain." The following excerpt is from Chapter 12 of the novel, which tells the story of the narrator's spontaneous rediscovery of the grace of Amitofu's (Amida) Name at the threshold of the experience of death.*

Before this long trip, after being diagnosed with lung cancer by the doctor, all I could do every day was to go to the park on the outskirts of the city. People said it was only in the parks that the air was slightly better in the polluted city and naturally the air was better still in the parks on the outskirts. The hill by the city wall used to be a crematorium and cemetery, and had only in recent years been turned into a park. However, the new residential area already extended to the foot of the hill which was once a cemetery, and if a fence wasn't put up soon, the living would be building houses right onto the hill and encroaching on their domain.

At the top of the hill was a desolate strip strewn with stone slabs left behind by the stone masons. Every morning elderly people from all around came to practice Taijiquan boxing or to stroll in the fresh air with their cages of pet birds. However, by nine o'clock or so when the sun was overhead they picked up their cages and went home. I could then be alone, in peace and quiet, and would take from my pocket *The Book of Changes with Zhou Commentary*. After reading for a while, the warm autumn sun would make me drowsy and I would stretch out on a stone slab and, with the book as a pillow, quietly begin reciting the hexagram which I had just read. In the glare of the sun, a bright blue image of the sign of that hexagram would float on my red eyelids.

I hadn't originally intended to do any reading: what if I did read one book more or one book less, whether I read or not wouldn't make a difference, I'd still be waiting to get cremated. It was a sheer coincidence that I was reading *The Book of Changes with Zhou Commentary*. A childhood friend who heard of my illness came to see me and asked if there was anything he could do for me. Then he brought up the topic of *qigong*. He'd heard of people using *qigong* to cure lung cancer, he also said he knew someone who practiced a form of *qigong* related to the Eight Trigrams and he urged me to take it up. I understood what he was getting at. Even at that stage, I should make some sort of effort. So I asked if he could get me a copy of *The Book of Changes* as I hadn't read it. Two days later, he turned up with a copy of *The Book of Changes with Corrections to the Zhou Commentary*. Deeply moved, I took it and went on to say that when we were children I thought he'd taken the mouth organ I'd bought, wrongly accused him of taking it, and then found it. I asked if he still remembered. There was a smile on his plump round face. He was uncomfortable and said there wasn't any point in bringing this up. It was he who was embarrassed and not me. He clearly remembered yet he was being so kind to me. It then occurred to me that I had committed wrongdoings for which people did not hold grudges against me. Was this repentance? Was this the psychological state of a person facing imminent death?

I didn't know whether, during my lifetime, others had wronged me more or I had wronged others more. I knew however that there were people such as my deceased mother who really loved me, and people such as my estranged wife who really hated me, but was there any need to settle accounts in the few days left to me? For those I had wronged my death could count as a sort of compensation and for those who had wronged me I was powerless to do anything. Life is probably a tangle of love and hate permanently knotted together. Could it have any other significance? But to hastily end it just like this was too soon. I realized that I had not lived properly. If I did have another lifetime, I would definitely live it differently, but this would require a miracle.

I didn't believe in miracles, just like I didn't believe in fate, but when one is desperate, isn't a miracle all that could be hoped for?

Fifteen days later I arrived at the hospital for my X-ray appointment. My younger brother was anxious and insisted, against my wishes, on coming with me. I didn't like showing my emotions to people close to me. If I were on my own it would be easier to control myself, but I couldn't change his mind and he came anyway. A classmate from middle school was at the hospital and he took me straight to the head doctor of the X-ray section.

The head doctor as usual was wearing his glasses and sitting in his swivel chair. He read the diagnosis on my medical record, examined the two chest X-rays and said that an X-ray from the side would have to be taken. He immediately wrote a note for another X-ray and said the wet X-ray should be brought to him as soon as the image had developed.

The autumn sun was splendid. It was cold inside and sitting there looking through the window at the sun shining on the grass, I thought it was even more wonderful. I had never looked at the sunshine this way before. After the side position X-ray, I sat looking at the sunshine outside while waiting by the darkroom for the film to develop. The sunshine outside the window was actually too distant from me, I should have been thinking about what was immediately to take place right here. But did I need to think a lot about that? My situation was like that of a murderer with cast-iron evidence against him waiting for the judge to pass the death sentence. All I could hope for was a miracle. Didn't the two damn chest X-rays taken by two separate hospitals at two different times provide the evidence for condemning me to death?

I didn't know when it was, I wasn't even aware of it, probably it was while I was staring out of the window at the sunshine, that I heard myself silently intoning, take refuge in Namo Amitofu, Buddha. I had been doing this for quite some time. It seemed I had already been praying from the time I put on my clothes and left the execution chamber, the X-ray room with the equipment for raising and lowering patients as they lay there.

In the past, I would certainly have considered it preposterous to think that one day I would be praying. I used to be filled with pity when I saw old people in temples burning incense, kneeling in prayer, and quietly intoning Namo Amitofu. My pity was quite different from sympathy. If I were to verbalize this reaction, it would probably be: Ah! Pitiful wretches, they're old and if their insignificant wishes aren't realized, they pray that they will be realized in their hearts. However, I thought it was ridiculous for a robust young man or a pretty young woman to be praying and whenever I heard young devotees intoning Namo Amitofu I would want to laugh, and clearly not without malice. I couldn't understand how people in the prime of life could do such a stupid thing, but now I have prayed, prayed devoutly, and from the depths of my heart. Fate is unyielding and humans are so frail and weak. In the face of misfortune man is nothing.

While awaiting the pronouncement of the death sentence, I was in this state of nothingness, looking at the autumn sun outside the window, silently intoning Namo Amitofu, over and over, in my heart.

My old schoolmate, who couldn't wait any longer, knocked and went into the darkroom. My brother followed him in but was sent out and had to stand by the window where the X-rays came out. Soon my schoolmate also came out and went to the window to wait. They had transferred their concern for the prisoner to the documentation of his sentence, an inappropriate metaphor. Like an onlooker who had nothing to do with it, I watched as they went into the darkroom, keeping in my heart Namo Amitofu which I silently intoned over and over again. Then, suddenly I heard them shouting out in surprise:

"What?"

"Nothing?"

"Check again!"

"There's only been this one side chest X-ray all afternoon." The response from the darkroom was unfriendly.

The two of them pegged the X-ray onto a frame and held it up for inspection. The darkroom technician also came out, looked at it, made an offhand remark, then dismissed them.

Buddha said rejoice. Buddha said rejoice first replaced Namo Amitofu, then turned into more common expressions of sheer joy and elation. This was my initial psychological reaction after I had extricated myself from despair, I was really lucky. I had been blessed by Buddha and a miracle had taken place. But my joy was furtive, I did not dare to appear hasty.

I was still anxious and took the wet X-ray for verification by the head doctor with the glasses.

He looked at the X-ray and threw up both of his arms in grand theatrical style.

"Isn't this wonderful?"

"Do I still have to have that done?" I was asking about the final X-ray.

"Still have to have what done?" he berated me, he saved people's lives and had this sort of authority.

He then got me to stand in front of an X-ray machine with a projector screen and told me to take a deep breath, breathe out, turn around, turn to the left, turn to the right.

"You can see it for yourself," he said, pointing to the screen. "Have a look, have a look."

Actually I didn't see anything clearly, my brain was like a great blob of paste and the only thing I saw on the screen was a blurry rib cage.

"There's nothing there, is there?" he loudly berated me as if I were deliberately being a nuisance.

"But then how can those other X-rays be explained?" I couldn't stop myself asking.

"If there's nothing there, there's nothing there, it's just vanished. How can it be explained? Colds and lung inflammation can cause a shadow and when you get better, the shadow disappears."

But I hadn't asked him about a person's state of mind. Could that cause a shadow?

"Go and live properly, young man." He swiveled his chair around, dismissing me.

He was right, I had won a new lease of life, I was younger than a new-born baby.

My brother rushed off on his bicycle, he had a meeting to attend.

The sunshine was mine again, mine again to enjoy. My schoolmate and I sat on chairs by the grass and started discussing fate. It is when there is no need to discuss fate that people talk more about fate.

"Fate's a strange thing," he said, "a purely chance phenomenon. The possible arrangement of the chromosomes can be worked out, but can it be worked out prior to falling into the womb on a particular occasion?" He talked on endlessly. He was studying genetic engineering but the findings of the experiments he wrote up in his dissertation differed from those of his supervisor who was the head of the department. When called up for a discussion with the party general-secretary of the department, he had an argument, and after graduating he was sent to raise deer on a deer-breeding farm on the Daxinganling Plateau of Inner Mongolia.

Later on, after many setbacks, he managed to get a teaching position in a newly-established university in Tangshan. However, how could it have been foreseen that he would be labeled the claws and teeth of anti-revolutionary black group elements and hauled out for public criticism. He suffered for almost ten years before the verdict "case unsubstantiated" was declared.

He was transferred out of Tianjin just ten days before the big earthquake of 1976. Those who had trumped up the case against him were crushed to death in a building which collapsed, it was in the middle of the night and not one of them escaped.

"Within the dark chaos, naturally there is fate!" he said.

For me, however, what I had to ponder was this: How should I change this life for which I had just won a reprieve?

BREATHING AND RHYTHM IN CHRISTIAN AND BUDDHIST PRAYER

William Johnston

William Johnston *was born in 1925. He is a Jesuit priest of Irish stock who has focused, both in his pastoral teaching and in his writings, on building contemplative bridges between Buddhism and Christianity. His books refer to the universal vocation of mysticism. He is the author of* The Still Point, Christian Zen, The Mysticism of the Cloud of Unknowing, *and* The Inner Eye of Love. *He is based at Sophia University in Tokyo where he has taught courses on mysticism and meditation.*

In the Hesychast tradition . . . there is not, as far as I know, any counting, but only the repetition of an ejaculation in unison with the breath. This ejaculation can take the form given above or it can simply be the repetition of the word "Jesus." Some writers say that with the inhalation Jesus comes in, and with the exhalation "I" go out, and in this way the personality is filled with Christ. . . . The ejaculation purifies the mind of all thoughts and desires and distractions so that it enters deep down into the psychic life in total nudity of spirit.

The practice of repeating an ejaculation is found especially in the Amida sect of Buddhism where the words "*Namu Amida Butsu*" (Honor to the Buddha Amida) are repeated again and again and again. Zen does not speak much about this so-called *nembutsu*, but I was surprised once while visiting a Zen temple to hear one of the young monks say that he made use of the *nembutsu*. He said that at first it was himself repeating the words "*Namu Amida Butsu*," but in time it was no longer "I" repeating the words, but just *Namu Amida Butsu* without any subject at all—for the "I" was gone. For him the *nembutsu* was a way to the nonself condition that is so characteristic of Zen. I was interested in this and recalled the thesis of Dr. Suzuki that silent nothingness and the *koan* and the *nembutsu* all lead to the same goal; namely, enlightenment. In all cases, the upper levels of psychic life are purified and cleansed, thus alloying the deep levels of unconscious life to surge into consciousness and give enlightenment.

Be that as it may, the repetition of an ejaculation can enter so deeply into the psychic life that it becomes almost automatic and continues even in the busiest moments. Some Buddhists claim that the rhythm of the *nembutsu* goes on even in time of sleep. A Japanese nun told me of how she once sat by the bedside of a dying sister. This latter had had an operation and was barely conscious; yet she kept repeating the words *"Jesusu awaremi tamae"* (Jesus have mercy on me) in a way that seemed quite effortless and almost automatic. This kind of thing is not, in my opinion, very unusual.

I myself believe that the repetition of an ejaculation or the consciousness of the breathing is somehow linked to a basic rhythm in the body, a rhythm that can be deepened and deepened until it reaches the center of one's being from which enlightenment breaks forth. Let me try to explain what I mean.

There is a basic rhythm in the body, linked to a consciousness that is deeper than is ordinarily experienced. When man was in his natural setting, working in the fields or fishing in the sea, this rhythm was probably easy enough to find, because man's rapport with his surroundings was harmonious. And in such a setting man was more open to cosmic forces, less inclined to atheism. Recall that the apostles were fisherman and that Christianity is closely bound up with fishing. But with the advent of urbanization this rhythm and harmony were lost; man became out of tune with his surroundings. That is where we now stand. Again it is a problem of ecology. We have to cope not only with air pollution but also with a rival rhythm that comes from the Beatles, the Rolling Stones, and a number of forces that jolt our psychic life. Excessive noise, it is well known, dulls not only the sense of hearing; but also the sense of smell and of sight. How much more, then, does it dull the deeper layer of psychic life! Small wonder if it deadens the profounder rhythm that should be within us.

But anyone who wants to meditate in depth must find this rhythm and the consciousness that accompanies it. And people find their rhythm in various ways. For some it is through the breathing, and this alone is sufficient. For others it is the breathing linked to an ejaculation. Or again it may be the repetition of an ejaculation without any thought of breathing whatever. Or again, some people find their rhythm by consciousness of the beating of the heart, and not infrequently an ejaculation is attached to this rather than to the breath. I have known people, too, who discover this rhythm simply by walking. A friend of mine goes for a walk every morning before breakfast repeating an ejaculation. As he walks, the ejaculation becomes automatic (it fits in with the rhythm) and just goes on, to such an extent that he becomes oblivious to his surroundings. He has not yet told me how he copes with the danger of traffic accidents, and I have not asked him. But this is what I mean by saying that an ejaculation fits in with the basic rhythm.

Perhaps all this has something in common with listening to music. Most people have had the experience of being haunted for several days by a beautiful melody they have heard. The music continues within and simply will not go away. In some such way, the Jesus prayer or the *nembutsu* continues in the psychic life of those who are in love with the object to which these ejaculations point. There is, however, one significant difference. Sometimes the haunting music may disturb us. We want to put it away and we can't do so; it is persistent, even at times tyrannical. Now the rhythmic ejaculation is never like that. Probably this is because it is much, much deeper. The music, I believe, does not enter the deepest layer of psychic life; it remains somehow external to us, and that is why it can jar and even cause discord—because it can be at odds with that other rhythm which is deeper. The ejaculation, on the other hand, wells up from the deepest point of our being and is not external at all. It is the expression of the deepest self.

Formerly many people seem to have found this rhythm through the rosary. Take the case of those old women living near the sea—women who saw their sons mauled and murdered by the cruel Atlantic waves—whose lives were spent in the repetition of the suffering. They were deeply enlightened.

For those of us who live in the city, the problem is acute. Life in the countryside in proximity to nature is undoubtedly a great advantage for one who wants to meditate, as the great contemplative orders discovered long ago. Yet I believe that the great noisy cities like Tokyo (which I love) are not an insuperable obstacle. Once the rhythm is found it transcends environment, and place ceases to matter. The ecology problem can be solved at this level too.

As I have said, the rhythm of breath or ejaculation leads to something deeper. All points to the center of the soul, the core of the being, the sovereign point of the spirit, the divine spark, the true self, the realm from which enlightenment arises. This is the truest thing that exists.

THE UNCEASING ACT OF LOVE OF SISTER MARY CONSOLATA

Father Lorenzo Sales

*The daughter of a baker, Pierina was the second of six daughters born of her father's second marriage in Saluzzo on April 6, 1903. In 1930 she became a Capuchin under the name **Sister Maria Consolata**. The name chosen by the young nun points to her spiritual function as consoler of the Sacred Heart of Jesus and of all those who are unaware of the love of Christ. On the day of the ceremony of taking the veil she received the following Divine command: "I do not call you for more than this: an act of continual love." This act of love is expressed in the jaculatory prayer: "Jesus, Mary, I love you, save souls." Sister Consolata died in 1946 in the Convent of the Sacred Heart of Moriondo Moncalieri near Turin. The following pages are excerpts from her confessor, Fr. Lorenzo of Sales' Jesus Appeals to the World.*

THE ACT OF LOVE AND VOCAL PRAYER

Let us examine more closely a few points about the unceasing act of love itself.

Above all, what can be said about the unceasing act of love in relation to the many and varied vocal prayers? Sister Consolata was a prayerful soul. In her writings she speaks again and again of her soul's immense need to become and remain absorbed in prayer. Her life is a practical example of how a soul can put into practice the Gospel precept: "We ought always to pray, and not to faint."[1] Her sanctity is a concrete proof of the omnipotence of humble, trusting, and constant prayer. The First Fridays of each month, for example, were her great feast days, for then she was permitted to pass as much as eight hours in adoration before Jesus solemnly exposed in the Blessed Sacrament. Jesus Himself had told her on March 31st, 1934:

Prayer shall be your fortress!

For this reason she clung ardently to the community exercises of piety, and this also from a love of regularity, observance, and good example. She had well understood and taken to heart the admonition which Jesus had given her one day:

---

[1] Luke 18:1.

Everything that distracts you from pious practices such as Holy Mass, Communion, the Divine Office, meditation, is not good, and proceeds not from Me!

But outside of these pious exercises which were made in common, and the Way of the Cross, which she made every morning upon arriving early in choir, and sometimes also in her cell in the evening, she practiced no other, or hardly any. Vocal prayer was for her spirit almost a torment. Her soul stood in need of one thing only: love. And in the unceasing act of love she found what is contained in other prayer forms. Jesus too reminds us: "When you are praying, speak not much, as the heathens. For they think that in their much speaking they may be heard."[2] Sister Consolata once wrote to her spiritual director:

"... The Gospel passage 'He that eateth My Flesh, and drinketh My Blood, abideth in Me, ... and shall live by Me"[3] brings me joy beyond measure, for it gives me the sweet certainty that by my act of love I am living and throbbing in the Sacred Heart and that I will live there eternally. I feel that I am living in Him, and that this act of love attaches me eternally to Him, soaring high above everything, above myself and everything that surrounds me. But the joy that derives from this intimacy is often disturbed by vocal prayers. Then my poor soul is shot through with distractions. ... As you see, Father, love has simplified everything; even a soul who is extremely active, enjoys complete repose by means of her unceasing act of love."

As Saint Thomas puts it: "The soul really and fully lives her life when she carries out the divine intentions in her regard."[4]

Sister Consolata's personal experience is that of every soul who has attained a high degree of unitive love. So it is not to be wondered at that she resolved: "I must not interrupt the act of love in order to formulate prayers. Jesus knows all my intentions!" Was she mistaken or correct in this? The divine teaching tells us that she was pursuing the right path; for, being fearful one day that her inability to formulate prayers was caused by laziness, she complained:

"O Jesus, I do not know how to pray!"

Our Lord calmed her by saying:

Tell Me, what more beautiful prayer do you want to offer Me? "Jesus, Mary,

[2] Matthew 6:7.

[3] John 6:57-58.

[4] *Summa Theologica* I, 16, 4, ad. 3.

I love You! Save souls!" Love and souls! What more beautiful prayer could you desire? (October 6th, 1935)

Mother Abbess, having noticed how Sister Consolata spent herself in work to the detriment of her health, once considered it opportune to dispense her from certain duties so as to afford her more time for prayer. The good Sister wished to obey, but felt incapable of praying more vocal prayers and so hastened to the feet of the divine Master: "O Jesus, teach me to pray!" This was His reply:

You think you do not know how to pray?. . . What prayer is more beautiful and more acceptable to Me than the act of love? Do you know what Jesus is doing in the tabernacle? He is loving the Father and He is loving souls. That is all. No sound of words, nothing. Only silence and love. So, do the same! No, my dear, do not add any prayers; no, no, no! Gaze upon the tabernacle, and love in that way! (November 17th, 1935)

Jesus referred again on December 12th, 1935 to vocal prayers in addition to those prescribed by the rule: *I prefer one of your acts of love to all your prayers!*

He also explained—and this is important and comforting to all who will be following Sister Consolata in that same path—that the invocation on behalf of souls, as contained in the formula of the unceasing act of love, extends to all souls:

"Jesus, Mary, I love You! Save souls!" This comprises all: the souls in purgatory and those in the Church Militant, the innocent and the sinful souls, the dying, the Godless, etc. (June 20th, 1940)

Let us repeat once more that the practice of the unceasing act of love does not in any way prejudice the prayers prescribed by the rule or those particular prayers to which a soul feels herself drawn. Grace should not be anticipated, but followed. Grace will suggest to the soul when it is opportune to substitute the unceasing act of love for this or that free prayer.

THE ACT OF LOVE AND MEDITATION

Sister Consolata was always faithful in observing community meditation and mental prayer. But she never succeeded in meditating according to any fixed method; this is, after all, also the case with other souls who incline by preference to the prayer of simplicity. "Young bees," writes Saint Francis de Sales, "are called grubs until they are able to make honey. Similarly, prayer is called meditation until it has produced the honey of devotion. Then it becomes contemplation. The longing for divine love makes us meditate; but once won, love causes us to contemplate."[5]

Sister Consolata had attained precisely this affectionate and unceasing union with God, so it is understandable that everything which books could say left her for the most part indifferent, and sometimes was more of a hindrance than a help. She writes:

". . . The vine branch does not produce grapes by itself, but only when it is attached to the trunk of the vine. Now this union with the trunk (Jesus) is favored by the unceasing act of love. Now Jesus no longer requires lengthy meditations and reading from me. For my soul they would be a waste of time. The important thing for me is to yield much fruit, that is to love much, to love unceasingly."

Jesus taught her in the same sense when she inquired of Him one day why she was unable to meditate or derive light, nourishment, and fervor from the beautiful books which were being read aloud; He explained that the same food was not suitable for every constitution, that a delicate stomach is unable to digest ordinary food which is beneficial to a robust one, and that to her He had assigned the Gospel. Certainly, the spiritual food of which a beginner stands in need is different from that of a proficient soul or one who has already arrived at the unitive life.

After a certain meditation on the end of man, Sister Consolata was racking her brain on how to direct her life intentions, when Jesus told her (September 1935):

You are too little to form intentions. I will decide the purpose of your life. Just love Me continually, and do not interrupt your act of love!

Still another time, and again in order to calm her concerning her inability to meditate, Jesus told her:

It is no longer the hour to meditate or to read, but now is the time to love Me, to behold Me and see Me in everyone, to suffer with joy and with thanksgiving! (April 3rd, 1936)

No matter what the theme of the meditation, the divine Voice and Light always recalled her spirit to the exercise of the unceasing act of love. One day she had been unable to hear the point of the meditation and sought to substitute the Gospel. On opening the book, she read: "Prepare ye the way of the Lord. . . . Every valley shall be filled, and every mountain and hill shall be brought low; and the crooked ways shall be made straight and the rough

---

[5] *Of the Love of God*, Bk. 6, ch. 3.

Father Lorenzo Sales

ways plain."[6] The meditation period was almost ended when Jesus gave her to understand:

The act of love does all this in a soul: it fills every void and lays low all pride. (October 10th, 1935)

Again, on July 25th, 1936, when the meditation was on the Gospel passage: "Watch ye and pray."[7] Jesus told her:

Do not worry! I am watching you. It is for you to love Me, and only that!

As one can see, everything was to bring her, and everything did in fact bring her, to the unceasing act of love. After a meditation on the prodigal son, she noted in her diary:

"Yes, Jesus gave me the most beautiful gown: love. He placed on my finger the ring of fidelity, and on my feet the sandals of confidence. And in return the Good God asks only for the unceasing act of love."

And after a meditation on Our Lord's words to Saint Peter: "Couldst thou not watch one hour?"[8] she wrote:

"I must remember this divine saying throughout the day in order to give to Jesus entire hours of love."

And again on August 20th, 1936:

"During meditation I understood that my act of love is like the treasure hidden in the field, and like the pearl described in the Gospel parable; in order to possess this treasure I must sell all. What remained to me still to sell? A few sentences which escaped me during recreation. I determined to be more faithful. I willed it and I kept my promise. After the victory I found myself much stronger in the exercise of virtue."

It was not, therefore, a case of her neglecting or failing to attribute sufficient importance to meditation. On the contrary. But for her, meditation did not mean an exercise of the mind, but a tranquil repose of her heart in love: to love, to love unceasingly, to remove every obstacle that impeded the perfect continuity and purity of love.

All this, we believe, will be of comfort and assistance to souls, particularly to those who have already progressed in the unitive life and who are experiencing the same difficulty with a multiplicity of vocal prayers and with methodical meditation; and also to all souls without exception on the days when the spirit is unable to concentrate on a point of reflection for reasons of

[6] Luke 3:4-6.

[7] Matthew 14:37.

[8] Mark 14:37.

aridity and so on. What is to be done then? Rack one's brain in order to extract even one good thought? It would be a loss of time. Let the mind wander? No. Instead, the soul can always love; and every act of love, even when done with an effort of the will, has always great value for merit and sanctification. Saint Thomas also teaches that the continuity of our love makes up for our weakness in contemplation.[9]

THE ACT OF LOVE AND SPIRITUAL READING

As with meditation, so also is spiritual reading in general of the greatest usefulness to most souls.

Sister Consolata never omitted the reading required by her rule, but beyond that she read little or nothing. In general, she felt no need to seek enlightenment from books. Referring to her first years as a Capuchin nun, she writes:

"I have never read ascetical books, and I read no books now. Besides the rule, the constitution, and directives, I keep only the *Imitation of Christ* and the Holy Gospels ready at hand. For spiritual reading I use *The Story of a Soul*, and this suffices . . . for my whole life!"

Actually, it did not serve her for her entire life, for Jesus later made her put that away also.

Aside from the fact that Jesus instructed her directly, there applies here what we have already said in connection with meditation: the purpose of such books certainly is to bring the soul to love God and her neighbor in a spirit of sacrifice. Now the spiritual life of Sister Consolata was already practically one unceasing act of love, a "yes" to everything. What could books teach her that would be any better? She writes:

"A book or a page, no matter how beautiful, makes me interrupt the act of love. Jesus desires my love to be entire and uninterrupted."

She did not change her opinion even when the divine Voice became silent in her soul. One of her Sisters once loaned her a book entitled *With Jesus Alone*. Sister Consolata kept it for several months, then returned it secretly so as not to have to confess to not having read it:

". . . One day, in a period of darkness, I sought enlightenment in the book *With Jesus Alone*. I was soon overwhelmed with doubts and understood nothing anymore. A good thing that my spiritual director put my little bark

---

[9] *Summa Theologica* II, II, 180. ad. 1.

on even keel again. I have learned my lesson and I give up the one book which has remained to me. The Holy Gospel will be Consolata's food henceforth for the rest of her life."

During 1936 she noted in her diary:

"Before beginning the holy exercises I had noticed in the library a life of St. Gerard Majella. The desire to know this saint who turned every stitch into an act of love, made me put that book aside until I could obtain permission to use it for my spiritual reading during those holy days. But even before I could ask Mother Abbess, Jesus made Himself heard in my soul: why not rather read His book, the Holy Gospel? In the lives of the saints one needs to read entire chapters in order to find words of eternal life, but in His divine Book every word would be food for eternal life for me. I accepted this divine inspiration and did my spiritual reading in the Holy Gospel. Every passage brought me enlightenment and nourishment."

Sister Consolata never gave up that book of the Holy Gospel! During the dark hours of the spirit she had recourse to it and always found the light she needed. She writes:

"Jesus makes me understand the Holy Gospel very well. Upon opening it at random my glance often happens to fall on the words of Saint Elizabeth: 'Blessed art thou that hast believed!'[10] Consolata also desires to believe, oh so deeply, in the Good God!"

Yes, to believe in the Good God by offering Him an unceasing act of virginal love, that is the sense in which Jesus made her understand the Gospel:

"I have found so much light in the Gospel. 'He that abideth in Me, and I in him, the same beareth much fruit.'[11] My great desire to be fruitful is satisfied by it. Not only that, but by remaining in Jesus through the unceasing act of love, my prayer too will be heard, for it says in the Gospel: 'If you abide in Me, and My words abide in you, you shall ask whatever you will, and it shall be done unto you.'[12] O my God, Thou hast exceeded all my expectations! I need only to observe Thy commandments with fidelity in order to be certain of persevering in Thy love. And to obtain this: 'Jesus, Mary, I love You! Save souls!'"

[10] Luke 1:45.

[11] John 15:5.

[12] John 15:7.

"In my mind I keep hearing the words of the Blessed Virgin at the wedding feast in Cana: 'Whatsoever He shall say to you, do ye!'[13] And because my spiritual director has told me never to deny Jesus one single act of love, I seek to do just that. This now comprises my entire life, and in carrying it out, life has become marvelously simple. Nothing else! No one else! In that way, virginal love can soar freely!"

"One passage in the Holy Gospel has given me particular confidence: 'All power is given to Me in heaven and on earth.'[14] 'O Jesus,' I said, 'use this Thy power in my soul and establish me in the unceasing act of love so that I may not lose one! Thou canst do it!'"

"'He that is not with Me, is against Me; and he that gathereth not with Me, scattereth.'[15] When I am not with Jesus in a continuous act of love, I am against Him, I am scattering."

"'If any man will come after Me, let him deny himself, and take up his cross, and follow Me.'[16] If I do not carry the cross of the unceasing act of love, I am not following Jesus, and therefore, I cannot follow Him to Calvary."

It is superfluous to point out that all these interpretations of the Gospel texts have no exegetical value; Sister Consolata simply adapted them to her own spiritual needs.

We have made particular mention of the Gospels, but Sister Consolata loved and delighted in all holy writings:

"I am ignorant in the extreme, and yet I often receive so much enlightenment during the recital of the Divine Office concerning the Latin words I pronounce, that I understand and enjoy them more than if they were written in Italian."

". . . If Jesus is silent now, the Father in heaven nevertheless does not fail to provide directly the food for His little bird; He nourishes me with choice grains by letting me find them in Holy Scripture, in fact He Himself hands them out to me. And at Matins last night, my thought was arrested during the first lesson by: 'Quis ergo nos separabit a caritate Christi?' (Who then shall separate us from the love of Christ?)[17] No. In union with the Apostle I joyfully repeat that no creature can now separate me from my unceasing act of love."

[13] John 2:5.

[14] Matthew 28:18.

[15] Luke 11:23.

[16] Matthew 16:24.

[17] Romans 8:35.

What is here said concerning spiritual reading properly speaking, applies equally to the reading in the refectory. One day Sister Consolata's mind was struck by this passage: "Find for yourself some task that will completely absorb you." On entering these words in her notebook, she added this comment:

"What must completely absorb me, is a continuous 'Jesus, Mary, I love You! Save souls!'"

On May 9th, 1936, she writes:

"Yesterday's mealtime reading told of Our Lord's desire for wholehearted and perfect victim-souls, and this morning the divine Light explained to me that if I were to cut even a small part from a magnificent peach, it would no longer be presentable at the royal table. Just so, if my soul omits some act of love through an extraneous thought or word, the victim will no longer be complete and perfect, and therefore, no longer presentable at the table of the Divine King."

THE ACT OF LOVE AND THE PARTICULAR EXAMEN

Concerning the particular examen of one's conscience, that indispensable means for maintaining and increasing spiritual fervor, Sister Consolata wrote as follows:

"... It is necessary for me to convince myself once and for all that to make a particular examen on any point other than the unceasing act of virginal love is for my soul only a waste of time and energy; it would mean leaving the road which God wants me to follow. Therefore, my particular examen shall solely and always be concerned with the unceasing act of love, the purity of mind. . . . I have come to understand that it is better for me to concentrate all my energies on that, and not to dissipate them in numerous resolutions."

One sees, she had simplified her spiritual life also in this respect. This does not mean that she did not appreciate sufficiently the value of the particular examen; on the contrary, it occupied a place of first importance in her spiritual life. She did not in fact limit it to the few minutes required by her daily schedule, but in a sense she prolonged it throughout the entire day. Jesus had taught her to renew her resolution of the unceasing virginal act of love at every hour throughout the day, and to this she would add a rapid examen of the hour just passed.

To that end she would enter in a little notebook which she always carried with her for that purpose, any infidelities in the continuity or purity of her love. In that way she had before her in the evening, when she made a comprehensive examen of the entire day, the clear and precise state of her soul. She would then ask pardon and would make reparation for her infidelity by making crosses on the floor with her tongue or by kissing the crucifix. After that she would take up again, calmly and trustingly, her song of love.

We do not say that such a method would be suitable for every soul, nor even a majority of souls. But for Sister Consolata, who longed to respond fully to grace, it was a necessity. To offer an unceasing act of virginal love in fact requires of the soul an extreme vigilance over herself, and the act is really impossible without controlling and renewing one's fervor as often as possible.

On the other hand, to conduct the particular examen and concentrate always on one point, made its practice easier; and the divine promises concerning the unceasing act of love, which we have already mentioned, gave her the certainty that through it she would attain all the rest, that is, the perfection of every virtue.

THE ACT OF LOVE AND THE SPIRITUAL RETREAT

The days of the monthly retreat were always for Sister Consolata, so to speak, days of spiritual provisioning. She made her retreats, therefore, with scrupulous fidelity and diligence, and since each Capuchin nun was free to choose for herself the most suitable day, she selected the First Friday of each month.

She began her preparation on the preceding evening during the Holy Hour in choir from eleven to midnight. She writes:

"During the monthly day of recollection Jesus would nourish and instruct my soul with some thought and engrave it upon my heart."

She also mentions some of these thoughts, as for instance: "The Son of Man is not come to be ministered unto, but to minister,"[18] or "He emptied Himself, taking the form of a servant."[19]

"What great enlightenment and resolutions!" she writes.

But here again, enlightenment and resolutions were always related to her particular vocation of love, that is, the unceasing act of love. At the close of the monthly retreat day or on the Sunday after, she would send a detailed report on the state of her soul to her spiritual director, as he had enjoined upon her and Jesus had approved. We quote in part from one such report,

[18] Matthew 20:28.

[19] Philippians 2:7.

which was written after the First Friday in September 1942, four years before her death, when her health was already failing:

"... Here I am, placing my poor soul at your feet, to receive in spirit your absolution and fatherly blessing, to gain new strength to carry on 'usque ad finem!'

"Your last letter has been my daily bread throughout the whole past month. I thank you for it from my heart! During August, it seems to me, love was more intense, although I must confess to the loss of two hours.[20] The unceasing effort to live the present moment helps me to center my attention on the unceasing act of love; it preserves my spirit in peace and frees it from all preoccupation over the morrow and what work to follow. On two occasions I indulged in useless thoughts, five times in useless talk, twice I did not suffer gladly. My charity, it seems to me, is in order. If a reproof escapes me or I resent some words, etc., I immediately ask forgiveness without a thought for myself, so that peace might always reign in every heart around me.

"In the kitchen my struggle for self-denial continues, but now everything passes between Jesus and Consolata, 'to tell Thee that I love Thee!'

"During these days I have great need to pray in order to maintain myself on the heights. I feel tired. ... Obtain for me a little generosity so that I may defeat my selfish nature and launch myself generously on the road of daily sacrifice ..."

THE ACT OF LOVE IN VARIOUS SPIRITUAL STATES

It is clear from what has already been said that the unceasing act of love was in truth the whole life of Sister Consolata, as indeed her whole life was one unceasing act of love. This was the case because she relied on the divine teaching and had faith in the act of love and its value. This value was above all intrinsic:

"I cannot communicate continuously, as is my need, but I have come to understand that an act of love brings Jesus into the soul, that is, it increases grace and is like a Communion."

She also knew its worth in regard to her own vocation and mission:

---

[20] Sister Consolata's day of unceasing love counted seventeen hours. To have lost two hours in a month is not much. Nevertheless, it must be pointed out that these omissions were not voluntary, but caused mostly by exterior circumstances of work, etc.

"The will of God, my vocation to attain to sanctity, is one continuous 'Jesus, Mary, I love You! Save souls!' . . . Every effort, every force and activity of the soul must be aimed at not interrupting the act of love. Nothing else; this alone! For that is my way, the way which Jesus has pointed out to me."

The act of love also has value because it eliminates from the spiritual life of so many Marthas the "turbaris erga plurima" (thou are troubled about many things).[21]

"Spiritually, Jesus demanded of me an absolute silence of thoughts and words, and of the heart an unceasing 'Jesus, Mary, I love You! Save souls!' The more faithful I am to this little way of love, the more is my soul flooded with joy and a true peace that nothing is able to disturb, not even my continual falls. For, when I bring these to Jesus, He makes me remedy them through acts of humility, and these in turn increase the peace and joy in my heart."

Finally, there remains the act's value for eternal life:

"How happy, active, and vigilant ought the certainty make me that my every act of love endures to all eternity!"

So there results one single, constant, and trusting prayer:

"O Jesus, grant that I may live entirely concealed in Thee, in complete self-effacement, so that Thou mayest always do what Thou wilt with me. Thou alone must remain, and an unceasing 'Jesus, Mary, I love You! Save souls!' Grant that of the seventeen hours in my day I may not lose one!"

We might also add that the act of love was her one and only weapon against the enemy. For one cannot assume that the devil would leave this saintly soul in peace and let her act of love go unpunished. Hers was a battle without respite, carried on now and then in the open, but she came out victorious from every encounter by means of the act of love.

"The invincible weapon which always assures one the victory, is the unceasing act of love. . . . (It) prepares the soul for the temptation, and it sustains it during the temptation; for love is everything! . . . Therefore, I must not let myself become discouraged by the enemy; the act of love must dominate the struggle, never must the struggle dominate the act of love."

We must not think that Sister Consolata spoke and acted in this manner only on the days in which she walked in the light of divine favor. No. She did so also when she found herself in spiritual darkness, walking in the simple path of faith:

"It was nine o'clock in the evening when I came out of the sacristy and found myself in complete darkness on the upper stair landing. It was a bit

[21] Luke 10:41.

hazardous to descend, but I clung to the railing, and by following it, calmly reached the bottom step. As I was descending I thought of how similar was the case of my own soul; complete darkness. But by clinging to the unceasing act of love, I will calmly arrive at my last hour. . . . Yes, the act of love is really everything; it gives light and strength to proceed. Woe to my soul if she did not have this anchor of salvation to which to cling at certain times! I cannot fathom the abyss of despair into which I would fall!"

As in the days of aridity, so in the days of suffering. Well did she experience it, for to her the heights of love were never separated from those of suffering; and yet she could bear witness:

"The unceasing act of love keeps the soul always in peace. I believe that it has a strong ascendancy over suffering and helps one to suffer joyfully. . . . The act of love is stronger than any pain. . . . I feel that the unceasing act of love maintains, and will continue to maintain, my little bark steady through all confusion, boredom, and tediousness."

Sister Consolata did not, therefore, achieve continuity of love without a great effort or in a short space of time. Herein lies her merit, that she persevered in spite of everything, began each day anew, and corrected herself after every fall. And this through years and years, with heroic constancy and humble prayer. She left no means untried, and let no occasion pass for renewing her resolution. "The sluggard willeth and willeth not."[22] Sister Consolata was certainly not a sluggish soul, nor did she deceive herself with mere wishing. She willed seriously and strongly. Her energetic determination, as we have said, was one of the most outstanding characteristics of her spirit. The same impetuous character that had earned for her the nickname of "thunder and lightning," also directed and sustained her will in the good cause. All who knew her closely, admired her strong and firm will for good. That was due above all to her unceasing act of love. Her "I will" is to be found in her every resolution and is always entirely sincere. This fact is evident on every page of her writings:

"I wish to respond fully to divine grace and let this act fill my entire day from the first to the last Sign of the Cross. I wish my every act, however insignificant, to be performed with oh so much love! . . . No thunderstorm or stroke of lightning shall interrupt one continuous 'Jesus, Mary, I love You! Save souls!' . . . To see and treat Thee in everything. . . . O Jesus, with Thine aid I will not deprive Thee of one act of love, not one! Yes, Jesus, that I will to do!

[22] Proverbs 13:4.

And in order that I may keep faith with this 'I will,' I submerge it and leave it forever in Thy Most Precious Blood!"

THE HEIGHT OF HEROISM IN THE UNCEASING ACT OF LOVE

It was always the same: effort and good will! Her iron will surmounted every trial, every renunciation, every sacrifice with firmness. She abhorred mediocrity, despised compromises, she had a heroic desire to reach the peak; and her heroism was continuous, as one may judge from the following words which she addressed to her spiritual director on August 28th, 1938; these might be termed her spiritual testament to all souls who wish to follow her:

". . . Father, at present I feel an infinite desire within me to live 'the Littlest Way' even at the price of heroism.[23] I feel that I can do it if I really have the will! And so, I will it with all my strength, and I begin! Father, I sense an imperious duty to live my Littlest Way to the full. I wish I could call out to all the Littlest Souls throughout the world, when I am on the point of death: 'Follow me!' I will, indeed I will to offer the unceasing act of love from my awakening until I fall asleep, because Jesus has asked for it; and He has asked for it because I am able to give it to Him if I trust in Him alone!

"But my weakness is extreme, and temptations are not lacking. I need to rise up alone against them all and must continue by sheer will power. No, I do not wish to lead a cowardly existence, I wish to live heroically! I desire it with all the strength of my heart and of my will, and I wish to continue so until death. Jesus, who died on the Cross for love of me, merits it, and for love of Him I wish to live heroically!

"But to live upon such heights does not please human nature and comes hard. I am in need of your prayers, Father, in order to persevere. On that peak alone do I find peace; there alone do I find joy and strength in suffering. If I live on these heights where there is only Christ Crucified, then I have need of continual sacrifice, as I do of the air I breathe.

"I see all this, I sense it, I understand it. That is why I do not feel right if I have not overcome every cowardice, even alone and in the face of all, and if I do not live my Littlest Way which I love so much! . . . O Father, pray that I may make my divine dream come true, else I shall be extremely unhappy! . . ."

These words reveal Sister Consolata completely, her soul and her life!

---

[23] That is, the way of the unceasing act of love.

TREATISE ON THE INVOCATION
OF THE DIVINE NAME

Shaykh Ahmad Al-'Alawī

Shaykh Ahmad Al-'Alawī was born in Mostaghanem, Algeria, in 1869. He never obtained any formal schooling, although he learned the Qur'ān from his father at home. He later earned his living as a cobbler, but he was deeply religious by nature, and thirsty for knowledge. His meeting with his spiritual master, Shaykh Muhammad Al-Būzīdī, was crucial in his spiritual awakening. Al-'Alawī had at that time been involved in developing magical powers such as charming snakes, but Shaykh Al-Būzīdī turned him away from this and awakened him to his true nature. After his master's death, Al-'Alawī was elected to succeed him as Shaykh. He first resisted this call, and for several months in 1909 traveled to Tunis, Tripoli, and Istanbul. Upon his return to Algeria, however, Al-'Alawī duly assumed his spiritual function and became so influential that, as early as 1923, he was reported as having in the region of one hundred thousand disciples. The Shaykh Al-'Alawī died in 1934. His emphasis on the way of the invocation is beautifully expressed in his statement: "Remembrance is the mightiest rule of the religion. . . . The law was not enjoined upon us, neither were the rites of worship ordained, but for the sake of establishing the remembrance of God." The epistle from which the following passages have been excerpted was addressed to a fellow Muslim who held the Sufi practice of the invocation of the Name of God in suspicion.

I observed during our brief conversation that you felt rancor, or so it seemed to me, against your brethren the 'Alawites not for any sin they committed, but because they ceaselessly pronounce the Unique Name *Allāh*. You feel that this deserves reproof or let us say chastisement, for according to you, they devote themselves to this Name whether it is appropriate to do so or not; according to you, it does not matter to them if they happen to be in the street in a place that is deemed unsuitable for such an utterance. This is true, you say, to such an extent that when one of them knocks on the door, he says *Allāh*, when someone calls to him, he says *Allāh*, when he stands he says *Allāh*, when he sits he says *Allāh*, and so on.

In addition, you are of the opinion that this Name does not merit being called a form of invocation as it does not, according to you, constitute a complete sentence (*kalām mufīd*), based on what the grammarians have determined as being necessary components of grammatical constructions.

I am answering you concerning all these things solely for the purpose of arriving at an understanding, and in order to determine the correctness of the 'Alawites' actions. The question is, is this permissible or not? I write this missive in the hope that it might provide a cure for the heart and rest for the soul.

To begin with, what you say about what grammarians' stipulations of necessary constituents of complete sentences is correct, except that you do not realize that when the grammarians laid down this rule it pertained to the classification of a form of speech that conveys a meaning to the listener. They had no thought of applying this criterion to forms of invocation, of judging its legality or illegality, of discussing the rewards due for accomplishing it, and so on. Were you to have asked them about this in their day or were you to do so today, they would undoubtedly answer by saying, "What we have stipulated in that regard is merely a technical formulation which we use in our field, for such formulations prevent ambiguity of meaning in our discussions." You are well aware of the fact that the formulations used by grammarians differ from those used by theologians, which differ in their turn from those used by doctors of the law, and these differ once again from those used by specialists in the origins of law and so on. In this way, every group uses its own terminology, which leads us to conclude that the grammarians were for their part concerned with the identification of complete sentences— that speech which benefits the person addressed in some way. They were not concerned with distinguishing lawful invocations from unlawful ones. In other words, conditions about the requirements of grammatical speech are meant in particular for him who wishes, by his words, to inform someone of something. The one who invokes, however, does it only to benefit his soul and in order to establish the meaning of the noble Name firmly in his heart, and other intentions of this kind. Moreover, the grammarians did not formulate these conditions so as to include the expressions of a grieving or saddened man, for the latter's intention is not that of the grammarians. The grammarian would hardly say to him, "I do not understand what you mean by your sighs and groans, for they are not a grammatical statement—they need some explanation," or the like. The intention of the saddened or grieving man is not to inform others of anything, but only to console his heart. In the same way, the intention of one who invokes the Name is to have it become imprinted permanently in his soul.

You know, brother, that every name has an influence that attaches itself to the soul of him who utters it, even if it is not one of the divine Names. For example, if a man repeats the word "death" he will feel an effect which attaches itself to him on account of mentioning this word, especially if he persists in it. This effect will undoubtedly be different from the one had by the mention of "money," "power," or "authority," even without considering this in the light of the noble *hadīth*: "Increase in remembrance of the Destroyer of Pleasures" (*hazim al-Ladhdhāt*), the reference here being to death. The word death is but one word yet it is said that among some of the first believers it formed an entire litany. Every man with a sense of the subtle is aware of the effect of what is mentioned on the soul, whether it be something serious or light-hearted. If we admit this, then we are bound to admit also that the Name of God has an influence on the soul, as do other names, each to its own degree. And brother, do not lose sight of the fact that a name is as noble as that which is named, inasmuch as it bears its imprint in the folds of its secret essence and meaning.

Now let us cease to consider everything set forth above, and concern ourselves solely with the judgment of the Lawgiver (God) concerning the pronunciation of this Name: we see that it must fall under one of the five categories of the law, namely the obligatory (*wujūb*), the recommended (*nadb*), the permitted (*ibāha*), the strongly discouraged (*karāha*), and the forbidden (*hurma*) for there exists no question pertaining to the words or actions that does not fall within one of these categories. Thus, before opposing the utterance of this name, one should decide under which category such an act falls. If we find that it is something forbidden or strongly discouraged then we are obliged to oppose whoever does it, for he has committed something worthy of reproach. If, on the other hand, it does not fall into either of these categories, then to reproach it is unjust, for the person concerned has uttered something permissible, even if it is not obligatory or recommended and even if it falls just within the bounds of the lawful. What is to prevent us from repeating something lawful, and how can you make the one who does so deserve reproach or punishment through stripping this name of all religious significance? However we think of this, we cannot classify it among the strongly discouraged or forbidden things, and it retains its value in accordance with its divine station.

You are the type who restricts himself to the levels that suit him; and who so honors that which is sacred to God has done well in the eyes of his Lord; "and who so honors the commandments of God has acted out of devotion of heart."[1] All that we have thus far set forth has been done for the sake of determining that the Name is unique, and without association to anything, be it even by way of implication. If we search for the truth, stripping it of its

---

[1] Koran 22:30, 32.

veils, we can see that its mention is permitted even for a grammarian, for it is in reality a noun in the vocative[2] which is classified as a complete sentence because it has a vocative particle meaning "I call." It is permissible and even common to omit this particle in Arabic. In fact very often the position of the words makes it necessary to do this—as for example in the case we are speaking of—because of the demands of Koranic knowledge and Islamic learning which are perhaps greater among the Sufi masters than among others.

. . . In addition to all that we have said previously . . . there is the fact that those who invoke thus obey the words of God: "Say: Invoke *Allāh*, or invoke the All-Merciful. However ye call upon Him, His are the most beautiful Names."[3] They have thus concentrated upon the first form of invocation ordered by Him. This is our saying *Allāh*. Through their single-minded effort and their total absorption in the solitary invocation of God "standing, sitting, and lying on their sides,"[4] and through their perseverance in the commanded invocation, the triumph of the divine in them compels them to drop the vocative particle, for the latter is used for one who is far, not for Him who is "nearer to us than our jugular vein."[5] There are verses from the Book of God which prove the truth of the inspiration of those who invoke thus. Invocations are of two types: those from the servant to his Lord, and those from God to His servant. There are examples of the first type where the vocative particle has been dropped, and of the second where it has been kept. . . .

God has clearly set forth the supplications of the servant as follows: "Our Lord, do not take us to task if we forget or err. Our Lord, do not make us bear a burden as you did those who came before us," etc.[6] So you see may God have mercy on you—that the invocations by the servant omit the vocative *yā* for the reasons set forth above. If you have understood this, then tell me, by your Lord: If we hear the people omitting the vocative *yā* in their invocations

---

[2] An example of this is the opposition by some people to those who draw out the final *h* of the word *Allāh*, saying that here the *h* is interrogative, but an interrogation can only exist in complete sentences. Here it has been introduced into a single word, and thus it constitutes a vocative. Ibn Mālik in his *Khulāsa* said: "The vocative has a remote object (signified by) *Yā* and *Ay* and *Aa*, and by *Ayyā* and *Hayyā*." Even if we assume it (the divine name) to be a sentence, no one could object to saying that the implication here is "O God, have mercy on us and forgive us" and the like.

[3] Koran 17:110.

[4] Koran 4:103.

[5] Koran 50:16.

[6] Koran 2:286.

and prayers to their Lord, are they still to be reproached? And do they do this because of their understanding of their religion, or because of their complete ignorance thereof?

Given all of our attempts to prove our point, I am yet aware that the opponent, or let us say the one who is searching for the correct answer, will continue to scrutinize the texts and proofs of the other side indicating the legality of invoking the Name alone and showing this practice to come from that of the earliest believers. . . . The strongest basis you have for this disagreement is the grammatical argument that the Name is not structured speech. We have shown the falseness of this statement by the proofs in this section; even if there were more texts in your possession concerning this, you should at least not be so quick to reject what people may have as arguments. Finally, whether each side is given an equal voice or not, the matter remains within the realm of *ijtihād*.[7] Thus, the statement of the opponent to the effect that the invocation of this Name in isolation is not permissible proves nothing to those who say the opposite. The crux of the matter is that your assertion of illegality is restricted to what concerns you in particular; but legislating and compelling others to do things is the prerogative of the Infallible, and no one else can say of his own accord, "this is permitted" or "this is not." Whoever does so should lower his voice where his ignorance of the subject exceeds his knowledge. This is a principle that holds for all other disputes, for the Sufi, like others, is obliged to bow his head and to refrain from holding other opinions in the face of the noble Law and the holy Book.

It is certainly possible that the opponent will attack us from another quarter, saying that we have no right to worship and seek reward for the practice that we do not know for certain the earliest Muslims performed. To this we would reply, yes, this is as you say. I hope for the sake of God that we are at least in unison on this point. However, I believe you will not forget, brother, and take note that it is in fact permissible to recite the divine Names and this is proven by the words of the Mighty and Powerful: "To God belong the most beautiful Names, so invoke Him by them."[8] They are single words, and although they are thus, neither this verse nor any other have stipulated as to how the invocation should be pronounced—that is, what form it should take, and so on. This, I believe, is simply out of consideration for the levels of those who are pious and on the path of God, for they will vary in strength

[7] Lit. "striving." The exercise of reason by an individual or group in order to form an opinion about a point not explicitly laid down in the Koran or *hadīth*.

[8] Koran 7:180.

and weakness, desire and awe, passion and yearning. People are at different levels and there are degrees of desire for God; and the innermost depths of men are known from the standpoint of their relationship with Him, Mighty and Glorious. From this we see that there were no restrictions concerning the forms of prayers and invocations among the earliest believers that could cause us to conclude that the Name was definitely not used as a form of invocation among them, or that they did not consider this Name as a form of invocation. For we do not know with certainty all that they uttered in their seclusion or in the world, or in times of illness or health. It is impossible for us to believe that the companions of the Prophet (may God be pleased with them!) did not repeat the Name of God, *Allāh, Allāh*, for He has protected them from such a possibility. Here I would like to put before you evidence which will decide the argument, and you may see then that this question has a wider import than you imagined. Muslim, in his *Saḥīḥ*, related on the authority of Abū Hurayrah (may God be pleased with him!) that the latter once saw a sick man groaning in the presence of the Prophet (peace and blessings of God be upon him!). One of the companions told him to cease his groaning and exhorted him to be patient. The Prophet then said (peace and blessings of God be upon him!), "Let him groan, for he is invoking one of the Names of God most high." Al-Bukhārī and Tīrmidhī also had on the authority of Abū Hurayrah that the Prophet said, "Let him groan, for the groan is one of the Names of God which brings relief to the ill."[9] Then—God have mercy on you—what would you do in such a situation if the sick man was pronouncing the Name of Majesty—*Allāh, Allāh*—instead of saying "ah!, ah!"? Would it be correct for this companion to forbid him this? Certainly not, for the exaltedness of the Name clearly precludes this possibility. The companion was reproached only because of his failure to understand the meaning of the word "ah," for it is one of the Names of God most high—and the Prophet (peace and blessings be upon him!) acknowledged that it is a form of invocation as such, apart from its being classified as a Name of God. This is undoubtedly a valuable lesson which should make men think well of those who invoke, however they do so. But even supposing you are not convinced that what we have presented to you as a logical argument is sound, yet justice permits one only to say that the question is one about which we must remain in disagreement. However sure its conclusion may seem to us by this argument, it remains

---

[9] At the time this *ḥadīth* was written down they ascribed the wrong source to it. The truth is that al-Rafii Imām al-Dīn related it in his *Tārīkh al-Qarawīn* on the authority of 'Aisha' and al-'Azīz confirmed its reliability.

a question of *ijtihād* and thus, how can you try to compel us, brother, to agree with your argument or submit to your *ijtihād* when we compel you to nothing of the sort? All this is one thing, and what is more, however much you assail your brethren the 'Alawites with reproaches, you cannot prevent them from following the way of those who invoke the Name alone, or from advocating this invocation for the leaders and guides of religion.

... In his *Sharh al-Mubāhith al-Asliyya*, Ibn 'Ajība[10] (may God have mercy on him!) relates that Abū Hāmid al-Ghazālī (may God be pleased with him!) said: "At first I desired to travel upon the path with many prayers, litanies, and fasts. Then when God saw the sincerity of my intention, He brought me to one of His saints who said to me: 'My son, rid yourself of all preoccupations save God alone. Withdraw into isolation, gather together all your strength and fervor, and say *Allāh, Allāh, Allāh*.'" And al-Ghazālī in his *Mishkāt al-Anwār* said: "As long as you occupy yourself with that which is other than God, you must remain with the negation, *lā ilāha*.[11] When you have become oblivious to all of creation by your contemplation of the Creator, then you have left the negation behind and attained the affirmation: 'Say *Allāh!* Then leave them to their vain talk.'[12]" He also said: "When you have left behind the remembrance of what never was, and devoted yourself to the remembrance of He who has never ceased to be, then when you say *Allāh* you will be delivered from all that is other than God." He also said, "Open the door of your heart with the key of the saying *lā ilāha illa Allāh*, the door of your spirit with the word *Allāh*, and invoke the presence of your innermost essence (*sirr*) with the word *Huwa, Huwa*.[13]" ...

Let us assume that the divine Law contains no indication whatsoever as to whether the repetition of the Name is permitted or not. If this is the case, then there is nothing at all to cause one to prohibit its repetition by the tongue, or its passage to the heart. In fact, it appears that there is nothing in the law to forbid the repetition of any name related by tradition and if this is so, then how can pronouncing one of the divine Names be prohibited? Far be it from the divine Law to contain such excesses and deviation and oblige the believer not to repeat the name of his Lord—not to say *Allāh, Allāh*, or what is the same, not to repeat any of the rest of God's Names, for He said:

[10] d. 1809.

[11] The two parts of the first Shahādah, or testimony of faith, are *lā ilāha*, "there is no god," *illa Allāh*, "save God."

[12] Koran 6:91.

[13] "He," the Name of the Divine Essence.

"To God belong the most beautiful Names, so call upon Him by them"[14] meaning petition Him by them and invoke Him by them. This is what we have understood and chosen for ourselves. You in turn have the right to choose for yourselves, but you should not oblige us to agree with your choice while we have not obliged you to agree with ours. I will end this section by quoting a passage that contains conclusive proof about the matter. I say this assuming the modesty and generosity of those who claim that this Name is in the category of strongly discouraged things. I ask forgiveness of God! The question of the strongly discouraged (*karāha*) or permitted (*nadab*) category of the word has been resolved, and it was stipulated that it ranks above the merely "permissible." Concerning this, al-Ajhuri, in his *Sharh* of Khalīl mentions the following on the authority of al-Mawwaq: "If there is a disagreement as to whether something is 'permitted' or 'strongly discouraged,' it is better to do it than not to. In the same way, if there is disagreement as to whether an action is part of the *Sunna*, or strongly discouraged, then it cannot be less than 'permitted' in any case."

. . . You also mentioned, or let us say objected, to the fact that they repeatedly utter the Name of Majesty whether or not it is appropriate to do so. They behave thus in the street and other such places. It appears to you that this attitude is lacking in reverence for the divine Names, and that this practice was never specifically ordered by the law. When one of them knocks on the door, he says *Allāh*, when someone calls to him he says *Allāh*, and other things of this kind, all of which you find inappropriate. Here I must add that however indulgent I am in my answer I am yet compelled, after asking your leave, to say that you have neglected to reveal the *hadīths* relevant to our case which have given you cause to reproach the 'Alawites for having done something wrong. For, if you had indeed read about such traditions you would not have tried to oppose us on the basis of suspicions that the earliest believers practiced differently. If you were able to find texts which corroborate what we have said, I am certain that you would have scrutinized them and pondered them in your heart, submitting to what they say, and placing them above your own opinion. This is only proper and fitting for someone in your position. Thus, here I will quote what should be sufficient, God-willing, to show that in the practice of the 'Alawites free, spontaneous invocation is not outside the realm of the *Sunna*; nor is it in conflict with it. We have concluded that it is the essence of the *Sunna*, and we base this belief on the command to "practice the invocation." This must indicate that

---

[14] Koran 7:180.

it is not to be restricted to a certain time or place, but can be practiced at all times and in all places. At each instant, man must build upon his moments of remembrance and rid himself of his inherent forgetfulness so that the former gains strength in his mind and remains fixed in his consciousness. In other words, the remembrance of God is praiseworthy whatever the circumstances, just as forgetfulness is blameworthy whatever the circumstances. Certainly the best course for both of us is to seek direction from the Holy Book and the *Sunna*. The passages which the Koran contains about the importance of the invocation and its warnings about being forgetful probably do not need to be quoted for clarification, especially to such as you. The *Sunna*, in turn, contains passages which are no less clear, but it will not hurt for us to quote a few of these *hadīths*, along with some practices established by the four schools of law, so that we know the will of the Lawgiver concerning us, and can act according to it, God-willing. Ibn Durays and Abu Yala[15] related on the authority of Abu Said al-Khudri: "It is incumbent upon you to fear God as much as possible, and to mention His Name at every tree and stone." The most important idea here is the generalization of time and place with reference to the practice of the invocation. . . . Nawawi relates something similar in his commentary on Muslim, the gist of which is that the Prophet (upon him be blessing and peace!) constantly practiced the invocation, regardless of circumstance or place. Anyone who researches legal opinions of scholars on this subject will find ample evidence indicating unanimous consensus in favor of this invocation. The Hanafi masters have related according to the *Nujūm al-Muhtadīn*, that the Qādī Khan said: "The invocation of God, as well as irreligious and dispersive gathering are permitted in the market place provided that the one in the first activity is preoccupied with glorifying and declaring the oneness of God, and the others are preoccupied with their worldly affairs." If you ponder—God have mercy on you!—the words "dispersive and irreligious gatherings" you will find that the 'Alawites are not so negligent as to belong to that category. In fact, the invocation has even been permitted in the hot baths, the place where one's private parts are uncovered and one cleanses oneself of filth. This is shown in a large number of texts such as: "Reciting the Koran out loud while in the bath is disliked, but it is not disliked to do so in a whisper, just as one can glorify God and pronounce the testimony of unity there, even in a loud voice." . . . If the invocation is permissible in the bath, what is the sin if the 'Alawites invoke in the street, for example? Given that a person unaccustomed to hearing someone invoke

[15] d. 1131.

in such places may be repulsed by it, it is nonetheless incumbent upon the impartial man, if he wishes to judge others, to do so according to the justice of God and His prophets and not according to what he would choose or approve, by himself. He should act without fear of the man who approves of one thing and disapproves of all other possibilities. For this reason, we must not be concerned with what a few have approved of, but should limit ourselves to choosing one of the possibilities contained in the religious law. The duty, then, for all who believe in God and the Last Day, is to look no further than these texts, and to act in accordance with their commands by choosing for their soul what God chooses for it. "When God and His Messenger ordain something for the believer, whether man or woman, it is not proper for him to choose for himself in the matter."[16]

. . . In drawing upon all these texts my purpose is not to favor the legal schools which either permit the invocation in the toilet or otherwise, but in order to demonstrate, brother, that some religious leaders have approved of the invocation even in the place considered to be the worst and most unclean by far. Thus if you happen to find someone invoking God while in such a place, do not consider it strange, or look upon him as an innovator, for al-Shāfiʿī and Mālik have stated it to be permitted, and they are sufficiently good examples of those who hold fast to the bond with God and to the *Sunna* of His Messenger (peace and blessings be upon him!). This and other texts clearly declare without a doubt that the ʿAlawites were wronged by your accusations for they have not gone, through imprudence, to the extreme limits of what is permitted. You have not heard any one of them say that he did not refrain from invocation even in the toilet or in other such unclean circumstances. The most that one can relate of the ʿAlawites is that if someone calls to one of them he says *Allāh* and if he calls out to someone he says *Allāh*, and so on. Someone may say that the Names of God are too exalted to be used as a means of gaining access to anything outside of the realm of the afterlife, nor should it be permitted to use them as a means of calling upon someone or attracting his attention. This would be correct, were it not for the fact that this same thing is permitted and even commanded in the religious law. If you were to look in the most obvious area for material which corroborates these arguments, you would find that what God wills of us in this matter is so clear that it comes close to being an order from Him. For example, just consider the call to prayer. As I am sure you know, it has been established as a means of declaring that the times of prayer have come, and as an exhortation

---

[16] Koran 33:36.

to all to fulfill their duty of prayer. It would be more precise and fitting, perhaps, to call out "the time of prayer has come" or "the time for prayer has commenced," or something that indicates the same thing. Why, in that case, is the whole testimony of faith recited and not simply a few words summarizing it? Furthermore, would you have asked why these Names of God have come to be used as instruments to call men to prayer? A similar example is saying "Glory be to God!" to inform the leader in prayer of a mistake, or to inform him of whatever necessity demands. It is said that the companions of the Prophet (may God be pleased with them!) used to awaken each other by the saying, "God is most great!" This is confirmed in both *Sahīh* collections in the story of the valley, where they slept past the time for the dawn prayer, and the first to awaken was Abū Bakr. ʿUmar was the fourth one to awake, and he began calling out "God is most great!" until the Prophet (peace and blessings be upon him!) awoke. Consider—may God have mercy on you!—how they used forms of invocation to awaken one another from sleep. This was how they acted in time of war or otherwise—indicating things by saying "God is most great!"

. . . Before we end this letter that, God-willing, contains blessings for you and for us, I would like to relate some *hadīth*s on this subject. I hope that you will give them the attention they deserve, as is your custom. There are two *hadīth*s which contain the essence of all we have said about the duty of devoting oneself to the remembrance of God, Mighty and Glorious, at every time and place and of filling up every moment with this remembrance. The first is related by Imam Ahmād, Abū Dāwūd, Ibn Abi al-Dunya, Nasai and Ibn Habban. In Abū Dāwūd's words: "The Prophet (peace and blessings be upon him!) said, 'Whoever sits in a place and does not invoke God there, his sitting is vain and frivolous in the eyes God.'" There Hafīz Abd al-ʿAzīm said the word *al-tira*, pronounced with a short *i* and a single *r*, means a fault and something which God counts against a person. The second *hadīth* comes from Abū Dāwūd and al-Hakīm, on the authority of Abū Hurayrah (may God be pleased with him!). He said: "No one will arise from a group in conversation where God has not been mentioned except they will be like the corpses of donkeys, and will lament their deed on the Day of Judgment."

THE LOVE OF RELIGIOUS PRACTICES

Simone Weil

Simone Weil *was born in Paris in 1909. Weil's parents were secular Jews. She was a gifted student and entered the École Normale Supérieure in 1928. After graduation she first taught at Le Puy. While teaching, Weil became involved in the local political activities, joining the unemployed and striking workers. Her political engagement took her away from teaching and she began working in a Paris factory in 1934. By 1936 she went to Spain to provide humanitarian support to the Republican troops in the Spanish Civil War. In the wake of her experience at war, Weil's interests and writings focused more explicitly on spiritual matters. She had her first profound spiritual experience at the Solesmes Monastery when hearing Gregorian chant. The second turning point in her spiritual destiny was when—in her own words—"Christ himself came down and He took me." Weil spent the rest of her life "waiting for God" and articulated the intellectual implications of her spiritual experiences in writing. Weil related her "Christic" perspective to pre-Socratic and Platonic philosophy, as well as to Indian philosophy. At the outset of the Second World War Weil was forced to flee to America with her family. After a few months in America, Weil left for England to join the Free French. She died of tuberculosis in 1943 in England at the age of thirty-four. At the time of her death, Weil was still relatively unknown and had published only a few articles. She has since been recognized as a major spiritual thinker of the twentieth century. The following excerpt, taken from* Waiting for God, *synthetically relates the whole religious experience to the way of the invocation.*

The whole virtue of religious practices can be conceived of from the Buddhist tradition concerning the recitation of the name of the Lord. It is said that Buddha made a vow to raise to himself, in the Land of Purity, all those who pronounced his name with the desire of being saved by him; and that because of this vow the recitation of the name of the Lord really has the power of transforming the soul.

Religion is nothing else but this promise of God. Every religious practice, every rite, all liturgy is a form of the recitation of the name of the Lord and in principle should have a real virtue, the virtue of saving whoever devotes himself to performing it with desire.

All religions pronounce the name of God in their particular language. As a rule it is better for a man to name God in his native tongue rather than in one that is foreign to him. Except in special cases the soul is not able to abandon itself utterly when it has to make the slight effort of seeking for the words in a foreign language, even when this language is well known.

GLOSSARY

advaita: The Hindu doctrine of non-duality; there is no other reality but *Ātman*, the absolute and infinite Subject.

Amida: The Japanese name of Amitābha, the Buddha of infinite Light.

Amitābha: Many aeons ago king Dharmakāra renounced his throne and attained to perfect enlightenment. He became the Buddha Amitābha and reigns over a celestial realm named the Pure Land. Following his vow preceding his entrance into *nirvāna*, all who turn to him with complete faith and trust will be reborn in the Pure Land.

arhat: "Worthy one"; the title given to those who have attained *nirvāna*.

Brahman: The absolute and supreme Reality in Hinduism.

cholem: A Hebrew vowel.

dhyāna: Sanskrit for "meditation."

Ein Sof: Literally, "without end"; in Jewish Kabbalah, the infinite and hidden essence of God, which remains unknown to humans.

Forty-first stage: In Japanese Buddhism it is said that a *bodhisattva* goes through forty stages of practice and reaches the forty-first stage of Buddhahood.

Gajendra: According to Hindu mythology the elephant Gajendra was so proud of his physical and mental strength that he thought he would be able to overcome a crocodile. But the crocodile fought relentlessly in the water, which is his element. Gajendra exhausted his physical strength until he turned his attention to Vishnu: at that moment, the God liberated him through His Grace.

gāthā: A small Buddhist meditation, often to remind the practitioner to be mindful.

Gāyatrī: A famous Vedic *mantra*: *Om bhur-bhuvah-svah tat savitur varenyam bhargo devasya dhimahi dhiyo yo nah pracodayat*. It can be translated: "Om.

Let us contemplate the spirit of the divine of the earth, the atmosphere, and heaven. May that direct our minds."

Gematria: A Kabbalistic system by which hidden meanings are discovered within words from the Jewish scriptures. Each letter of the Hebrew alphabet corresponds to a number; numerical values of words are totaled up, and these words are then said to correspond with other words sharing the same numerical value.

Girdhar: Krishna in the form of a cowherd. Mīrābāī worshipped the God in this form as her divine lover.

gunas: The three cosmic qualities found in Nature: *sattva* (clarity), *rajas* (passion), and *tamas* (heaviness, inertia).

Hanumān: A monkey god; a noble hero and great devotee of Lord Rāma whose story is related in the Hindu epic, the *Rāmāyana*.

Hiranyakasipu: The king of the demons; Vishnu, in the form of the lion Narasimha, defeated him.

kīrtan: The musical chanting of sacred *mantras*.

lakh: A Sanskrit term meaning "one hundred thousand."

Naraka: In Hindu mythology, a hell state.

Nārāyana: A name of Vishnu. Ajamil, though he had forgotten his true nature and gone astray, was saved from death when he called his favorite son, Nārāyana, to his side. Such is the power of the Lord Nārāyana's Name.

Narsingh: An *avatāra*, or incarnation, of Vishnu, who appears neither by day nor by night, but at dusk, and neither as man nor as beast, but as half-man, half-lion.

nien-fo: Remembrance or mindfulness of the Buddha through the repetition of his Name.

Notarikon: A Kabbalistic way of permuting words in the Jewish scriptures; it utilizes the procedure of devising new words from combinations of the first and last letters of special words.

Prahlad: The son of Hiranyakasipu, the king of the demons, who remained faithful to Vishnu in spite of the threats and sarcasms of his father.

Rāma: A major *avatāra* of Vishnu; the hero of the Hindu epic, the *Rāmāyana*, in which he defeats the demon king Rāvana.

Rāvana: The demon king of Sri Lanka; antagonist of Rāma in the *Rāmāyana*. He is described as having ten heads and twenty hands.

sādhanā: In Hinduism, the path and discipline of spiritual realization.

Shekhinah: In Jewish Kabbalah, the Divine presence or immanence.

shinjin: The act of taking refuge in the Buddha.

starets: Equivalent of the Greek *geron*, "old man"; a senior monk to whom other monks and laypeople turn for spiritual direction.

Sukhāvatī: The Buddhist Pure Land of the Western Paradise.

Sunna: The tradition of ethics, action, behavior, and social etiquette founded on the imitation of Muhammad, the Prophet of Islam.

tallit: A prayer shawl that is worn during the morning Jewish services.

tapas: Sanskrit for ascetic practice.

Tathāgata: Literally, "thus gone"; a name referring to the Buddha, following his entrance into *nirvāna*.

tefillin: Phylacteries, or leather objects, used in Jewish prayer and containing scriptural verses.

Tetragrammaton: The four Hebrew consonants, Yod-He-Vav-He (יהוה), which form the supreme Divine Name.

wasan: A Japanese word for collected volumes of verse.

Yod-He-Vav-He: *See* Tetragrammaton.

ACKNOWLEDGMENTS

The editor is especially grateful to Barry McDonald and Seyyed Hossein Nasr for their precious advice and helpful suggestions during the process of choosing the excerpts for this anthology. He would like to thank the following authors, editors, and publishers for their consent to publish the articles in this anthology. Special thanks to Gray Henry and *Fons Vitae* for allowing us to include excerpts from Leslie Cadavid's translation of the "Treatise on the Divine Name" by Shaykh Ahmad al-'Alawî.

I. FOUNDATIONAL TEXTS:

Bhagavad Gītā, "He Who Thinks of Me Constantly": *Bhagavad Gita*, translation by Winthrop Sargeant, Albany, State University of New York Press, 1994, pp. 353-362.

Chaitanya, "I Shall Repeat Thy Name": Bankey Behari, *Minstrels of God*, Bombay, Bharatiya Vidya Bhavan, 1970, pp. 258-259.

Kabīr, "Recite the Name of the Lord": Vandana Mataji, *Nāma Japa: The Prayer of the Name*, Delhi, Motilal Banarsidass, 1995, pp. 208-209.

Mīrābāī, "I am Fascinated by Thy Name": Vandana Mataji, *Nāma Japa: The Prayer of the Name*, Delhi, Motilal Banarsidass, 1995, pp. 209-210.

Tulsīdās, "Comfort in this World and the Next": Bankey Behari, *Minstrels of God*, Bombay, Bharatiya Vidya Bhavan, 1970, pp. 274-275.

Sukhāvatīvyūha, "Glorify the Name of the Lord Amitābha": *Buddhist Texts Through the Ages*, edited by Edward Conze, New York, Harper & Row, 1964, pp. 205-206.

Hōnen, "The Buddha of Boundless Light": *Honen, the Buddhist Saint, III*, translated by Harper Havelock Coates and Ryugaku Ishizuka, Kyoto, Chionin, 1925, pp. 371-373.

Hōnen, "Taking Refuge in the Right Practice": *Hōnen's Senchakushū*, translated by Senchakushū English Translation Project, Honolulu, University of Hawaii Press/Tokyo, Sōgō Bukkyō Kenkyūjo, Taishō University, 1998, p. 63.

Shinran, "Passages on the Pure Land Way": *The Collected Works of Shinran, I*, translated by Dennis Hirota, Hisao Inagaki, Michio Tokunaga, and Ryushin Uryuzu, Kyoto, Jōdo Shinshū Hongwanji-Ha, 1997, pp. 295-298.

Zohar, "The Holy One Speaks His Name": *The Secret Garden: An Anthology in the Kabbalah*, edited by David Meltzer, Barrytown, NY, Barrytown Limited, 1998, p. i.

Abraham Abulafia, "The Light of the Intellect": Abraham Abulafia, *Or HaSeichel*, in Moses Cordovero, *Pardes Rimonim* ("The Orchard of Pomegranates"), 21:1, http://www.tabick.abel.co.uk/abulafia.html

Abraham Abulafia, "The Question of Prophecy": *The Secret Garden: An Anthology in the Kabbalah*, edited by David Meltzer, Barrytown, NY, Barrytown Limited, 1998, pp. 121-123.

Isaac of Akko, "Gazing at the Letters": *The Essential Kabbalah*, edited by Daniel C. Matt, San Francisco, Harper, 1996, p. 120.

Isaac of Akko, "Climbing the Ladder": *The Essential Kabbalah*, edited by Daniel C. Matt, San Francisco, Harper, 1996, p. 121.

Philokalia, St. Philotheos of Sinai, Ilias the Presbyter, St. Symeon the New Theologian, and St. Gregory of Sinai: *The Philokalia, II*, translated and edited by G.E.H. Palmer, Philip Sherrard, and Kallistos Ware, London and Boston, Faber & Faber, 1979, pp. 25, 45, 71-73, 264, 275-276.

The Way of a Pilgrim, "Unceasing Interior Prayer": *The Way of a Pilgrim*, translated from the Russian by R.M. French, London, S.P.C.K., 1954, pp. 8-18.

The Cloud of Unknowing, "Strike Down Every Kind of Thought": *The Cloud of Unknowing*, edited by James Walsh, SJ, Ramsey, NJ, Paulist Press, 1981, pp. 131-134.

St. Bernardino of Siena, "The Sermon for Palm Sunday": *The Invocation of the Name of Jesus: As Practiced in the Western Church*, translated by Kilian Walsh OCSO, Spencer, edited by Rama Coomaraswamy, Louisville, KY, Fons Vitae, 1999, pp. 79-81.

St. Jean Eudes, "The Name Admirable Above All Names": *The Invocation of the Name of Jesus: As Practiced in the Western Church*, edited by Rama Coomaraswamy, Louisville, KY, Fons Vitae, 1999, pp. 95-96.

Jean-Pierre de Caussade, "The Sacrament of the Present Moment": Jean-Pierre de Caussade, *The Sacrament of the Present Moment*, translated by Kitty Muggeridge, San Francisco, Harper, 1989, pp. 77-78.

Ibn 'Atā' Allāh Al-Iskandarī, "The Key to Salvation": Ibn 'Atā' Allāh Al-Iskandarī, *The Key to Salvation: A Sufi Manual of Invocation*, translated by Mary Ann Koury Danner, Cambridge, UK, The Islamic Texts Society, pp. 73-78, 88-93.

II. CONTEMPORARY DOCTRINAL ESSAYS:

Frithjof Schuon, "Modes of Prayer": Frithjof Schuon, *Stations of Wisdom*, Bloomington, IN, World Wisdom, 1995, pp. 125-128.

Frithjof Schuon, "Communion and Invocation": Frithjof Schuon, "Communion et Invocation," *Études Traditionnelles*, Paris, May 1940, translated from the French by Gillian Harris and Mark Perry; with permission of the Schuon Estate.

Titus Burckhardt, "Rites": Titus Burckhardt, *Introduction to Sufism*, San Francisco, Thorsons, 1995, pp. 99-105.

Martin Lings, "The Method": Martin Lings, *What is Sufism?* Berkeley and Los Angeles, University of California Press, 1975, pp. 78-82.

Leo Schaya, "The Great Name of God": Leo Schaya, *The Universal Meaning of the Kabbalah*, Baltimore, Penguin Books Inc, 1973, pp. 145-165.

Marco Pallis, "*Nembutsu* as Remembrance": Marco Pallis, *A Buddhist Spectrum*, Bloomington, IN, World Wisdom, 2003, pp. 103-123.

D.T. Suzuki, "The Shin Teaching of Buddhism": D.T. Suzuki, *Collected Writings on Shin Buddhism*, Kyoto, Shinshū Otaniha, 1973, pp. 51-57.

Archimandrite Lev Gillet, "On the Practical Use of the Jesus Prayer": Lev Gillet, *The Jesus Prayer*, Crestwood, NY, St. Vladimir's Seminary Press, 1987, pp. 93-105.

Mir Valiuddin, "Some Important *Dhikr*s": Mir Valiuddin, *Contemplative Disciplines in Sufism*, London and The Hague, East-West Publications, 1980, pp. 37-39, 61-65.

III. CONTEMPORARY TESTIMONIES:

Thomas Yellowtail, "Always Praying and Thinking of God": *Yellowtail, Crow Medicine Man and Sun Dance Chief: An Autobiography*, edited by Michael Oren Fitzgerald, Norman, OK, University of Oklahoma Press, 1994, pp. 126-127.

Sri Ramakrishna, "Pray to God With a Yearning Heart": Mahendranath Gupta ("M"), *The Gospel of Ramakrishna*, New York, Ramakrishna-Vivekananda Center, 1996, pp. 246-247.

Swami Ramdas, "Constant Repetition of the Divine Name": Swami Ramdas, *In the Vision of God, I*, San Diego, CA, Blue Dove Press, 1995, pp. 6-7, 243-244, and Vandana Mataji, *Nāma Japa: The Prayer of the Name*, Delhi, Motilal Banarsidass, 1995, pp. 222-223.

Mahatma Gandhi, "Prayer": Vandana Mataji, *Nāma Japa: The Prayer of the Name*, Delhi, Motilal Banarsidass, 1995, pp. 224-226.

Vandana Mataji, "*Japa-Sādhanā*": Vandana Mataji, *Nāma Japa: The Prayer of the Name*, Delhi, Motilal Banarsidass, 1995, pp. 265-266.

Ramana Maharshi, "*Advaita* and *Japa*": Robert Powell, *Talks With Ramana Maharshi: On Realizing Abiding Peace and Happiness*, Carlsbad, CA, Inner Directions, 2000, pp. 42, 46, 58, 74, 227.

Acknowledgments

Swami Abhishiktananda (Henri Le Saux), "The Prayer of the Name": Abhishiktananda, *Prayer*, Westminster, John Knox, 1973, pp. 51-58.

Gojun Shichiri, "Sayings on *Tariki*": D.T. Suzuki, *Collected Writings on Shin Buddhism*, Kyoto, Shinshū Otaniha, 1973, pp. 101-110.
Gao Xingjian, "*Namo Amitofu*": Gao Xingjian, *The Soul Mountain*, New York, Perennial, 2001, pp. 69-74.

William Johnston, "Breathing and Rhythm in Christian and Buddhist Prayer": William Johnston, *Christian Zen*, New York, Fordham University Press, 1997, pp. 81-84.

Father Lorenzo Sales, "The Unceasing Act of Love of Sister Mary Consolata": Father Lorenzo Sales, *Jesus Appeals to the World*, New York, Society of Saint Paul, 1949, pp. 161-181.

Shaykh Ahmad Al-'Alawī, "Treatise on the Invocation of the Divine Name": *Two Who Attained: Twentieth-Century Muslim Saints, Sayyida Fatima al-Yashrutiyya and Shaykh Ahmed al-'Alawi*, introduction and translations by Leslie Cadavid, Louisville, KY, Fons Vitae, 2005, pp. 49-73.

Simone Weil, "The Love of Religious Practices": Simone Weil, *Waiting for God*, New York, Perennial, 2001, pp. 117-118.

BIOGRAPHICAL NOTE

PATRICK LAUDE was born in France in 1958. He took an undergraduate degree in History, and a graduate degree in Philosophy, at the University of Paris-Sorbonne while a Fellow at the École Normale Supérieure in Paris. He came to the USA in the early eighties and obtained a Ph.D. in French literature in 1985. He is the author of numerous articles and several books dealing with the relationship between mysticism, symbolism, and literature, as well as important spiritual figures such as Jeanne Guyon, Simone Weil, Louis Massignon, and Frithjof Schuon. His works include *Approches du Quiétisme* (Tübingen, 1992), *Massignon intérieur* (Paris-Lausanne, L'Age d'Homme, 2001), and *Divine Play, Sacred Laughter, and Spiritual Understanding* (New York, Palgrave-McMillan, 2005). He is also the co-editor of *Dossier H: Frithjof Schuon* (Paris-Lausanne, L'Age d'Homme, 2001), and the co-author—with Jean-Baptiste Aymard—of *Frithjof Schuon: Life and Teachings* (Albany, SUNY Press, 2004). His previous publications with World Wisdom include: *Music of the Sky: An Anthology of Spiritual Poetry* (2004), and *Singing the Way: Insights in Poetry and Spiritual Transformation* (2005). He is currently Professor of French at Georgetown University.

INDEX

For a glossary of all key foreign words used in books published by World Wisdom, including metaphysical terms in English, consult: www.DictionaryofSpiritualTerms.org.
This on-line Dictionary of Spiritual Terms provides extensive definitions, examples and related terms in other languages.

Titles in the Treasures of the World's Religions series

The Essential Vedānta: A New Source Book of Advaita Vedānta,
edited by Eliot Deutsch and Rohit Dalvi, 2004

For God's Greater Glory: Gems of Jesuit Spirituality,
edited by Jean-Pierre Lafouge, 2006

*The Golden Chain: An Anthology of Pythagorean and Platonic
Philosophy,* selected and edited by Algis Uždavinys, 2004

*In the Heart of the Desert: The Spirituality of the Desert Fathers and
Mothers,* by John Chryssavgis, 2003

Not of This World: A Treasury of Christian Mysticism, compiled and
edited by James S. Cutsinger, 2003

Pray Without Ceasing: The Way of the Invocation in World Religions,
edited by Patrick Laude, 2006

Zen Buddhism: A History, Part I: India and China,
by Heinrich Dumoulin, 2005

Zen Buddhism: A History, Part II: Japan,
by Heinrich Dumoulin, 2005